LOVE
IS ALL
AROUND

THE MAKING OF
THE MARY TYLER MOORE SHOW

LOVE
IS ALL
AROUND

ROBERT S. ALLEY
&
IRBY B. BROWN

Delta

A DELTA BOOK
Published by
Dell Publishing
a division of
Bantam Doubleday Dell Publishing Group, Inc.
666 Fifth Avenue
New York, New York 10103

Photos on pages iii, 78, 86, 228, 231, and citations in Chapter 8, reprinted with permission from *TV Guide*® magazine. Copyright © 1988 by Triangle Publications, Inc. Radnor, PA.

Photos on pages 2 (photoright), 3 (photoright), 31, 64, 233, 237, photographer John R. Alley.

Library of Congress Cataloging in Publication Data

Alley, Robert S., 1932–
    Love is all around : the making of the Mary Tyler Moore show /
Robert S. Alley and Irby B. Brown.
        p.   cm.
    ISBN 0–385–29773–4
    1. Mary Tyler Moore show.   I. Brown, Irby B.   II. Title.
PN1992.77.M285A45   1989
791.45'72—dc19   89–31311
                                                                              CIP

Printed in the United States of America
Published simultaneously in Canada

December 1989

10 9 8 7 6 5 4 3 2 1

Designed by M 'N O Production Service, Inc.

RRH

Inscribed in grateful appreciation to our friend
Jay Sandrich,
gifted director of 119 episodes,
for his unflagging support and encouragement
and
for Ilia and Norma

ACKNOWLEDGMENTS

Collaboration on this project is not limited to the two of us but includes cooperation of the generous people who labored those seven years to produce *The Mary Tyler Moore Show*.

Old friends demonstrated a youthful enthusiasm for our inquiries. Grant Tinker, presiding over a new studio, GTG, and its first season of television offerings, allotted hours to talk with us and advise. Jim Brooks and Allan Burns, together and separately, gave that kind of guidance that only the creators could provide. Jay Sandrich, as always, opened his schedule to us and made important calls of introduction that afforded access to numerous other persons in the original MTM company.

New acquaintances gave us added incentive as they broadened our understanding of the show. The cooperation, encouragement, and interest of writers Bob Ellison, David Lloyd, Steve Pritzker, Susan Silver, and Treva Silverman provided new meaning to the episodes that had become so familiar to us. In the time we had with producers Stan Daniels, Lorenzo Music, and Ed. Weinberger we gained a fuller understanding of the process of cooperation that was the MTM hallmark. Marge Mullen, script supervisor and occasional director, gave us an overview that was very enlightening. Ethel Winant, recovering from a serious illness, sat patiently as we pressed dozens of questions that only she, as casting director, could answer. James Burrows, now the distinguished director of *Cheers*, talked about his breaking in with the show and its effect upon him. The talented actors—Ed Asner, Cloris Leachman, Betty White, Gavin MacLeod, John Amos—who gave voices and faces to our favorite television ensemble helped to frame our vision of the show. The late Robert Wood, ten years ago, afforded us a unique view into the CBS world of 1970.

A word must be added concerning the obvious omission in this list. After an initial agreement to talk with us, Mary Tyler Moore decided that she would prefer not to participate in this endeavor. We know the book would have been much the better with her contributions, but we respect her decision. Our determination to proceed, in spite of this disappointment, is a result of three considerations. First, there is a gaping hole in television history as long as such a study remains undone. In this, time itself becomes a factor.

Already John Chulay, Robert Wood, and Ted Knight are gone. Second, we love the show on its merits and we know personally most of the principals involved in its creation. Third, we are dedicated to a special kind of look at this very special series. We intend this book to be nostalgic and celebratory, to be sure, but we also want something seldom offered by those writing in this genre on the "most popular art"—substantial analysis of process and content. So we have pressed on, to paraphrase Bob Wood, with a "primary, exclusive, one-on-one mission" to provide the finest record we could give of this remarkable moment in television history.

Closer to home we wish to acknowledge the support of our colleagues at the University of Richmond and, in particular, the thoughtful comments of Professor Suzanne Jones. We thank Shirley Ann Fisk and Wendy Thompson for valuable assistance. And a special note of gratitude is due Jean Davis, who always finds time in her busy schedule as secretary to the Department of English to answer all calls for help.

Finally, thanks to four patient and helpful students—Lisa Amdur, Melissa Cube, Alan Duckworth, Katherine Turner—whose class in Los Angeles often became the sounding board for our ideas.

CONTENTS

FOREWORD

As one who was extremely proud of *The Mary Tyler Moore Show* and of those who made it work, I am exceedingly pleased at the prospect of a book that celebrates its success. Bob Alley and Irby Brown have spent long hours absorbing the story of *The Mary Tyler Moore Show*. Their research includes their own personal knowledge, gathered since 1975 when we first met. They know the show and, more important, they respect and admire it. Perhaps best of all, they *enjoy* it, the fun of it. The account they offer blends remembrances by the principals with their own perspectives. I couldn't be happier with their celebration of an important moment in television history.

GRANT A. TINKER

To Mary and Frank Tinker - In deep appreciation for making my T.V. debut possible - It really was fun - Fondly Betty Ford

INTRODUCTION

Caveat emptor, as they used to say around the Coliseum, "Let the buyer beware." The purchasers of this book—and we hope there are millions of them—should know at once that it is an unabashed labor of love, a celebration of a show that we place among the finest crafted works in the history of television. Our research shows that general critical opinion seems to agree with this assessment.

We tried, skeptical reader. We really tried to find some things to balance all the sweetness and light. Instead we found unsolicited testimonials that sounded pretty much alike:

"We all loved each other."

"There were almost never any harsh words, and when they came they were uttered for the good of the show."

"I had never known such a smoothly working cast and crew."

"There has never been a group that worked this harmoniously since."

"I had no idea that the rest of television wouldn't be like this, but so far this show stands alone."

We were at first dismayed to find Tinseltown, with its fabled sin and corruption, turning into Sunnybrook Farm before our very eyes. Who among the increasingly suspicious American public would believe this?

As old Hollywood types—we have been visiting, studying, and teaching there off and on for more than a decade—we generally know when we're being conned. And it was obvious that we weren't. People like Grant Tinker, Jay Sandrich, Allan Burns, and Jim Brooks, whom we have known for years, had always been straight with us. And we got the same news about the golden MTM years of 1970 to 1977 from the writers, producers, and actors whom we met for the first time in preparing this book.

Sure, there were a few contradicted details, but they got resolved when we asked people to compare notes. And there were acknowledgments of bruised feelings and even a few raised voices during the seven years. But none of this mattered very much then, and certainly not now. The daily life on and behind the set of *The Mary Tyler Moore Show* was happy and productive. Period.

So what are a pair of poor authors to do to generate interest in their book, for a public ravenous for anecdotal strife amid the lifestyles of the rich and famous? We have no long-kept secrets of the stars to expose, no revelations of hatred and retribution to proclaim. We can't even say bad things about the aesthetic quality of *The Mary Tyler Moore Show*. It was a very, very fine show, and if we could poke around until we found our collective Homers nodding during one of the 168 episodes—well, there isn't much point in belaboring a little misfired joke here or there.

So we are celebrating. Celebrating the twentieth anniversary of the beginnings, the plans that began with Grant and Mary in the fall of 1969, grew quickly in the next few weeks to include Allan Burns and Jim Brooks, then Jay Sandrich, and found success in the first broadcast on September 19, 1970. From then until March 19, 1977, Saturday night on CBS was about as good a place to be as anywhere.

In pitching the idea for this book to our agent and to the publisher, we stressed three enthusiasms of our own, which we felt would be shared by readers: the wonderful joy of the show itself; the large and faithful audience that would welcome nostalgic moments with Mary and Rhoda and Phyllis, Ted, Lou, Murray, and Sue Ann; and the more formal introduction to this audience of a group of talented creators who we knew were delightfully witty and wise. Our own meetings with the writers were full of pleasure— not only for us, quietly revelling in the wonderful material pouring forth for our book, but for them, as they remembered the good old days.

We hope that we have done at least some small amount of justice to these women and men, the writers, producers, directors, executives, actors, and crew who hunkered down week after week and year after year to hone each half hour to the level of their enjoyment and our own. Evidence of their collective creative genius is best seen in the shows themselves, and we have referred to hundreds of details from them to prove the point but also to offer the pleasure of nostalgia. Further proof of talent is demonstrated by the continued success of these people the reader is about to meet, people whose careers still bloom in some of television's most ambitious and successful undertakings. You will recognize many of the names, but others will be introductions. We think there is pleasure in recognizing that in the cutthroat business that is the stereotypical picture of Hollywood, good people are occasionally rewarded, hard work is recognized, and talent is nurtured.

Brava and bravo to the women and men whose success we enjoy again in these pages. As Lou Grant said in the final episode, "I treasure you people." And so do we.

LOVE
IS ALL
AROUND

THE BEGINNINGS

AN IDEA TAKES FORM

The *Mary Tyler Moore Show* was an accident of time and circumstance. The time was 1969, some three years after *The Dick Van Dyke Show* left the air. Mary Tyler Moore had won two Emmy awards for her acting in that series, a television milestone that continues, in syndication, to grace living rooms across the nation.

Mary and Grant Tinker married during the run of the Van Dyke series. Tinker remembers that Mary "signed a deal with Universal and did some indifferent movies." One of those was the 1967 film *Thoroughly Modern Millie,* in which Mary shared the bill with Julie Andrews.

But before the movie career Mary was off to Broadway to star, with Richard Chamberlain, in a musical version of *Breakfast at Tiffany's,* a crushing disaster for Abe Burrows, Edward Albee, and producer David Merrick, who closed the show before it had an official opening night. One reporter described the audience as "alternately bored and shocked." Dwight Whitney, in *TV Guide,* wrote in 1970 that Mary wanted to return to television but "the industry now found it all too easy to believe that Mary wasn't really all that zingy but had merely ridden to her Emmys on the coattails of Dick Van Dyke."

It was, then, ironic that Van Dyke invited Mary to appear on his CBS musical comedy special in 1969. As Tinker remembers, "Mary and Dick did this very fine special, *How to Succeed in the 70's Without Really Trying.* At CBS they had sort of forgotten about this lady who

1

Jim Brooks.   Grant Tinker.

played Laura Petrie. Mary was gangbusters in that special. I don't think Dick threw it to her, but he certainly gave her plenty of funny things to do." Tinker speculates that CBS said, "My God! We've discovered a star." Suddenly the network wanted Mary for a series. "We said they could have her only if they'd give us a series commitment. And they did." The commitment was for thirteen episodes under the complete control of Mary and Grant.

Tinker reconstructed those early events in a recent conversation. "I had worked with Jim Brooks and Allan Burns separately at Fox. Jim had created a show called *Room 222*. He and Gene Reynolds were doing it. And then Jim wanted to go away and do a movie. I was the program guy, supposed to supervise that stuff, at Fox. So Jim did leave to do the movie for television. I knew Allan because he had joined us to write several episodes of *Room 222*. I asked him if he would produce it while Jim was gone, and he did and I couldn't tell the difference between what he did and what Jim did. Both were obviously superior talents. So when the Mary commitment came along, I asked them to collaborate. I had nothing specific at all in my mind. They just sat down together and worked it out."

As the two writers recall, the slate was so clean, they did not even have a name for the series. "We had this remarkable situation where we had an office and an on-the-air commitment and nothing else." They had been given a budget for a one-camera show. As they reflected on the beginnings they insisted they knew nothing about

Allan Burns.   Jay Sandrich.

the business end, "so it wasn't only having to find the show creatively, it was physically making the show happen every week,
something we were not trained at doing." They found Lin Ephraim
to handle business affairs; otherwise, "there was nothing, just space,
and of course an enormous amount of support and encouragement
from Grant." But that support, of necessity, had to be somewhat
quiet. "Grant at that time had to kind of moonlight. He worked as
Vice President for Development at Twentieth Century Fox and this
was not a Fox show. His involvement couldn't be public, but behind
the scenes he was able to do a great deal. From the beginning the
company was Mary and Grant." Brooks noted that while Mary had
a manager, Arthur Price, he had other clients. "So Allan and I were
the only two employees of MTM."

Grant Tinker told us that Mary had wanted to name the company
GAT, "because she knew I would run it. But it's called MTM,
deservedly, because she got the commitment."

The work of this new team in the fall of 1969 resulted in a concept
that they "pitched" to CBS executives in New York. "Obviously we
didn't want to put Mary in a domestic situation comedy because she
had just done probably the most successful such comedy of all time
with Dick Van Dyke. We didn't want to repeat that and that sort of
limited us. We said, 'Okay, here we have a woman thirty years old.'
In 1970 we felt we had to explain why a woman was thirty and
unmarried. In a way that demonstrated how limited our own think-

ing was at the time with respect to women. Our explanation—she probably has to be divorced."

They were convinced they had to explain "thirty and unmarried." As Burns recalls, "We thought, 'Ah! here is our chance to do a divorce.' " "Mary," Brooks says, "loved the idea of being divorced. That part struck her as a very new territory."

Quickly the idea emerged in a plot that showed the ex-husband's parents as loving Mary and seeing their son as a jerk. "They sided with her in the divorce. We got around any problems with blaming 'Laura Petrie' for a divorce by making it clear that it wasn't her fault. It was his fault and his parents were saying it was his fault so therefore she was off the hook. So we could do all those divorce stories." The next problem was to find Mary a job. They proposed that she be a stringer, a "leg" person, for a gossip columnist. Joyce Haber was big at the time.

"We discussed our ideas with a vice president of CBS in Los Angeles. He looked very startled when we told him we were going to have Mary be divorced. We told him all these ideas we're telling you. He asked the question, 'Wouldn't people think she had divorced Dick Van Dyke?' And we said not if her name isn't Petrie, and not if we let the audience see this guy she divorced, maybe make him a character to be seen from time to time. That didn't seem to satisfy him. He looked very unhappy, but we seemed to talk him around to backing us up and he said, 'I'll be behind you on this.' "

Armed with this assurance, Allan and Jim flew to New York to pitch their idea to CBS brass. Accompanying them was Arthur Price, Mary's manager, whom Grant had asked to represent him. Burns remembers that the New York meeting "was in a very womblike room. Not a single window. Very dark. All these pin lights coming straight down. It was very theatrical. Of course the CBS people had been informed we were going to come in with this idea so they were ready for us and they had this huge, fat man in research who gave us his famous list of forbidden subjects—divorce, Jewish people, people from New York, and mustaches—which explains the reason Tom Selleck has never been successful!" Also present were Mike Dann, head of programming, and that Los Angeles VP who was "behind us all the way."

"Mike Dann was leading the attack but he pretty much left it to the research guy. I remember us asking, 'How can that be? Americans don't hate divorced people because there is almost nobody in this country who isn't touched by it in a rather intimate way. How can you hate people who are divorced?'

"They said, 'We cannot tell you you can't do it but we urge you to reconsider.' Grant had very wisely made a deal where he had gone on the hook on the deficit issue so that he was coming at it as a very independent producer and wasn't asking them to cover his deficits. He could pretty well call the shots the way he wanted to. Of course CBS did have the final hand to play and it was clear that Dann was saying, 'We'll really kill the show off, we'll put you on at a bad time.' In fact CBS did just that, even after the concept was changed. The show was put on in a place where we were destined to die." Along the way that Los Angeles CBS vice president "promptly bailed out on us. The minute he saw any kind of flak was going on, he bailed out."

Jim and Allan left the sunless room at CBS thinking that they had maybe done fairly well. In any event their feeling was, "We don't have to do this, we can do something else." The two men are not sure why they were that cocky about it. "We left the room and Arthur said, 'I'm going to talk some business with those guys.' And we went out and waited by the elevator. We found out only a long time later that the executives told Price to 'Get rid of those guys.' To his credit, Arthur never came out and told us what they had said. He and Grant never threw that at us. We always appreciated that. Neither he nor Grant ever said 'We saved your asses.' "

The writers had to decide whether to change the concept or refuse to budge and likely leave the project. Tinker informed the two men that they would do the series or no one would. If they agreed, they had only a week to create a new concept. Allan's recollection "is that we thought it would be very damaging to Mary and Grant if we followed our first reaction, 'Let's leave!' We thought, to have the producers quit is going to make it look like a reflection on them. Somehow it was going to come out that we quit because of Mary and Grant and they had been so good and decent to us, so supportive since this started, that we owed them at least a try. We thought we would take a week or two and see if we could come up with something else. We just thought if we could come up with a concept that we would feel wasn't compromising ourselves too much, we would give it a try."

"We did get a better idea," adds Brooks.

On January 10, 1970, Brooks and Burns completed the "Format for *The Mary Tyler Moore Show*." A twenty-one-page treatment, it begins with a description of Mary's apartment, the large room with its picture window that became familiar as one of the chief settings for the series. A comparison of this format with the opening scenes of the first episode some eight months later (September 19th) reveals a startling maturity of concept at the outset. The two versions are virtually identical in description of characters and in actual dialogue.

From the beginning Burns and Brooks developed a basic idea of setting: "We wanted to trap the characters indoors. We wanted the audience to feel comfortable about a series that seldom ventured outside. Early on we thought of Seattle because of the constant rain there." But they quickly decided instead on Minneapolis, where, Brooks says, "the major industry is snow removal." Over the years almost all of the episodes took place within the comfortable but modest working-woman's apartment or the newsroom of WJM-TV. Mary did move in the fifth season to a high rise, "to spice up the proceedings and give us a little more variety," says director Jay Sandrich.

And so the stage was set for the first scene of the first show, in which Mary, newly arrived in the city, will compete with Rhoda Morgenstern, who lives on the third floor of the converted Victorian mansion, for the most desirable apartment in the building. We are instantly aware that Mary has the edge, since her friend, Phyllis Lindstrom (originally Marna in the format), has outsmarted Rhoda in obtaining a lease for Mary. As she shows Mary the apartment, Phyllis demonstrates much of the character that Cloris Leachman was to embody so hilariously for the next few years: She has rented the apartment in Mary's name without consulting her; she is engaged in a constant struggle for superiority over Rhoda, whom she inexplicably despises; and she dominates her daughter, nine-year-old Bess (Marna, Jr. in the format), who is a ripe candidate for psychoanalysis, at least of the *Reader's Digest* variety.

In this opening scene Mary is primarily uncertain, obviously off base in the game of life as she is currently playing it. She is uncertain about her ability to pay the $130-a-month rent; she is uncertain about her claim to the place, since Bess announces that she thought this was to be Rhoda's apartment; and she is uncertain how to react to the news that Phyllis has already signed her up.

This uncertainty, elaborated and refined during the next few critical years, remained Mary's perhaps most distinguishing trait. In fact, as the series developed, the producers coined several words which became shorthand for describing and directing this aspect of Mary's personality. One of these, "grention," referred to Mary's special brand of puzzlement; another, "fumphering," came to describe her inarticulateness and tendency to sputter in especially tense situations.

Into this little maelstrom of conflicting feelings jumps Rhoda. Her first appearance is a dramatic—and very comic—one. Phyllis draws the drapes to demonstrate the superior view, only to reveal

Rhoda diligently washing "her" picture window. Her first words to Mary are "Hello. Get out of my apartment." It seems that she has already spent a month's salary on brand-new carpeting; she has bought a couch; and now she has cleaned the window—all for *her* apartment.

Typically, the expository information is cleverly handled. It is at this point that we learn about Mary's background, as Phyllis introduces her to Rhoda. She claims that Mary has the greater right to the apartment because she has just been dumped by her doctor/fiancé, whom she supported through medical school, internship, and residency. Throughout this piece of Phyllis-logic, Mary is remonstrating in her uncertain way, trying to indicate that she was not quite so passive, not quite so abused by the man, and is not quite willing to use this unfortunate background as the basis for wresting the apartment away from Rhoda.

But when the aggressive Rhoda pushes this confrontation we see another side of Mary emerge. She, too, can fight. She proclaims that she is not a "pushover," that she can indeed "push back." We know that she will get the apartment.

This is a remarkable opening scene, establishing a setting, a time, a tone, and three essential characters. There will be a great deal of embellishing, but we already know that we have a young career woman in search of an apartment, a job, and people who will help build her new life. We suspect that this overbearing landlady, Phyllis, and this aggressive tenant, Rhoda, will reveal softer, more ingratiating sides.

In fact Rhoda, in particular, was to become an unlikely but intimate friend. Burns remembers their discussions of how to develop the relationship between a self-assured, independent Jewish girl from Manhattan and this nice, quiet WASP girl from Smalltown. Although the two women will have preconceptions about each other, they will discover similarities of situation and purpose out of which their friendship will be forged. But they will never be remotely alike.

An essential ingredient often mentioned in the format, then picked up in the dialogue of the first episode, is the toughness beneath Mary's stereotypically passive demeanor. "She was partly," says Brooks, "a quivering *chick*—as that term used to be employed—too open and trusting, a sort of Norman Rockwell creation." But the creators also liked to think of her as a "Presbyterian militant," who could certainly "push back" when the situation demanded it, even though she might be reluctant to do so. Furthermore, in their original conception, "we never made a point of it, but in our eyes

Mary was not a virgin. She wasn't a man-hungry animal like Rhoda, but very definitely she had an active, fully rounded sex life."

Hearing their description of the two women, we can sense why Brooks felt compelled to say to us in 1988 that "it was a different time." In 1970 the writers had equated "essentially feminine" with "quivering fear." They often referred to the two friends as "girls." And sure enough they do "explain" why Mary is single. It would be interesting to know what kind of characteristics would have been assigned to Mary had she been divorced. Finally, in the early descriptions virginity is equated with wholesomeness. This clearly was not a belief held by the creators, but just a claim that might be understood as a traditional attitude.

Along the way in these depictions the writers have told us something of their own views on society in 1970. They were prepared to brand the seventies as lacking openness, niceness, and trust. Perhaps they were prescient. Against this perception of the coming decade they delineate a character, Mary Richards, who they describe as open and nice, having traits in sharp contrast with the world. In that world, openness, they said, would be for parklands; niceness for Betty White, who could make a living out of it. Little did they imagine that four years later White would be cast as Sue Ann, who would become etched in our minds as a conniving, sex-craving manipulator.

The next scene is of Mary's job interview at WJM-TV, where we get a glimpse of the newsroom staff in its earliest development. Full of anxiety she enters their terrain, responding to a job advertisement. As Lou ushers her past Murray (first called Richard) and into his office, he begins the interview with a totally unexpected question. As he reaches into his right-hand desk drawer he asks whether she would care to join him for a drink. She properly declines, but he insists, and so she asks for a brandy Alexander. Somehow this is much funnier than the original Tom Collins of the format. Without comment, Lou matter-of-factly returns the two shot glasses and whiskey bottle to the drawer, closes it, and suggests coffee.

Mary hands Lou an application just as he tells her that the job has been filled. She is disappointed and, with some spirited resentment, asks why he made her feel so comfortable if the job was no longer available. She has made her point: as she struggles awkwardly into her coat to leave, Lou blurts out that the station does have another job to fill. Burns remembers that at one point Lou had a line suggesting that he wanted a man for this other job, but they could at least talk about it. No one seems to remember why the line was dropped.

The three principals in Rhoda's apartment.

What follows is one of the classic scenes of series television. As it evolved through minor changes from the format, it began with Lou asking Mary's religion:

Mary: Mr. Grant, I don't know quite how to say this, but you're not allowed to ask that when someone is applying for a job. It's against the law.

Lou: Wanna call a cop?

Mary: No.

Lou: Good. Would you think I was violating your civil rights if I asked if you're married?

Mary: Presbyterian.

Lou: Huh?

Mary: Well, I decided I'd answer your religion question.

This begins the pattern of disjointed questions and answers, in which her marital status and typing ability get hilariously mixed ("Fifty-five reasons why you aren't married?" "No, fifty-five words per minute"). Finally, Lou tells Mary just to answer his questions. Her answer suggests some of the aforementioned Presbyterian militancy: "You've been asking a lot of very personal questions that don't have a thing to do with my qualifications."

In the uneasy silence after this outburst, Mary seems to wonder whether she should have uttered this mild reprimand. The stage is set for the most often quoted interchange from the series:

Lou: You know what? You've got spunk.
Mary: Well . . .
Lou: I *hate* spunk.

But she gets the job of associate producer. It pays $10 less a week than the secretarial job for which she had applied!

Brooks and Burns summarize their feelings about the series in words that echo their conclusion to the original format. "Mary's relationships with Rhoda and Lou," they say, "were the key to the whole thing. With Rhoda especially it was the constant blend of affection and conflict. With Lou it was kind of mutual protection of each other."

They never lost sight of the comedic intent of their series, even though they had designed it to focus on this woman who was "making it on her own" in a world dominated by men. "We thought of the difficulty of being thirty, single, and female in the very tough world of the 1970s, and we wanted to find the comedy—but also the meaning—in that."

The writers now had a concept, an empty office, one cast member, no staff, no scripts, and only eight months until the opening week on CBS.

2

THE CASTING

As any viewer can testify, casting is the key to a successful series. Somehow you just feel right about the mix of characters and are prepared to give them a chance to become part of your family. If the scripts are poor, then the cast may be unable to sustain the show, but the chemistry of the people is the ingredient that gives the scripts a chance. Obviously, the better the writing, the better the actors' chances of creating the magic that captures the audience. Allan and Jim knew they had the best in Mary, but could they ever hope to match her *Van Dyke* cast of Rose Marie, Carl Reiner, Morey Amsterdam, and Richard Deacon? It was suggested they hire Ethel Winant to do the casting, a particularly bold choice since Ethel was at the time a vice president at CBS. Brooks and Burns, while noting that Dave Davis and Mary took part in the casting, assign the majority of credit to Winant. "She was wonderful. She was stalwart and fought a lot of battles for us, our casting battles when people would say to us things like, 'Ed Asner is a fine dramatic actor, but . . .' " Burns adds, "We owe a debt to Ethel. She is a great lady of the business. She was a tower of strength and courage."

Winant remembers her first meeting with Brooks and Burns. Allan and Jim "called me and asked me to lunch." She reminded them that she was head of casting for CBS. "I'm your enemy. I'm the one sitting over here at the network, and I'm the one that's going to say yes or no." She pointed out that "when you cast a

11

show you become a part of it and it's hard to keep your objectivity." Winant recalls that she "could make executive decisions, could say, 'Yes, this person is the one who's going to be in this show.' It was a lot easier to do that than to cast a lot of shows."

Interestingly, CBS appeared to have no problem with Winant taking the job. "When I took on this special casting assignment, the network was thrilled, because they felt that this would give them more control. I was the person they thought they wanted to make decisions for the network. And so if I was casting the show, that made them feel that somebody was looking after the network's interests, somebody who was not an employee of the company and wouldn't be intimidated. I didn't have to think, 'Gee, if MTM gets mad at me, they'll fire me.' And it was good for me, because I was never afraid of losing my job if I disagreed or if I said, 'No, you can't cast that person,' or 'You must see this person'—things that many casting directors are afraid to do, because they don't want to create a problem. They don't want to be abrasive or push too hard. They need the job."

Ethel Winant "just loved Jim and Allan. They were so young, they were so enthusiastic. I read the first script and I just loved it. The characters were wonderful. I thought it was the best script I had read. So even though it was against my own rules, I did want to cast it. The characters were wonderful. So I said yes."

The task of casting is never easy, but with Burns and Brooks, who would see anyone, at length, who wanted to audition for a part, it sometimes seemed as if decisions would never be confirmed. As one friend notes, "Allan and Jim were young, polite, and decent. They cared about people and they wanted to be fair. So they interviewed everybody."

Winant describes the two young writers/producers as they worked with her on the task. "We must have seen a hundred people, because Jim and Allan wanted to see everyone. And they were so nice. They read everybody. They were wonderful to each person. Everybody who left that office thought they had gotten the part. Jim and Allan would spend hours, and if it was a terrible reading, they would try to make it better.

"It was very hard sometimes—as with a person who was plainly twenty years too old, whom they saw because a friend or an agent had convinced them they should see that person. It didn't matter. They treated everyone so marvelously. Agents would call me the next day and say, 'Wow, I haven't heard from you.' 'Your client was terrific,' I would say, 'gave a wonderful reading, but you know they're not quite right for the part.' And the agent couldn't believe it. I spent several months on it.

"Some of it was easy. Cloris was clearly Phyllis, to me. I could have cast Phyllis immediately. I knew Cloris was Phyllis, I just knew it. One of the hard things was that Jim and Allan saw her not as a comedienne. She'd been doing the mother on *Lassie* and all these dramatic roles. I knew she could do comedy, because I had worked with her in New York in the theater. But she hadn't been doing comedies on TV. Then, too, this was before *The Last Picture Show*, and the world wasn't standing in line to hire her. But she was just wonderful. So I decided on her and knew that it was just a matter of waiting it out.

"I prayed that she wouldn't get another job. Cloris would never have the patience to wait. But luckily she was free-lancing, so she was off in Mexico for weeks, doing some terrible movie. And every time she came back to town I'd bring her in. Finally, after I had brought her back about five times, Jim one day said to me, 'Ethel, do you think we should hire Cloris for Phyllis?' And I said, 'Yes, I think that would be nice.' And he said, 'Well, perhaps we should do that.' It got to be such a joke; every time we'd have a reading I'd bring her in. And of course she got the part."

Cloris Leachman is a close friend and admirer of Ethel Winant. Commenting upon her first impressions of the *Mary* environment, Leachman remarks, "I went in and read for them. I was very impressed with the care and the intensity of their caring, and the absolute joy that was around them. They were bright and you were immediately not in a judgmental situation, which doesn't bother me anyway, but it was instant. I felt that without question this was the thing I ought to do."

Winant also quickly identified another cast member in her mind. She was convinced Gavin MacLeod should play the part of Murray Slaughter. "I knew that was going to be very late casting, because Jim and Allan were convinced early that Gavin should play Lou Grant. They never thought of him as Murray because they had seen him as Big Chicken on *Hawaii Five-O*. But I knew that was a matter of time, that eventually we could bring Gavin in and he'd get the part, because he was so right for Murray."

Gavin MacLeod was unaware of Ethel's thoughts on his playing Murray. He does remember the day of casting. "My agent told me Brooks and Burns wanted me to read for the new show. I had worked with Mary on *The Dick Van Dyke Show* and I was crazy about her. I saw the script, and while I thought the Lou Grant character was fabulous—that was the part I was called to read—something drew me to the Murray Slaughter character. I saw myself more as Mary's peer than as her boss. To be honest, I thought I was right for Murray. Well, I read for the Lou Grant part with Ethel and Allan and Jim there. On the way out I said, 'Would you mind if I read for Murray?' They were surprised but said fine. I did it and Jim just fell on the floor laughing. As I left Ed Asner was out in the waiting room pacing back and forth. That afternoon my agent called to say they wanted me to play Murray."

Allan Burns differs slightly in his memory. "Actually that character was pictured as a sort of fiftyish guy based on someone Jim had known at CBS in New York who was gay. He was a newswriter and very funny. He kept a pair of figure skates in the bottom drawer of his desk so that he could go out and ice-skate in Rockefeller Center at lunchtime. In the first episode or two we planned to have Murray go into the drawer and there'd be a pair of ice skates. He was going to be overtly gay, but we decided not to, I'm not sure why. We had in mind casting Charles Nelson Reilly but he was in a play in New York and wasn't available.

"Gavin came in to read for the part of Lou, and the first thing he said when he came in was, 'I'll read for this, but I'm right for Murray.' We told him, 'No, we want you to read for Lou.' After he read it we thought, 'No, he's just not right for this.' And then he said, 'Now can I read for Murray?' He did and we looked at each other and said, 'That's it, that's what we want.' "

Ethel expounds further on the willingness of Jim and Allan to see everyone and at some length. "We saw hundreds of people for those parts in between. Not only because Allan and Jim wanted to see everybody, but also because they got ideas from people. They were so creative. They were building an encyclopedia of actors for the series. And they were seeing different ways to develop each character. Every actor brings new things to the role. Jim and Allan would see how it was if you played it older, younger, if somebody was hard, if somebody was soft, if the balance changed. It was extraordinary. They really cared, and everybody who came in they really learned from, even if they were terrible."

When Winant speaks about the casting of Ted Baxter, she recalls that it was different from the others. "Leonard Stern was casting a pilot. I wanted to cast it, because there was a girl I wanted to play the lead in it. I knew nobody else would ever cast her. There was a part in it that had no lines but that needed a very distinguished-looking actor. It was hard because to get somebody that had that kind of style but who is never going to say anything is not easy. Ted Knight was great-looking, but he wasn't working very much. I thought he would be wonderful for the part in that other show, would be able to do it very well. It would be great for him to have a series, because it would pay the rent and he could go on doing off-Sunset plays and at least have some money in the bank. Dave Davis was the line producer on that pilot. I didn't think I'd even bring anybody else in for the part; I'd just bring Ted in. And Dave said to me, 'He's wonderful, but we shouldn't use him in this because there's another show that's going to come up for which he would be wonderful. I can't tell you what it is yet, but this part isn't worth it, just wait.' 'Oh, great,' I thought, 'first of all, it isn't going to be all that easy to get somebody great. And secondly, I'm doing an actor I like out of a job.' But David was so adamant about it, and he felt so strongly about it, that we didn't use Ted for the job; and of course when I read the *Mary* show I knew he'd seen Knight as Ted Baxter. And he was right. It was worth waiting for."

Ethel notes how this simple event radically changed Ted's life. "As an actor he had really come upon hard times and was doing one- or two-line parts, or, if you had a bunch of army officers, he was the colonel, or a distinguished-looking judge who could say 'Guilty.' That was the sort of thing he was doing. And then he got this part and, of course, became a superstar. But it took us a long time, because I had some concerns that playing Ted as mature as he was—he wasn't written that way, he was originally sort of a contemporary of Mary's—that you might feel sorry for him, that he might be sad. As opposed to having this young guy, who was much like the character in *Broadcast News*, arrogant but a stupid journalist. But Ted gave wonderful readings and Jim and Allan were so bright that, after having lots of other people read, including many who were younger, they made adjustments in the script. That's why Jim and Allan were so terrific. When they saw somebody they really liked, they'd still go through other readings, then they'd come back and make the changes necessary to use him. They wouldn't try to make him play something he couldn't; they wouldn't misuse him. And of course it was extraordinary for Ted."

Burns and Brooks recall their initial questions about Ted Knight. "I guess the only one we argued about was Ted because our concept had been younger and we just had a different impression in our heads. It took an internal debate and us getting rid of our preconceptions about Ted."

The character of Rhoda was central to the initial concept, but, as Winant remembers, "We didn't have Rhoda cast just a week or ten days before we were going to shoot. I was really in trouble. We had had a couple of people we saw and had back—people like Linda Lavin. I must add, the reasons for rejection had nothing to do with her talent. We just couldn't cast it; it was such a difficult role. Sometimes the actors would come into the room and they'd read wonderfully, but when they would read with Mary it just wouldn't work because that relationship was so difficult. If she was too mean and too hard, you'd hate her because she was being so mean to Mary; and if she wasn't, there was nothing for Mary to play against. You couldn't have two Marys. I had failed; I had just not come up with anyone to play that part. And I was scared. I didn't know what I was going to do. We were getting down to the wire and our choices were not good. I'd reached the point where I had my department in New York looking at everybody there and my department in L.A. was doing the same. And if anybody looked good, I'd either fly to New York or fly them to L.A.

"I was going to the theater every night in the hope that something would happen. And finally one night I went to see the first act of a group of little sketches at the Melrose Theater in L.A., and then for the second act I had arranged to go to another theater. I had to cover all these plays. And in that first play I saw Valerie Harper. She did a sketch, and I thought, 'Oh my God, she's perfect.' She seemed right. She was the right type, the right age, and she was very good. The sketches were produced by an agent from New York and I was in such a hurry because I knew I had to get to the other theater, so I just grabbed the program and left to see the second act of the other play.

"The next morning I decided to call Valerie in. Usually in showcase the program will have the name and address of the actor or they'll at least give you the agent's name. But in this program there was only the name. I called the theater and said I was trying to reach Valerie Harper and they said, 'Oh, that was a four-walls rental and we don't know how to reach her. There was this group of people that came in from New York and there's this guy and we don't know who he is.' I said, 'Somebody must have written a check. Do you have the check?' But I couldn't find anything. I was crazed. I finally had found Rhoda and I couldn't find the actress. It made me feel I had just discovered this major star—and promptly lost her! I thought, 'Well, she's got to be a member of something,' and so we called Equity and we called the Screen Actors Guild and she wasn't there. We called New York and we couldn't find her. According to the program, she had understudied in New York.

By that time Winant was desperate and her secretary was going crazy. "Meanwhile we were seeing more and more people, but about three or four days later my secretary came in with an envelope that she gave to me and said, 'Could this be the Valerie Harper you're looking for?' The guy who had produced the play had now sent out packets to everyone who had attended—we had signed this little book—and there was a picture of Valerie and a phone number. So I got her in and set up a reading for her. The day she came we brought some girl in from Vegas, we'd flown her in, we were that desperate, and she was terrible and she also had behaved very badly. And Valerie had to wait something like three hours, and I was terrified that she'd leave, or that something would happen and she'd go away. She was my last hope. But she said no, she wasn't in any hurry, she had nothing to do all afternoon. She was happy to be there.

The reading was successful ("a miracle," recalls Winant), but there was one problem, a feeling that Valerie Harper was too young, pretty, and sophisticated for the role. Jay Sandrich saw the solution. He called Valerie and suggested that she "dress down" and "not wear makeup" when she returned for the second reading. Winant summarizes, "They loved her; she got the part."

The part of Lou Grant was critical. There appear to have been three options available after a long search. As noted earlier, Winant preferred to cast MacLeod as Murray rather than Lou. Winant remembers that Brooks and Burns wanted a well-known comic for the role. "That was the first choice, and I would have died. He was wrong. And Arthur Price wasn't going to have him, but for a different reason. Artie wanted to protect the show and he didn't want somebody who was going to be terribly disruptive. He wanted to protect Mary, and the series. It was Mary's first show and he represented Mary."

It seems that this was the most contentious of the situations surrounding casting. Brooks and Burns recall their thoughts. "We couldn't cast the part of Lou Grant for months, and one of us had the bright idea that a famous stand-up comedian should play that part. We said, 'He's got everything we're looking for. He's kind of crotchety, he's the right age, and we fell in love with the idea. We sort of put it out there to Grant and everybody that that's what we were going to do. We got a call from Arthur Price, who said, 'Listen, have I ever told you guys what to do?' We said, 'No.' He said, 'I'm telling you that if you cast this man, you will regret it the rest of your lives. He will destroy the relationships you need in a three-camera show.' "

Brooks continues, "It was very important for Mary to cast nice people. We kept on talking about that. She had had that experience with *The Dick Van Dyke Show* and she wanted to continue it. I don't think we cared. That hadn't been our value system. We had just come off of a series where it was a little cranky. It wasn't on our list of priorities the way it was with Mary—that people should be nice."

Winant was arguing on another level. "I always knew that part could not be played by a comic, that if Lou Grant were not played by an actor, the show wouldn't work. Lou Grant had to be played by an actor who had good timing. He had to be a real character, not a comic. It was hard, because comedy writers work very hard and then they want to hear their jokes and it's harder to get an actor always to find the joke, to play it as opposed to just doing schtick.

So when you're young and new, and a comic comes in and reads your lines, you get every laugh. But you could destroy your show for your laugh. What's terribly hard is to hear your lines and know that they're not getting laughs and have the patience to wait and let the actor find them.

"Thank God for Grant Tinker. We sat there with this list and Ed Asner was on it. Grant came in and said, 'Ed,' and somehow they heard him. They were tired of me saying 'actor, actor, actor.' But Grant had seen dailies of a Movie of the Week featuring Ed Asner. He picked up a list and said, 'Well, here he is, Ed Asner could do it.' Asner came in and they loved him in spite of a terrible reading. They loved his quality."

Indeed, Burns and Brooks agree that it was a bad beginning. "He read badly the first time and it was very awkward at first. We were very naive. With Ed it was so bad, we did not know what to say. We knew he was a good actor and when he left we kind of shook our heads because we had thought he was going to be it and he was really terrible. We thought, 'Maybe it's us or maybe we don't know what we're doing wrong, but we're not getting what we want.' Just then our secretary stuck her head in and said, 'Ed Asner's back. He came back and says he would like to talk to you.' He walked in and said, 'I was so shitty I can't believe it and you just sat there and let me read that bad. You were polite to me and I left. I know I can do this part.' He said, 'Just tell me what the hell it is you want!' " He came back. He read with Mary. Burns recalls that he and Brooks were thrilled but Mary reacted, "You're kidding." In the end she accepted their judgment.

Ed Asner's version of the casting completes the picture. He does not recall the leaving and returning, but the evidence is clear that the first reading created uneasiness, calling for a second effort. "My recollection is that Ethel Winant, when asked by Allan and Jim, 'Can Ed Asner do comedy?' replied, 'He can do anything.' She'd seen me once or twice, so she was a brave soul. In fact, she was one of the few executives at CBS who believed in the show.

"I was given the script. I had come to L.A. in 1961 and had experienced constant growth, and then in 1967 and 1968 came a cropper. The year 1969, though, turned into my best year. At the same time I had changed, I had been bitten, I had been stymied by a drop in employment. So I came to *Mary Tyler Moore* and the script just after my best year, but having been chastened just previous to that. I read the script and I was dazzled by it. It was the best piece of writing I'd ever seen. Any comedy I had ever done before this I was always very insecure in, because I could always get to the comedy but never repeat it. Plus the fact that in those days, the golden age of comedy was yet to come, at least for us. Success meant being stubborn and pursuing bigger and bigger guest spots on hour shows. The general feeling was that you never got discovered on a comedic show. So we paid no attention to comedy, my agent and I, in those first nine years. This script came along, just blew the scales off my eyes. So I went in to read, with not a great deal of confidence.

"Allan and Jim asked me to read and afterward they said, 'That's a very intelligent reading. The next time, do it all-stops-out.' I did what they told me. I acted crazy, paranoid, schizoid, you name it, and they're sitting over there laughing their heads off. They said to do that next time. And I said, 'Well, I'm not sure I can do what you want, so why don't you read me now—that way—and see if I can do what you want me to do. If I don't, then don't have me back.' They were flustered by that. They had another appointment they had to get to but they said all right. So I did it and they laughed their asses off. And they said, when we have you back to read with Mary, read it just like that. How did I read it? I had no idea what I'd done. So, I came back a couple of weeks later, read with Mary. They laughed their asses off again. After I left Mary said, 'Are you sure?' And they both nodded. She was as nonplussed as I was with my entire approach. We did the hiring scene from the first show. I think primarily they were seeing how far I was willing to drop my pants, how inventive or imaginative or crazy I could get, in case they wanted me to go that far."

At long last the casting was complete and the ensemble was there—to be directed, scripted, and thrust at a dubious network.

3

FILMING FOR
THE ON-AIR COMMITMENT

DARKNESS AND DAWN

The months between January and June 1970 were filled with activities surrounding casting and writing. But there were also political realities that would affect the future of the *Mary* series in dramatic ways. CBS brass was in the process of changing the guard. The old order of Mike Dann (1963–70) was giving way to the leadership of Robert Wood (1969–76). As head of programming, it was Dann who, in 1969, commissioned Mary and Grant to make the thirteen episodes. As we have learned, Dann and his associates reacted negatively to the team of Brooks and Burns in the fall of that year. Tinker's refusal to capitulate to their wish that the two men be replaced was, it appears, sufficient to poison attitudes in New York concerning the project. In spite of the producers' willingness to abandon the divorce theme, an atmosphere of contention remained. Thus, while Brooks remembers spending "maybe three times the normal period casting," because "we felt we had an advantage having an on-air commitment and could start, knowing we had a show," the first warning of trouble came in February.

Ethel Winant was particularly sensitive to network attitudes since she was a CBS executive. She recalls, "CBS announced its fall lineup on February 22, Washington's birthday. We were working on the show when they announced the schedule and gave it its terrible time period. Jim and Allan were almost suicidal."

Marge Mullen, who served for the seven years as script supervisor, recalls, "Everybody knew we'd have a tough time overcoming this. But I don't believe you can think about that, especially when you're doing comedy. You just try to do the best show that you possibly can and hope that the network will reslate it or somebody will say, 'This is too good to sacrifice at this time, let's find a better slot.' Unfortunately, the networks don't usually do that; they don't come around fast enough."

Winant has a particularly significant perspective on the clash with CBS, since she was working both sides of the street. The announcement in February "was Mike Dann's schedule. He had laid it out for the fall and *Mary* was scheduled on Tuesday night after *Hee-Haw*. It was in a terrible time period."

Burns has a vivid memory of the circumstances. "We had been put on in the death slot at 7:30 P.M. Tuesday. We came after *Hee-Haw* and we were in between it and *To Rome With Love* with John Forsythe, which was being bucked up by the addition of Walter Brennan. We were going to be in that time slot, in the hammock between those two shows against *Mod Squad*, which was a top show the past season, and the *Don Knotts Show*, which everybody thought was going to be the smash of all times. What CBS had done was say, 'You're dead, you're dead as a doornail,' and we knew it. We were given that slot in February, I think, and prior to our shooting show one. We were not set to shoot until June. The time slot was based on our scripts, which they hated."

Their basic point, that they were in a death slot, is accurate. However, all the principals in the events have, in fact, slightly flawed memories. The CBS schedule released on February 20 put *To Rome With Love* at 7:30, *The Mary Tyler Moore Show* at 8:00, and *Hee Haw* at 8:30 on Tuesday night.

The problem that developed between CBS and MTM was exacerbated by the fact that, as the scripts were written during the early months of 1970, they were sent to CBS for examination. Winant notes, "Nobody liked the scripts. The development people hated them. They didn't think they were funny. They couldn't understand them. They were used to a different kind of comedy."

So even as the show was being cast and a production company was taking shape, tension had been building. Winant recalls, "CBS executives would call over every day and scream, 'Fix the scripts.' These wonderful scripts. One day Allan had just had it and he responded to one of the callers, 'Well, there's one of your executives over there who likes the scripts. Ethel Winant likes the scripts.' I came back to the network that day and was summoned to the front office. They asked, 'Did you tell Allan Burns and Jim Brooks that you liked the scripts?' and I said, 'I guess I did.' They asked why I did that. And I said there were two reasons—'I liked the scripts and I'm casting the show. I don't think it would be very productive to tell them I don't like their scripts, particularly since I do.' "

When Ethel went back to her CBS office Jim and Allan called to tell her they thought they might have gotten her in trouble, even gotten her fired. She replied, "No, it's not going to get me fired, but it's not going to help my reputation." Indeed, Winant saw those months as very, very hard. "The show was treated like a stepchild. The network was convinced they were stuck with it."

Throughout the months before filming began CBS programming executives continued to express dislike for the material they were reading. But there wasn't anything they could do since Grant and Mary had the commitment. Winant comments on the MTM team, "Mary was tough. She just wouldn't back down. CBS tried to get her to give up the writers, to fire Jim and Allan, to bring other people in, to write the show more conventionally. They thought the show was too unconventional, the characters were too strange. Mary and Grant supported their producers and Jim and Allan were tough about their material, as well they might have been."

In the spring, under these tense conditions, CBS directed Grant Tinker to supply a three-minute filmed segment of the first episode for promotion with network affiliate stations. They rented a studio, hired two cameras, and produced the interview scene. That scene was the jewel of the show in its final version, but this time there was no chance to rehearse, the lighting was unprofessional, and Ed Asner's acting was still a little too heavy for this comedic scene. With no time to reshoot, Jay, Grant, Allan, and Jim decided not to risk a promotional fiasco.

It was June when the first episode was ready for filming. The stories related by the nervous participants in that week's drama paint a portrait of a series destined for disaster. Knowing that CBS was unhappy and that the show had been placed in a death time slot, the company gamely assembled for the first time on Tuesday before an audience to provide a few scenes for network viewing.

It had been a difficult week. Brooks and Burns recall an incident that demonstrates the tension leading up to Tuesday night. Jim Brooks begins the description of the event. "During rehearsal the actor playing the guy with whom Mary had had the affair threw the script on the floor, derisively. He just threw it down. He had gotten a big cast laugh from the other people at the table. They laughed that he had done that to the script, but we went crazy and just almost annihilated him. I think that was a very healthy thing to happen to the whole life of the series at this critical point. It was one of those things that happen and it was entirely spontaneous, one of those accidents that really helped us. It meant that after this everyone understood that scripts were to be respected. They always got changed, but the script was always a part of that show that the cast tried to make work, tried to make the existing script work before changing it."

Burns: Also it meant that we asserted ourselves as the ones who would run the show.
Brooks: We took control of the show.
Burns: The actors were not going to do that.
Brooks: Everything about Mary herself doesn't want control.
Burns: The question was whether *we* wanted that kind of control.

Of course they did—either in their own persons or in the delegated form that they later passed to such peer producers as Ed. Weinberger and Stan Daniels. But at the time the actor's derisive gesture was troublesome, a moment in a tense week that exacerbated the problems.

A far more ominous circumstance surrounding the fateful Tuesday-to-come concerned the filming itself. In an especially animated conversation, the two producers shudder over their memories of a crazy innovation:

Burns: Somebody asked us if we would test a new system of cameras.
Brooks: Oh my God!
Burns: We wanted to do a run-through with an audience and test these cameras before we did the actual show.
Brooks: That's why we did the run-through?
Burns: Yeah. It was a disaster. I think we were going to do it anyway, then we decided to do it with that camera system. Even the scenes that later on became so classic— four days later without touching a word of it, they went through the roof—were dismal.

But that wasn't enough. In an effort to control the Tuesday night experience and make everything just right, Brooks and Burns had decided to do the audience warm-up themselves. As we shall mention several times later, *The Mary Tyler Moore Show* was blessed during its seven years with a series of excellent comics who would succeed brilliantly in putting the studio audience in the mood to laugh—a very important ingredient in the spontaneity and fun of a live show, especially when a show is being filmed and might require three hours of shooting before an audience. It is a cruelly demanding job, not one for amateurs. Jim and Allan were amateurs.

Brooks: That night the two of us did the audience warm-up. You know when Gleason freezes on television? I was the lucky one, because that was me. Allan, unfortunately, could articulate human speech, so he had to stumble along.

Burns: We were too naive. We thought as producers we had to do the warm-up because producers in the past had done them. Those were people who loved to do it and we were petrified. We were terrified.

Brooks: It was horrendous.

Burns: Our story editor, Lorenzo Music, said to us, "I could do that and you wouldn't have to worry about it." It was his kind way of saying, "You guys are so shitty." As the evening dragged along, the fact that we were bombing so badly in warm-up was bothering us as much as the fact that the show was bombing. It was just awful. Our production manager, Lin Ephraim, who looked like Mandrake the Magician, told us he could do better, this most serious guy in the world. And we were almost prepared to let him. We decided we were even worse than we thought.

Sometimes people are too hard on themselves; there is some fun in looking back after success and seeing the dismal beginnings. But in this case the truth seems literal. As for the show itself, Marge Mullen calmly corroborates the dramatic description of failure:

It did not go very well. The first big laugh didn't come until the second scene when Lou Grant says, "I hate spunk." To us it was all funny, because we knew where the actors were going, but the audience didn't. The only character they knew coming in was Mary. They remembered her from the *Van Dyke* show. But they didn't yet know her in her new role. Valerie had worked in New York, but the West Coast audience didn't know her. Cloris had been out of the business for quite a while and also came from New York. Ed Asner had not done comedy.

Enter Jay Sandrich, the director of 70 percent of the *Mary Tyler Moore* episodes. Of all the decisions made by the producing team, none was more significant than this choice. On the *Mary* show Jay

was constantly on the floor directing camera movement and place-
ment, as well as constructing the ambiance for and providing direction to the actors. It was there, with writers and producers sitting
just behind him, that he exercised that brilliance that often created
tension with the imagination and genius of Jim Brooks. Tinker
speaks of those moments in positive terms as he remarks, "The
show always looked great when it went on, but there were lots of
wonderful disagreements about the material—Jim versus Jay, for
instance. Those were the most celebrated contretemps. It was exhila-
rating to hear those two guys arguing over a joke or a line or a piece
of business. And Allan, that great and honorable guy, an amazingly
organized executive for such a creative person, would be the
mediator."

Jay's full involvement came in that fateful June week. He remembers, "When it came time to do the first show somebody approached
us and said, 'We'll put it on tape for you so the audience can see it
because we have a new system of filming and taping at the same
time.' The system split the image. It would go to film and at the
same time there would be a television image. For some reason we
agreed to try this gimmick. We weren't going to do the series with
this system. The Tuesday filming was just a test. The cast was not
quite ready, the shots had not been planned out, and I don't think
Ed Asner was quite at the same place as an actor that he was on the
following Friday.

"Then, too, the audience disliked Valerie because, I think, in her
opening scene she was yelling at Mary. I don't think they particularly liked Ed in the second scene, the one that became such a
classic. It didn't get any laughs because, for whatever reason, Ed
was playing it a little too mad. It just didn't work, so that run-
through was a disaster. The audience didn't laugh because, I think,
we as a group of actors just weren't ready yet, plus the shots
probably were bad. We all sat around afterward and I think the
major change that was made was suggested by Marge Mullen, who
was the script supervisor. She said, 'Why don't you have Phyllis's
daughter, who was a little girl, say, "Gee, I really like Aunt Rhoda"?'
And that was it. We were in trouble if Rhoda was unpopular with
the audience. Her relationship with Mary was going to be the main
key to the whole series."

Ethel Winant offers her close-up feelings of Black Tuesday. "It
was a terribly hot and humid day, 102 degrees, and the smog was a
first-stage alert, or worse. The air-conditioning wasn't really working on the stage because it was too hot. It was designed to take the
temperature down from ninety maybe to eighty, but not this, and so

the stage was impossibly hot. When I got there to see the run-through everybody was standing outside, but not because of the heat. It was because there had been a bomb scare. A bomb scare, can you imagine! Finally we all got to go back in. They were trying something with a video camera on top of a film camera. These huge, heavy cameras made it impossible for the audience to see anything. Those great lumbering cameras were between you and the actors.

"Nobody from the network came, as evidence of how supportive they were. This would normally be called the pilot, but since there was no pilot it was the first episode. The sound system was terrible, the audience couldn't hear what was going on. They didn't laugh. They had this little break where you go outside and the actors go to change. It was so hot, people left. The friend I was with asked, 'Is Mary married in this series?' I said, 'Bob, the entire first act is about her not being married.' He said, 'You know, I didn't hear anything.' And I thought, 'No wonder we're having such a hopeless audience response.' I, of course, had read that first act out loud so many times that I knew it by heart. So I could hear the lines, but he didn't hear anything.

"At the end of the show I was so impressed because Mary came out and thanked the audience for hanging in, for staying. I would have been in my dressing room in tears at the end of that awful evening."

With this beginning, things looked very bleak indeed.

After Brooks and Burns dismissed their office company on Tuesday evening, they set to work on revision. Elsewhere in the city another drama was unfolding. Tinker relates, "Mary and I went home after doing this vital run-through. It had been a disaster, it had gone very badly, nothing worked, and Mary and I went home in silence. About midnight she started to cry. She was distraught and said, 'I can't do it, this is the most embarrassing thing, it's going to fall on its face.' She was as upset as I've ever seen her, and she's very professional, as everybody knows. I'd never done what I then did. I picked up the phone and called, knowing the guys were still there struggling with the rewrite. I called down there and talked to Jim and Allan. I said, 'Mary's hysterical. You guys are not doing it right. Fix it!' I didn't have any good advice to give them, I just said, 'Fix it!' They didn't reassure me with their comments, which were something like 'Yeah, we know it's not working and we're trying.' But when we did do the shooting on Friday, it went remarkably well. So they had fixed it. And Mary by that time had pulled herself together. They're the only ones who knew about that phone call. And I'm the only one who saw this wonderful, dedicated actress going to pieces before my very eyes. The rest of them just saw the professional that she always has been."

Brooks and Burns reflect on that call. Burns recounts, "I remember after the disaster getting a call from Grant—an angry phone call—asking, 'When are you guys going to start acting like producers?' He started throwing Carl Reiner at us. And we reminded him that not all producers are Carl Reiner. He's a hail-fellow-well-met kind of guy who always sees the bright side of things. And we told Grant that we were very shy and introspective people and he'd have to deal with us on those terms, because we were never going to be Carl Reiner. I think we exploded, 'If you want Carl Reiner, Grant, get Carl Reiner.' That's how upset we all were." Now they understand that Grant made the call because "Mary had been hysterical on the ride home. We didn't know about that until later. He protected us so much. Mary was upset because of the fact that their fortune was riding on the show." Burns adds, "They had gone out on the hook for the show and I think they could have been wiped out financially. I think they were in deep financial trouble if the show hadn't gone. So they had every reason to be upset."

As they moved toward that Friday, Sandrich recalls there was "almost no rewriting. I doubt that there were more than three or four lines changed. We all felt it was good and I will give Mary and Grant the utmost credit; they didn't panic. You know, we just said to ourselves, 'We like this, we think it works.' I was saying, 'I don't think the cast was as good as it can be or will be.' They were nervous, it was a rehearsal, and we did it because we wanted to put the show in front of an audience before the final filming so we could find out things—whether we were too long, whether the script needed rewriting. As an artistic group, we found that this show worked. And Jim and Allan felt confident in their material. It's an amazing thing—there were no recriminations, nobody blamed anything on anybody, nobody called for wholesale changes. There was a show of confidence in the actors, materials, and—thank God—the director!"

Winant also remembers the soaring moments on Friday that followed the abysmal ones of Tuesday: "I was feeling so bad, because I had loved working with these people, with their caring, and their patience, with the endless time they had taken with everything. On Friday my friend Paul King from Current Programming at CBS asked if I was going back again. I said, 'Yes,' and he said, 'I'll go with you and then we'll go have dinner.' I thought that was really nice; he was being supportive. And it was so much better. You could hear and you could see and it worked wonderfully. It *was* a wonderful show. They had abandoned the second-camera thing and they had fixed the sound system. And they had cleaned it up; they had tightened it."

Brooks and Burns add that the change in warm-up comedians was another essential step in climbing from the dark into the light: "Lorenzo Music was now doing the warm-up. The show that had been this humongous bomb on that Tuesday night, on the Friday night when we did it, it was a hit. We knew it. Everything scored. It was just amazing."

Amazing it was. But, as Sandrich reminds us, "that Tuesday was a very frightening evening—an evening that none of us will ever forget. I've been in many a situation like that on pilots where the first audience just doesn't particularly laugh. And insecure people will panic. Mary and Grant didn't."

MTM now had a completed episode, one they felt was first-class. They had made it through the last major trauma that the company would experience, but still faced the death slot on Tuesday night.

Winant joined the other CBS executives to preview the new product. She relates, "Mike Dann had been fired and was replaced by Fred Silverman. However, it was Dann who had laid out the fall schedule." No one had seen the film so Silverman flew to California to see the print. "Even though we were all friends, I'd never seen it. Not a frame. The last time I had seen the show was in the studio. I was so nervous, I was terrified. All these people had come to hate the show, and now the new boss, who had been told the show was a loser, but it had to go on the air because CBS had this commitment, was sitting there. We all assembled and they rolled it and it was wonderful. Not only was it well performed but it was well edited and the music and the visuals were terrific. It's such a stylish company; they really knew what they were doing. Dave Davis had done a marvelous job with the titles. They were snappy and exuberant and set a great tone.

"I think I was probably the only one who laughed during the screening. I mean there was dead silence. Of course when the lights came up everyone waited for Fred to react and he didn't say anything. I was mumbling, 'Wasn't it good, yes, ummm . . .' Fred picked up the phone and said, 'Get me Bob Wood in New York.' And we waited. He got Wood at home. It was probably nine o'clock at night in New York. Fred said, 'Bob, we have to change the schedule. I've just seen *The Mary Tyler Moore Show* and it's a terrific show. We have to move it to Saturday night. I know it's August, and I know it's late, but we've gotta do it because we can't throw this show away.' And I could hear Bob Wood saying, 'Jesus, this guy is going to drive me nuts.' But they did change the time."

After the series went on the air Silverman badgered Winant about getting Mary married. "You can't have this loser woman remain unmarried," he said to her. "He thought Valerie was a little too hard-edged. But I have to give him credit. It's easy to bash Silverman, and a lot of the things he said about the show were unnerving, like getting Mary married. But he looked at it and he knew it was a good show."

Burns and Brooks focus on Wood when they discuss the rescheduling. Brooks volunteers, "There is a hero who never gets mentioned—Bob Wood. He was, I guess, so self-effacing that he never took credit and never got credit, but he's the only man in the history of American entertainment that I've ever heard about who took enormous success and got rid of it because he thought it wasn't right qualitatively and replaced it with a new day just by taking shows off that were enormously successful. It was the time when CBS had twelve of the top twenty shows. He was riding that kind of streak. He made our show and saved us just by changing our time period. He made *All in the Family* and saved *All in the Family*. He changed television. He deserves the recognition that Pat Weaver and all those other great broadcasters have. I've never seen him get his due."

Burns adds an interesting point of view concerning the relationship between one's personal political and social stance and professional responsibility. "Wood was a great guy. He was very much of a conservative politically, who put a lot of very liberal shows on. He had just come aboard and was beginning to feel his way. He was made president of CBS in rather a surprise move. Nobody expected Bob Wood to do what he did. He impressed everyone."

And who was this Robert Wood? He was a longtime CBS employee, starting out with the network radio station KNX a week after graduation from USC in 1949. When he accepted the presidency of the CBS Television Network on February 14, 1969, he possessed a vision that was at odds with the programming vice president, Michael Dann. Wood wanted to replace the bucolic image of CBS by addressing more contemporary themes. Dann objected, insisting upon retention of, among other shows, *The Beverly Hillbillies* and *Hee-Haw*. This radical disagreement led to Dann's departure by early 1970. Wood later jokingly referred to this period in his career as "a modern St. Valentine's Day massacre."

The genuine irony of this situation lies in the fact that Dann bequeathed to Wood the cornerstone of the new image, *The Mary*

Robert D. Wood, president of CBS-TV, 1969–76.

Tyler Moore Show. As we have noted, Dann came to hate the show. Wood, who seemingly knew little of the negotiations with Tinker and Moore, became aware of this gem only in the summer of 1970. He made a totally unprecedented schedule change, so delighted was he with this Dann legacy. His admiration for the MTM series sprang from his television creed: "Your primary, exclusive, one-on-one mission is to put the finest shows on the air." As he worked on the CBS offerings in the last half of 1970, he was "trying to take some of the wrinkles out of the face of television."

Nobody had ever taken a network schedule and shaken it like this anywhere near as late as August, only one month before the program was to debut. Burns and Brooks remind us, "We later became the cornerstone. This was pre-*M*A*S*H*, pre-*All in the Family*. We were on with a show called *Arnie*—*Arnie* was our lead-in and *Mannix* came after, which was not exactly perfect in terms of the kind of audience we'd attract. But at least it got us looked at. We opened with a thirty-seven share."

Braced by the Wood decision, a new enthusiasm gripped the whole community at MTM as they worked to complete the first thirteen episodes. When the September 19 issue of *TV Guide* reached the public with a cover story about *The Mary Tyler Moore Show* announcing "You've Come a Long Way, Baby," the remarkable reversal was complete. Tinker and Moore were vindicated in not "getting rid of those guys."

Then came the reviews. Again there was some cause for concern. Burns recalls the *Time* review in particular. "It was a devastating review. I remember reading it on a Monday night and the next morning I was driving on Melrose Avenue, which is the way I used to get to the studio. Mary went that way too. I remember pulling up to a stoplight and Mary had stopped in her car; she was driving a Jag coupe. I glanced over and saw Mary and she saw me. I thought, 'Oh, Jesus, she's read the review,' because the look on her face was such devastation. It was a stupid review. At least Cecil Smith loved us in the *L.A. Times.*"

Time had indeed done a number on the show. Richard Burgheim wrote, "*The Mary Tyler Moore Show*, on opening night at least, was a disaster for the old co-star of *The Dick Van Dyke Show*. She plays an inadvertent career girl, jilted by the rounder she put through medical school, and working as a 'gofer' at a Minneapolis TV station. Her bosses, a drunken clown of a news director and a narcissistic nincompoop of an anchorman, do an injustice to even the worst of local TV news." (When the series left the air in March 1977 *Time* ran a full-page essay entitled "Goodbye to Our Mary," singing the show's praises.) *The New York Times* was less expansive but far from complimentary. Jack Gould observed, "Situation comedy fell apart on both NBC and CBS. . . . Mary Tyler Moore is caught in a preposterous item about life as an 'associate producer' in a TV newsroom."

So the series, which had won the first-night audience and vindicated the trust of its creators, now faced the hurdle of critics.

Reacting to this challenge, Tinker and Moore, Brooks and Burns, Davis and Sandrich—the talented individuals rapidly becoming an ensemble—forged ahead.

To illuminate this extraordinary display of talent, to attempt to isolate its uniqueness, we turn in a series of portraits, first of the writers and then of the actors. We begin with the writers, because that's where it all begins.

4

THE HEART OF THE MATTER
CREATING THE SCRIPT

In the beginning is the blank page. "The old tabula rasa," as Maxwell Smart might say. And the writer writes, and the page is filled. And the evening and the morning are the first day. Then the rewrite. And the evening and the morning are the second day. Considerably more than six days later, and probably without one for resting, the writer may be ready to sigh, "Behold, it is very good," and submit his work to more critical reading.

One of the most entertaining and informative books on the agony of creating words as a business is William Goldman's *Adventures in the Screen Trade*, the result of two decades of work in Hollywood as a screenwriter. He enumerates the "Powers That Be" as stars, studio executives, directors, and producers. *Not* writers. "In terms of authority," he says, "screenwriters rank somewhere between the man who guards the studio gate and the man who runs the studio (this week)."

In television, commentators agree that the good writer is the rare bird and the commodity most sought after by the medium. Also the least appreciated, the most cavalierly dealt with, and the most underpaid. The Great Writers' Strike of 1988 demonstrated how fragmented and undernourished is the Writers Guild, although the several months of work stoppage did demonstrate some tenacity and muscle, winning some of the concessions demanded. The unhappy sidebar to the strike is its exacerbation of the poverty of all but the lucky few writers who work regularly. Many have been unable to recover from the high principles for which they and their guild stood.

MTM, however, holds a rather remarkable record in the industry: It regularly treated its writers well. This unusual treatment was due not only to Grant Tinker's benign influence but to the fact that Jim Brooks and Allan Burns were themselves writers and always accorded writing its preeminent place in the creative process.

Throughout these pages Burns and Brooks play a dominant role, but above everything else they were and are writers. So as we turn to this crew of talented, irreverent storytellers, the two creators hold center stage. Together they crafted fewer than a dozen of the scripts, but their ideas would cascade into the story conferences. Whenever either Brooks or Burns was there, the scripts changed. A line here, a movement there, a funny concept made hilarious by the unexpected. Everyone who was present attests to the continuing impact of the two men on every dimension of the tale to be told, week after week. Yet there seems to have been no resentment, no territorial imperatives rampant among the cadre of writers who frequented Sound Stage 2 for those seven years. At episode 168 Brooks and Burns were still there to shape the close of a seven-year phenomenon.

They always retained control over the dialogue, even down to last-minute changes during the final filming. They were what Hollywood terms "hyphenates," using their producer titles to give them the clout as writers. And all the writers on staff came to share this privilege. This is an aberrant pattern and could be unnerving to visiting directors, who were not used to such active and frequent interference from the sidelines. Imagine the discomfiture of, for example, Jackie Cooper, who as director of episode 99, "You Sometimes Hurt the One You Hate," complained about the process over which he usually had control being abrogated time and again by the writers/producers interrupting at will, calling actors, director, other writers—anyone whom they deemed appropriate—over from the set to the sidelines for a conference. And changes might be made by them on the spot—to be recorded by Marge Mullen and then incorporated into the script.

Jay Sandrich adapted to this "harassment" in his own special way. A very strong personality, with the iron will typical of a good director, Sandrich developed for himself the kind of authority customarily wielded by directors of feature films rather than television, traditionally a producer's medium. His clashes with Jim Brooks, another strong-minded individual, were loud and numerous, sometimes unnerving to those around them. To put a writer's perspective

Allan Burns, Ed. Weinberger, Ed Asner, Jim Brooks, Mary Tyler Moore, Treva Silverman.

on it, Ed. Weinberger says that "only in a few television shows is the producer not essentially the director. In those shows the director is very strong. Jay is one, with strong points of view. He had made his stamp on our show and did not back off from any confrontations and you couldn't walk over him, nor did you try to or even want to."

The writers who flourished under this system of active involvement by virtually the entire creative team claim that it was part of the special genius of the show. No writer seems to have felt neglected or underappreciated by the other groups who worked on the series.

The writers' weekly schedule for creating *The Mary Tyler Moore Show* was not much different from that of any other comedy. On Monday the actors would gather around a table to read the script. Right away they would start "fiddling" with it (David Lloyd's word) and this process continued on Tuesday. David had a special deal, which Bob Ellison and others still envy: He was freed up to work at home and had to come into the studio only during the major rewrite night, Wednesday. Ellison and others were there five days, and the script consulting and wrangling was a continuous process. On Wednesday night there was a full-fledged run-through, immediately after which any major fixing was expected to occur. Thursday and

Friday were a series of run-throughs with the technicians who handled the cameras, lighting, and sound. The director continued to work with the actors to polish dozens of details. All of this was working toward a Friday afternoon deadline of 4 P.M. when the cast, production staff, and writers assembled for the final run-through. Everything had to be in order by six o'clock, when the actors departed for a quick snack, makeup, and costume prior to the 7:30 filming before an audience.

Brooks and Burns, Weinberger and Daniels were constantly present during all phases of rehearsals and even filming, for whatever adjustments seemed necessary.

It's time to rhapsodize again about the unique blend that was Brooks and Burns: the one, as Lloyd has said, the genius whose flights of brilliance characteristically lifted them all out of earthbound moments; the other, a master of comedy and character, who "kept us all honest." When the second generation of producers edged forward in the third season, although never to the total exclusion of Brooks and Burns, they continued the tradition of overseeing the dialogue and collaborating with the ensemble. Nobody seems to remember, even under the most insistent probing, when personal ego overrode the "best decision"—best, that is, for the final product. Moments of inspiration in life are very few, as we all know, whether we are writing, teaching, designing wallpaper, making love, or playing chess. But there was something like a regularity of happy discoveries that flourished under the leadership of Brooks and Burns, then Weinberger and Daniels.

An important ingredient in the mystery of the Brooks/Burns genius was their ability to deliver the unexpected. And this, we believe, became the most important characteristic of the show. The typical sitcom joke follows a form as predictable as—well, let's not be patronizing—the conclusion to *A Midsummer Night's Dream*. Part of the audience's enjoyment comes in anticipating the expected. Like a child hearing about Goldilocks for the forty-seventh time, we don't want surprises, we want expectations fulfilled. Nothing wrong with that formula. Except, perhaps, that it gets a little tiresome if you watch too much TV.

But *The Mary Tyler Moore* punch line often swoops in from an unexpected place. Example: Mary is preparing to go to jail rather than reveal the source of a controversial story (#97, "Will Mary Richards Go to Jail?" written by Daniels and Weinberger to open the fifth season). In his office Lou Grant takes her through a litany of high-minded beliefs and wellsprings of action, all deriving from the gods of journalistic integrity. She repeats, in her own hesitant way, his great thoughts; then, in her most vulnerable manner, she adds, "There's just one problem." She pauses, then, her composure shattered, she wails in that famous quaver, "I don't want to go to jail, Mr. Grant!"

We haven't seen that coming. But it's just right.

The unexpected may also be seen on a larger scale. The plot line careens regularly between realism and absurdity and we are never sure exactly where it will dip or rise toward one or the other. Again, in episode 97, when Mary has been told that she will indeed be jailed, Sue Ann comes up with the totally outrageous idea of throwing a party, "with a prison motif." This is not just a gag line—the party actually takes place and becomes a rich mine of fine comedic material. From the party Mary is led off to jail by the federal authorities with Sue Ann's special farewell ringing in her ears: "I will be right here to help you find your way back into decent society."

A long-delayed but always-expected plot was the romance between Mary and Lou Grant. It finally came, in the next-to-last episode of the series, "Lou Dates Mary," written by David Lloyd, who remembers, "There was clearly a possibility of romance but we never spelled it out. Finally we went for one show where they tried to date each other and realized that it is just not going to work. We set it up by having her reminisce about all the guys she had been dating, who had let her down in so many ways, and she was talking about the kind of man she really admires and realized that Lou Grant exemplified him. And, I said, fine, let's confront this and see what happens if they were to date." The term "confront this" says volumes about the writers' methodology, taking characters and forcing them into unfamiliar situations to yield the unexpected.

In the story Lou and Mary are very nervous, making a shambles of the special meal she has cooked in her apartment for the great event. Finally, they decide to force the issue, test their limits, and attempt a kiss. Here the brilliant, unexpected resolution: simultaneously, they begin to giggle. They realize that the romance won't work, but the tension is eased. The notion is precisely right and is perhaps the grandest coup of the whole series: Prepare the audience over a period of seven years for a possible romance between two characters, build in an integrity that makes the consummation of such a romance impossible, tease the audience with the contradiction, and then resolve it in the most unexpected but simplest of ways. Their love for each other is perfectly shown by their amusement.

"Of course a real romance between Lou and Mary couldn't work," Lloyd says. "But I'm sure the notion of something, the undropped shoe, came from Jim Brooks initially. The possibility of such a romance had been referred to right along year after year and probably in the last year Jim said, 'Let's embrace this; we have got to deal with this.' But clearly it couldn't work." The Allan Burns joke is often quoted: "The last show would end up with them in bed; then blackout, a long silence, and Mary's tag line, 'Oh, Mr. Grant!' But of course this was only a joke, never a plot possibility."

One more example of the unexpected will suffice for the moment. It occurs during the final episode, when the cast, enveloped in a sentimentality that is genuine but rescued from archness by being partly self-conscious, breaks into a chorus of "It's a Long Way to Tipperary," a song long associated with sentiment but ludicrous in this context. Ted Knight has, with exquisite stupidity, chosen it to say his farewells on the Six O'Clock News. As the team from Station WJM fade into recent memory, they file out, singing a song from the trenches of World War I.

As the episodes accumulated and the years rolled by, the ensemble of actors, producers, director, and technicians melded their talents in a way that precludes giving credit to any one group. The reader will note that in the foregoing sentence only one of the job descriptions is singular. Directing seventy percent of the episodes, Jay Sandrich continually provided a creative voice and a vital means of communication between the cast on one hand, for whom he often spoke, and the producers and writers on the other hand, who exercised their craft in very close proximity to the actors day after day. Brooks noted, "While we did communicate with the cast directly, it was usually through Jay." It was Sandrich who was able to meld various acting styles into a finely tuned unit. Burns, who sees television as a producer's medium, views most TV directors as "itinerant journeymen," except for Sandrich, "whose involvement with our show was unique." Brooks concludes, "Jay is the champ. There are no directors who do what he does."

In the ensemble certainly the writers had to understand the special needs of the characters as they were established and evolved. It was the writers who had to begin the process of putting those delightful words into those increasingly famous mouths. It was these writers who had to keep us, the audience, tuned in with fresh surprises each week.

Statistically, over the span of seven years there were sixty-three writers, but most of these wrote only one or two episodes (see Chapter 8), and the count is further inflated by the fact that many were writing teams. There were five writers who contributed four or more scripts who are not included in our analysis that follows. Dick Clair and Jenna McMahon teamed to write four scripts, including

The Emmy Awards, 1977. Allan Burns, Jim Brooks, Ed. Weinberger, Stan Daniels, David Lloyd, Bob Ellison.

the exceptional episode about Phyllis's brother, who is gay (#65). Elias Davis and David Pollock added four more, the last of which, #90, provided continuous cause for laughter as Mary and Rhoda find themselves producing a new show hosted by Sue Ann and Ted. Finally, Martin Cohan wrote eight scripts in the first three seasons, most of them focused on Mary. His last contribution, #72, gave us a splendid cameo appearance by Louise Lasser as a loan officer. Exceptions noted, the more accurate picture is of a seven-year series in which 108 of 168 episodes were written by only eleven writers. That's almost two thirds. Further, the controlling hands of Brooks, Burns, Weinberger, Daniels, or Ellison (as writers, producers, executive producers, story editors) were a constant factor. As Bob Ellison puts it, "The chemistry of the writing staff was as good as the chemistry of the actors."

Each of these extraordinary writers made a unique contribution to the series, and yet each was adept at teamwork. A rapport developed that became an important ingredient in the show—in its content, its method, its spirit, and its success. To enjoy the show and to understand it, conversations with the writers yield many of the secrets of its particularity.

THE FEMININE VOICE: TREVA SILVERMAN

The earliest major writer, in addition to Brooks and Burns of course, was Treva Silverman, a fledgling in 1970 and friend of the produc-

ers. Jim and Allan had called her in the fall of 1969, and she recalls
the conversation:

Jim:　　Hi, Treva, what are you doing?
Treva:　You mean right now?
Jim:　　No, I mean with your life.

Silverman, who is quite introspective ("I psychoanalyze everything, including a cloud that passes my window"), could have
supplied Jim with a very long answer to his question, but she
remembers only his getting to the point right away. He and Allan
asked her to hold her schedule open. "We're writing *The Mary Tyler
Moore Show* pilot and we think you'd be terrific for it and it would be
for you; you'd have fun doing it."

And so she did, beginning with the script that was aired as the
second show—although there were two other scripts already written
that aired later, as well as some that were scrapped—and continuing
until the fifth season. During that time she is credited with fifteen
scripts, although she participated in story conferences and rewrites
that extended her influence beyond her own scripts.

Her first, "Today I Am a Ma'am" (#2), concentrated on Mary and
Rhoda. "I gravitated to writing for Valerie from the very beginning.
I think it was because she and I shared an important characteristic,
self-deprecating humor. Whatever it was, writing for her was just
instinctive for me." When she came onto the show Silverman was
quitting smoking as one of two New Year's resolutions. The second
was a promise not to gain weight. And so her first episode dealt
with a diet and losing ten pounds and not eating, centering on
Rhoda but applying, she was sure, to the entire female population
of America. "I thought the script was pretty funny. And then I
realized that I didn't know what the actress who was going to play
Rhoda looked like. I had written the script just assuming that everybody is on a diet, but I thought, 'Jesus, what if by some horrible
accident of fate she's anorexic or something.'" A call to Pat Nardo,
then the secretary for MTM and later herself a writer for the show,
resulted in a heart-stopping moment. "I asked Pat who was the
actress. The name Valerie Harper didn't give me any information, so
I blurted out, 'Is she fat?' Pat said, 'No,' and my heart sank. But
then she said, 'No, not fat, *zaftig*.' That means plump but in a very
sensuous, nice, attractive way. Thank God!"

As a contemporary woman of the seventies, Silverman felt able to
give to Rhoda a lot of the feeling of being an underdog. But then,
because the show was long-running, she was able to give her alter

ego a change in personality. "Valerie and I both got deeply involved in the Women's Movement. I think it was probably good for the show that I hadn't been involved before I was hired. That meant that I began by writing for Rhoda during her self-deprecating phase, and so I had the automatic attitudes about having to get married. Is he cute? Is he married? We women would marry anybody because we're kind of hard-up. It's the guys who really have the pick. Rhoda felt that. I felt that. I think Val felt that too. But as time went on we no longer felt that." All of them started learning, as women and men did all over this country, and this enlightenment became a part of the character of Rhoda. "I took more pride in being a woman, and that was reflected in Rhoda's growth."

But of course no successful scriptwriter can concentrate on only one character, and Silverman is thoughtful—and remains analytical— about them all. Like the other writers, she feels a keen *reality* about the show, something different in kind, not just degree, from most other shows. One way to express this quality is the feeling "that each character seems to be talking on a one-to-one basis to some-body in the audience, kind of firsthand, just as if you were talking to your friend and were describing something very funny." She recalls being asked by a friend how it felt to sit down knowing that she was writing for millions of people and she was "astonished; I hadn't realized that I was writing for a gigantic audience. And I never wanted it to be brought up again!" Such a terrifying idea has to be sublimated immediately and definitively. "Instead, I think of this as character writing, a very personal thing that we were communicat-ing. This show was so intimate. People watching it took it in a really personal way."

Perhaps this approach is easy to see with Mary, understated and personable as she was. "The way the show was created by Jim and Allan, each of the characters was created to have a conflict, with Mary in the middle, like some game where you're always in the middle. At least in the first year, Rhoda and Phyllis were automati-cally in the conflict with Mary in the middle; the same with Lou and Ted, with Murray and Ted." By the time the show had gone on for a little while, the audience knew that when Ted walked in and Lou was there, there would be tension, with Mary somehow mediating an argument, or at least being uncomfortable.

With Ted, however, the reality quotient may be harder to under-stand. Silverman admits that the egotistic anchorman was larger than life, and maybe that was part of the secret of his popularity. "But I always felt that the reason he worked out so beautifully was that, even though he was larger than life, everything was so truthful about him. Enlarged, but truthful." When she wrote Ted she used a mixture of people she actually knew, automatically asking what they would do in this situation. But, more personally, "I used a part of *me* that was the most self-centered, narcissistic part." There is, in other words, some Ted in all of us. Further, Ted is likable because "he never left a trail of unhappiness behind him, because he never knew that he was being insensitive. If he ever knew it, it would be cruelty." Instead, he was more like a baby or an animal. "A dog switches his tail in happiness and off goes your expensive antique vase. You're miserable and the animal is just perky and smiling. That's Ted, saying the most outrageous things, but with such joy and obliviousness to the effect that he is having."

Thoughts of Ted lead to another Silverman theory, this one about the tone of the show. Most jokes, it is customary to say, rely to some extent on hostility. As Allan Burns put it in another context, "Most comedians come out of adversity, the Lower East Side of New York, or Brooklyn, or somewhere where things were tough."

And their audiences are potential killers, no longer on the street but arrayed menacingly in a nightclub, sipping their drinks and coldly waiting to murder the lonely performer with their silence.

An audience does tend to force jokes with a harder edge. But Silverman refuses to assign the audience as primary cause. "So much depends on the egos involved—the producers, writers, and actors. There are many people who gravitate to comedy, any sphere of it, who need immediate gratification. Like when you're watching a nightclub comedian and nobody's laughing, he'll instantly start putting down the audience because he's so angry that he hasn't gotten the immediate laugh. There are people who can withstand the pain and discomfort of writing a novel, which takes up maybe two years; that means that for two years they don't get satisfaction, they don't get feedback. And then there are people who choose to write something they can write in three days. Let's say they're writing a stand-up comedian routine. They have to get feedback immediately. If the child actor or the adult actor needs it from the audience, he or she will be tempted to make the joke and the line bigger so he can hear the audience say 'Yes, we think you're funny and we like you.' This is the greatest mistake that he can make because it has nothing to do with the millions of people who are watching.

"Many people can write or speak only one-liners; they can never withstand the discomfort of writing a novel. I think that a lot of the people involved with *Mary* were, to put a poetic twist on it, novelists. We were a group of people who could withstand the need for immediate gratification. Nobody exaggerated. Anything. Everybody was as truthful as he or she could be."

A corollary to this theory: In most sitcoms, the jokes are centered in hostility. But in *Mary* the dominant note was good-naturedness, the jokes centering more on insight than hostility. In *Taxi*, on the other hand, the Danny de Vito character is so angry—never offensive, because there is such joy in the anger—but angry nevertheless. Practically every episode in *All in the Family* is based on hostility, Meathead versus Archie. The banter in *M*A*S*H* is like that, a cover for anger, fear, frustration. But *The Mary Tyler Moore Show* never had this kind of aggression. Instead it featured what Treva Silverman calls "insight into behavior": "It was so relaxing not to have to write that kind of aggression, as perfect as it was for those other shows. And we were the only ones doing our gentler kind of humor."

She sees the jokes as "very real, and not jokes as such.They were things that maybe the next morning couldn't be quoted because they were so in context with what was happening emotionally."

There *were* some one-liners, most of them assigned to Murray and coming directly out of his character, but with Mary and Rhoda or Mary and Lou, the humor was less quotable, coming from a richer source. Silverman's word is "organic."

Another part of the easy familiarity of the show was the constellation of characters that several writers and many observers have seen as typical of a family. According to this theory, Lou—Mr. Grant—is the father figure, somewhat stern but loving and even accommodating to the "children" in his charge. There is no mother; Phyllis attempts the kind of authority that strong mothering accomplishes, but she is too eccentric. Some who believe in this theory might agree with Silverman that Phyllis is more the crazy aunt. Mary, of course, is the daughter, vulnerable, growing up and finding herself, wanting to make it "on her own" but still needing the nurturing presence of others. Murray is the older, wisecracking brother, in competition with Ted, putting him down; Rhoda, the sister who really loves Mary and wants her to be independent. And finally Ted, the little brother, the baby of the family, psychologically diapered, so to speak. "And so," concludes Silverman "it was all very warm. People could have fights, but like a family they knew they would always get back together again." And we, the audience, knew that too. We identified with this surrogate family and saw there some of the strengths and weaknesses of our own.

The ideal of the family was certainly in the forefront in episode

Lou and Edie's separation.

76, "The Lou and Edie Story," for which Treva Silverman won the
Emmy in 1973–74 for Best Writing in Comedy. She remembers the
genesis of the show: "At a story conference I said that I would like
to see Lou in pain. We had never seen him in pain; he always took
things very casually. [Treva may have forgotten the twenty-first
episode, during the first season, when Lou and Edie had a serious
confrontation about her going back to school. It ended with a reconciliation, but the pain of the confrontation is still clear enough.] And
I also thought I'd like to see him in a sexual situation." All of her
women friends responded to the easy masculinity that Ed Asner
projected onto the character of Lou Grant. "It's a special thing when
a heavy man gives off an aura that is truly sexy; it's particular in that
you think you're the only one noticing the sexuality. All my women
friends would say how cute and adorable and sexy he was. And I
thought so too."

As the show finally took shape Lou's pain derived from a tension
in his marriage leading to separation, then divorce. Silverman's first
job was research into the background of the show: Who *was* this
wife, as she had been written about before? What had she been
reported to say? To do? What had others said about her? Treva was

surprised to find that by the fourth season Edie was an important presence in the show. "There was 'Edie says this' and 'Edie says that,' so Lou obviously had her on his mind a lot."

What followed was a major group decision. They would begin what had to be a continuing story, with separation, then divorce, then how Lou would conduct himself as a bachelor. Whom will he go out with? In whom will he confide? Will he get involved with people? They wrestled over the sale of his house. Would he sell it? What would that mean to him? Silverman remembers this as "the first commitment to following through on a major story change. We had never done a thing like that." Here her earlier analogy with the novelist seems appropriate. The writers would bide their time, developing over many seasons the implications of their decision to divorce Lou and Edie. It wasn't to be handled in one episode or even one season. Later in the fall of 1973 Lou has his first date (#80) and a little later is found haunting Mary's apartment in a depressed state of mind (#83). By January 1974, Lou is considering selling his house (#89) and a month later has his second date, with Rhoda (#94). Time passes and Lou finds a new female companion in the fall of 1974 (#100), but it is not until the opening episode (#121) of the sixth season that Edie remarries.

The decision to force Lou's divorce was not an easy one. In opening up certain avenues of exploration with the Lou Grant character, the creators were cutting off others. And perhaps more important was an attitude strongly expressed by Jay Sandrich. Silverman remarks, "Usually Jay and I were on the same wavelength with subject and attitude and everything. But not this time. He told me it was a big mistake to write about anybody leaving Lou, such a beloved man. 'They're going to hate Edie's guts,' he told us.

"We were all reacting to this story from deeply personal feelings. I was the quintessential single woman in the seventies and I felt that this was an opportunity to say a lot of things about what was happening to women then. So my writing about Edie *not* coming back to Lou was thrilling to me." Jay, on the other hand, was himself going through a divorce at that time and had to feel a special discomfort with the subject. Jim was divorced and not so much dating as having women for friends, being pals with them and finding out a lot about the contemporary woman, what she was thinking and what she was up to and scared of and all that. And Allan, a happily married man, was also extremely intuitive about this subject, without having all that accessibility to women. He just really knew deeply how women feel. Ed Asner was a bachelor, at that point not wanting to settle down at all; he was happy to be footloose. At least these are my readings of where we all were at the time."

Perhaps she is right, perhaps not. But what an interesting point of view. "Everybody in his or her personal life brought attitudes and ideas to the show, reflecting in the show where we all were in our lives." Here is the reality quotient again—although it takes a great deal of talent to transform personal experience into interesting, significant, and "real" fiction.

But of course the show was never a vehicle for exposing its creators' inner lives to the vast American public. All the writers remember the fun of it. "I'll tell you a little secret about the 'Obituary Show' [#92]. When Mary and Rhoda get the giggles, I was writing them as if they were stoned on grass. Getting the munchies and all that stuff." But that was just Silverman's little personal joke, a writer's trick, and not a social message!

How about those social messages, though? Treva is on record as not writing for millions of people, not speaking from a platform. And yet she was a developing feminist, with serious ideas about her life and the American Experience. She has to admit that many people tell her that they were influenced by Mary and Rhoda during those times. "While *All in the Family* was making vast inroads into the public's thinking, with issues tackled directly, I think our show took the more difficult path and was more subtle, again in an *organic* way." She remembers episode 55, "when Mary's parents are visiting. Her mother, as she leaves the apartment, calls to her husband, 'Be sure to take your pill.' In unison Mary and her father answer, 'I will.'

"That almost gets by and then people say, 'Did I just hear what I thought I heard?' And very casually we hear that Mary takes the pill. We've just exonerated all the women who ask, 'Oh, suppose my mother finds out?' A show on CBS about people she loves and respects, here's a woman taking the pill. And that was influential in a very private way, I think."

She remembers another story detail that others might refer to as a pro-social message, but which she feels is infinitely more casual and therefore effective. Phyllis's brother was dating Rhoda (#65). Phyllis really didn't like Rhoda and was worried about the possibilities of heavy dating, even marriage. Somebody at the last minute, when a planned ending didn't work, came up with the idea that the brother was gay. And the episode ends with Phyllis's comic sigh of relief, "Thank God!" "Just a remark," says Treva, "more a character remark than a joke, as an ending for a show. That says volumes about what the show was like. You see, there wasn't a point about homosexuality being made, but there *is* a point—that being gay is nothing and has no importance. What is important is that Phyllis will not get Rhoda as a sister-in-law."

Almost any writer connected with this show might have come up with that line. Its importance is that such a thought would occur only to a person with a certain sensibility, a certain liberal, perhaps we can say *humanistic*, attitude.

Silverman made her important contribution to the show during the first four seasons. She was instrumental in shaping the entire seven years, however, including the development of the characters and their stories as she had helped to give them direction. "*Mary* was a huge turning point for me. I had found a wonderful vehicle and had gotten very intense about my writing. It had helped me find out some things about myself. But it came time to move to something else. I had to decide what I was going to do with my life. Everybody asked how I could leave *Mary* then, before it was over. But I always wanted to live in Europe, so I left. It seemed the time, when I was feeling very high, very responsible and growing and learning."

THE CONTRACT WRITER: STEVE PRITZKER

Another early recruit to the writing staff was Steve Pritzker, whom Brooks and Burns had known from *Room 222*. Since then he had been writing on an assignment basis by choice. In the second year Davis and Music were given the title of story editors, but never a large staff, and Pritzker didn't want any of that, having experienced it on *Room 222*. "You get locked in a room and have to turn out a story virtually by yourself each week—at least you have responsibility for it." He was very apprehensive about this assignment, though, "because the audience was going to be there. It was scary." The three-camera show had fallen out of favor by that time and *Mary* was going to reintroduce it, along with the audience. "Norman Lear gets credit for bringing back the audience, but these guys did it before him."

An important difference between one-camera and three-camera shows is the greater control exercised by the writer/producer in the latter. "With one camera, you just write it and ship it." The director takes control and there tends to be much less rewriting.

He also remembers the phenomenon of calling shots from the sidelines. "We [writers and producers] used to call a halt whenever we felt the need, for consultation and changes. It was a bit chaotic, but it absolutely worked for us from the first day. That made a big difference in the nuances." Like Treva Silverman, he sees their jokes as more realistic than those in other shows, more full of subtleties. "The audience is laughing at people rather than at jokes."

Concerning these people, he remembers how remarkably easy it was to write them, all of them, although he regrets not having a chance to write a show where Ed Asner did more because "I really liked that Lou Grant character." He didn't write a show in which Phyllis was central, either, just because his assignments didn't go that way, but he found her wonderfully funny. "Rhoda was the kind of lady that I had been fixed up with many times in my life, so I related to her immediately as someone whose attitude I under-stood." Because he was doing character humor and he was thor-oughly familiar with the characters, once he knew an attitude from which to write, he felt 75 percent of the way home. He is still awed by how well the show worked over the seven years. "It was because it was all laid out from the first."

From the moment when he joined the show, possibly because of his close relationship with Brooks and Burns, Pritzker had a lot of give and take with the actors. He was there for story conferences, rewrite sessions, run-throughs, the whole thing, "and I had a voice in those; I remember being listened to carefully." Story conferences were quick, usually done in one day. "I would take notes. Each scene was so clearly lined up that I would know what to write and just sit down and write it pretty quickly. An amazing amount of it would go right through to the show." Like other youthful partici-pants, he was shocked later, on assignments for other shows, to find that most of them didn't get done with this degree of ease.

"The director and actors were good, though. Some of my mate-rial, taken verbatim, would take spins that I hadn't anticipated. Same words, but transformed. I saw Ed Asner one time come in and say 'Hello' and get a laugh with it." Although he has undoubtedly filtered out some tense moments, his dominant impression is echoed by others: writers felt genuine affection for the characters they were creating and for the actors who were bringing them to life.

"The actors always added to what you had written. You could count on everybody on that show to deliver an attitude and to show up and do it. I never felt they had off nights, like the Lakers! There was basically one shot, requiring actors to get up and do their thing. And they usually did it. Mary was especially amazing; she practi-cally never made a mistake."

He sees much of the ease of accomplishment deriving from the beneficent style of Grant Tinker. He supported the creative people to a degree that is virtually unheard of elsewhere, then or now. "I came out of business school, and management is something I looked at, and I think Grant was a remarkable manager, in giving a kind of blanket approval to what his people wanted to do, as long as it wasn't obviously in bad taste. I think that attitude brings out the best in people. I've talked with Brandon Tartikoff about that, and it was the same when Grant went to head up NBC later." Everyone tends to be an expert in television and everyone has an opinion about every show. "But Grant always resisted the desire to tinker [the dreadful pun seemed accidental, but who can tell, with a writer, even a very good one?]. I haven't run across anyone else who's done that, who wouldn't give a note, at least a few notes, so he can say, 'I'm here and I gave notes. That's why it's good, because of my little notes.' Network and studio executives say things like 'You know that little thing where he forgets his hat? That was me, it made the whole show!' " Grant not only left his creative team alone, but he went on the line to protect them when there was trouble, usually from the guys who wanted to make it better.

But after all this talk of "ease," Pritzker warns against misunderstanding. They did not begin with perfection and freeze-dry themselves, miraculously adding water every week. Mary, for example, who had all her lines almost immediately, together with the right thing to do, was not locked into a final cut from the first day. Of course she listened to suggestions, and accommodated herself to many changes each week. Further, the characters evolved, sometimes in ways unforeseen, but always in response to some nudge from the writer/producers. He remembers a show in the second season when Ted is afraid he'll lose his job if he takes a vacation and someone substitutes for him. So we learned that underneath all this pomposity there was a vulnerable human being. "After that you realized that this bravado was a bluff for a very insecure man." Likewise with Rhoda, who changed from a shrewish to a more vulnerable woman, but was always very funny. And Lou Grant, as he developed marital problems, revealed a dimension of insecurity, even fear. An easy show, he claims, but not without its creative challenges. The point is that meeting those challenges was fun to do and the results rewarding.

One of the challenges involved the integrity of theme and atmosphere. Unlike its best-known peers, M*A*S*H and All in the Family, The Mary Tyler Moore Show did not deal explicitly with political or social topics. Yet, in creating a contemporary woman, its writers had to reflect modern concerns. "The feminist movement was happening and this was a show about a woman discovering herself. There was Betty Friedan, as well as a residue of issues left over from the sixties. I think Valerie Harper may have been the only one of us who had read any feminist literature, but I think every one of us had undergone some consciousness-raising during that time. Under the influence of Jim and Allan, both of whom are very knowledgeable, very well read, we integrated certain contemporary ideas into the show."

Mary herself was a fine, unforced example of the New Woman. "When I was growing up, women who never married were always talked about in my house with a tone of pity, as if they had failed in the major area of life. Unless you were Bette Davis or Joan Crawford. Actually, I thought unmarried women were very interesting people and got duller after they got married. To me, Mary represented a new attitude, that you could be single and still be a whole person, that you didn't need to be married to have a complete life. To me that was the strongest statement the show made."

Like the others, he doesn't remember any discussions of values, just what was appropriate to characters. He recalls a value-laden show, however, in which Mary stays out all night, to the consternation of her parents, whom she must tell to get off her back and let her find her own identity, live her life, be herself.

"You're dealing with a lot of important stuff there, with people trying to make their own decisions and be strong enough not to be a hypocrite with their parents." This is Pritzker's perspective on the episode also cited by Treva Silverman when we learn Mary is on the pill. It is perhaps instructive to see that two writers come at the importance of the show through different details, yet both agree on its essential significance. "With Jim and Allan I felt there was a clear sense that an adult woman should be dealing with her parents on a free and open level, not hiding anything, as hard as that might be. Not so simple then. Not so simple now."

His least favorite show is one where the message was too explicit. It was episode 47, "Some of My Best Friends Are Rhoda," which dealt with anti-Semitism. In it Mary Frann guest-starred as a snobbish and prejudiced country-club type who woos Mary as a friend but rejects Rhoda *Morgenstern*.

"In this show," Pritzker says, "the message is too transparent—anti-Semitism is bad. If you don't already think so, this episode is not going to change your mind. It's all too preachy." And certainly atypical.

THE WRITER/PERFORMER: LORENZO MUSIC

Like Treva Silverman and Steve Pritzker, Lorenzo Music was on the show before the first episode was shot. And like many others, he came from a background other than situation comedies: His first career was as a stand-up comic in nightclubs, but he moved early on into a second, as a writer for variety shows. He had won an Emmy for writing *The Smothers Brothers Comedy Hour*. He was the writing partner of Dave Davis, who had been hired by MTM with the title of producer but primarily for his talent in postproduction, especially editing. "I was brought on because I was Dave's writing partner. They didn't really need me: They created a space. CBS and Grant Tinker didn't need me, but Jim and Allan said they'd pay me a little bit out of their salaries, so I came on board, for a whole lot less money than I was accustomed to. It was a gamble on my part, that sitcoms were a classier way to go, that more opportunity lay for me there." Of course he was a proven commodity as a writer and could be expected to be another source of scripts. And so he was—eight of them, seven in colloboration with Dave Davis. The first year he was assistant to the producers and then he moved, along with Dave, to story editor. They shared an office. "What I learned about writing alone was that I didn't want to. My one solo script, episode 12, 'Anchorman Overboard,' turned out well, but some of the lowest points in my life were on that script. It's what I hear about hanging—there's supposed to be a moment where there's pleasure, but after that it's nothing!" He operates best in a room with a bunch of people using all the energy to be clear about what's working and what isn't.

The first script that he and Dave wrote was aired as episode 8, "The Snow Must Go On," in which the WJM news team is snowbound at the office. He had joked that part of the reason he was hired in the first place was that he was from Minnesota and "I knew about snow. How long it stayed on your shoulders when you came inside." Well, he also knew about being stuck in a typically heavy Midwestern snowstorm. "You can't get home. That's a tiny fact, but it contributed to the reality of the script. A lot of people in the snow country recognized that one fact as a true one, and apparently that gained their trust, so they thought if that was true, then other things about the show must be true too." This was, after all, a realistic show, and Pritzker feels that its basic truth was the reality of Mary Richards herself. Jim and Allan were "intelligent enough to know the truth about this young woman, this Mary Richards. And they were artists enough to transmit this reality to single women, who watched and said, 'I'm Mary; she's me.' And the rest of us followed their larger truth and contributed with our own, perhaps smaller ones."

On an even more self-deprecating and more typical note, Music remembers that the first act of their script was eighty pages. "We didn't know that the whole script was going to be thirty-five pages. Nobody knew how long things would take. We were experimenting."

He likes to see himself as part of the ensemble and not just the writing/producing team. "Dave Davis knew how to do joke editing. That's as important as knowing how to do joke writing or acting or directing." So all the elements from the beginning were in place for writing through postproduction. If any one of those elements failed, the joke didn't work. A lot of very experienced people were thrust together, as in a theatrical endeavor. They enjoyed their work and appreciated the quality and care. They knew that they were in a good thing and were appreciated. It was this sense of mutual responsibility that informed the work of the writers, of the director, the cinematographer, other technicians, the actors. "Dave and Jay got into arguments a lot, over where to put the camera and how fast things should move, even in the acting, what kinds of things should be shot again. Too many will exhaust the audience and the actors, not enough will be fatal for the final product. We put in a very vital, high-energy week, culminating on Friday when we performed the show for an audience. And we had all contributed—to the show, to each other. I've never seen anything like it before or since.

"Although we respected job titles, we also didn't! In other words, if someone wanted to pull someone aside, he did. Nobody pulled rank, unless some klutz was standing in front of the camera and shouldn't have been. We were a family, even though I'm sick of the word, in that we were free to be positive and negative with each other. There was no holding back. There's so much tension in the world that the free expression of ideas encouraged there was all the more precious." He believes that this freedom was fostered by Grant Tinker, a familiar father figure who ruled by giving.

In analyzing the role of the Friday night audience, Music sees yet another part of the family, engaging with the actors in the weekly taping with increasing goodwill as the characters became more familiar and accepted. "On Monday, with our first run-through of the script, everyone was the audience. If we didn't get it or felt that something was wrong, we were the audience that judged that and started changing it right there. The next audience was the run-through on Wednesday night. Again, there we all were, sitting in chairs, watching as the actors ran through, sometimes still holding scripts. And if we as an audience didn't like it, didn't laugh, we changed it. So by the time we came to Friday, with the outside audience, we were ready."

He remembers one particularly difficult moment when the inside team, as audience, couldn't find a joke. In the episode Rhoda was not working and was being a burden on Mary, really depressing everybody around her. "Phyllis came into the apartment with Mary, and there was Rhoda, eating candy, watching television, half sleeping, and with a hairdryer on her head, the kind with the tube leading to a plastic bubble. They were talking about not pushing her too hard because she was in a sensitive place, and yet they knew they had to encourage her to get off her butt and get a job and get back to her life. And Phyllis, who so often did the outrageous, impulsive thing and didn't care for Rhoda that much, was annoyed, but so was Mary, who was always hypersensitive and under a lot of pressure from herself to do the right thing. Well, they came into the apartment and didn't know what to do. [They also did not know that Rhoda had just gotten a job.] We tried this and that and nothing seemed right. So I had a moment of inspiration. I just walked over and pulled the tube from the blower, put it to my lips, and yelled, 'Get up!' This was the perfect thing for Phyllis to do, a visual joke that was right out of her character. And the audience loved it."

The audience for the first episode, as we have said in Chapter 3, did *not* love the show. Music easily explains the problem from his point of view. First, the audience was not familiar with the characters—somebody says something about boobs and Ted Knight comes in and says, "Hi, guys." The first audiences don't know he's a boob and so they don't have any reason to laugh there. But by the second year they would laugh delightedly at that sequence.

A second problem with the early audience was that no one was setting them up properly. As we have seen, Jim and Allan attempted the audience warm-up at first. Both admit they were terrible at it, and so they hired a comedian. But then they hit on the happy discovery that they had a stand-up comedian in their midst. "I could stand in front of an audience with nothing to say and say it for an hour and a half without any trouble. It's a little less terrifying than being a stand-up comedian on an empty stage; I had all this action around me to help. Another thing that made it easier for me than for others was that I knew the script and what it was trying to do. I knew when we took an act break where the script was going next, so I could set the audience up with the few facts that were necessary and they would get the story when the next scene came on. Whatever character traits needed reinforcing were easy for me. These people were strong characters and there were so many of them. That's tough for an audience to follow, especially at the beginning. Remember we did about ten shows before anyone saw it on the air. People were coming in to see the actress Mary Tyler Moore, whom they liked, but she was not defined as the personality we all now know and love. That took building."

So Music was the perfect one to "conduct" the audience. He knew the show and he knew how to handle himself before a crowd of strangers. He thought of himself as a sort of Ed Sullivan, with a lot of terrific acts, which he stood in the middle of and announced. He was, of course, infinitely more.

He has one more thought about the audience after it became familiar with the show. "When we knew what the audience expected, we wanted to surprise them. That is common in comedy, but to do it with a story and with character, not just outrageous jokes, is more difficult. Without taking away from anyone else, Jim Brooks was the most inspired at this. He has a strong psychological background and he is a genius. Me, I was just trying to get a laugh and make a buck."

Again, not true, but a good line. Because he was doing a great deal more than just getting a laugh and making a buck, Music and Davis were asked by CBS to create a new show. That was *The Bob Newhart Show*. They left for this new assignment after the second season of *The Mary Tyler Moore Show*.

THE WOMAN'S PERSPECTIVE: SUSAN SILVER

Susan Silver was not a regular or frequent contributor to *The Mary Tyler Moore Show*. She is credited with five scripts, dating from near the end of the first season to early in the third season. But her contribution to the show was significant, and her story helps to make a point about the feminine point of view reflected by the entire series. [See Chapter 9, the Epilogue] "As I recall," she says, "there were more women working on that show than on any other, and there was a different feeling about the story." In fact, seventeen of the sixty-five writers were female, accounting in whole or in part for thirty-seven, or 22 percent, of the shows. Beyond these statistics, of course, remains the feminine presence at story conferences and all during the work week—and not just keeping the coffee mugs brimming.

Silver had been in the casting department for Rowan and Martin's *Laugh-In*, but her ambition was to write. She had arranged management of her hoped-for career with Garry Marshall, who had set up a company for his father to handle talent and especially to work with fledgling writers. Garry Marshall was becoming one of the triumvirate of producers (the others would be Norman Lear and the MTM group) who pretty much ruled television comedy during the seventies. His *Odd Couple* was followed by *Happy Days*, *Laverne and Shirley*, and *Mork and Mindy*, among other successes.

"I just knew that I could write for *The Mary Tyler Moore Show*, which I saw as the first that was really from the woman's point of view. I knew that Garry was a friend of Jim Brooks. So I got a meeting. I went in there with six stories and they promised that they'd give me a shot if they got picked up for a second thirteen shows. Of course they did, and my first assignment came in October 1970." Her first script, "A Friend in Deed," aired four months later, on February 20, 1971.

She always wrote from direct experience, even denying that she has any great imaginative powers. "I really never made anything up. I always said that if nothing happens to me on Tuesday, then I'm in real trouble about a Wednesday meeting because I won't have anything. Besides, I thought it was cheating to make something up." This somewhat poetic explanation of her talent points not only to the reality of her stories but to another special quality. "They thought all my stories were incredible, just really original, and I realized then that men have different experiences, and all the stories that I came up with I think most women could relate to because it had happened to us in our lives. But to them it was all new. Up until that point there were so few women writing that our perspective hadn't been shown and they thought I was a genius."

She touches on a crucial point. Because there were enough women on staff and because they were listened to, they brought to the show a true and realistic attitude recognizable to men and women alike as right for Mary and her friends. Sometimes the input was small enough to seem negligible. "Jim Brooks and Lorenzo Music were always at my story meetings, and at one point one of them supplied a piece of dialogue, Mary saying 'Let's go clean up.' And I told them that women don't say that. They say 'Let's take a shower.' " A small thing in itself, perhaps, but magnify it by a thousand such casual differences and a different quality emerges.

Often, however, the elements were larger. Silver wrote a show about Rhoda, out of a job, hanging around Mary's apartment (#36). Coincidentally, a job became available at WJM, but Mary didn't want Rhoda to have it. "This is a real thing that happens with women. You love your best friend, but you don't always want her in your territory." Susan Silver has a theory, derived in part from research for a project called "What Men Don't Tell Women." "Men's friendships are different from women's. They're based on talking about things outside, about sports, politics, business, sports. They learn to play on a team. They'll play with somebody they don't like if he can pass the football. Women don't have that early team experience. If we don't like somebody, we don't like somebody, and we don't want to work or play with her. It's a different feeling. And so we have to deal with friendships where you're really close to somebody and yet have to acknowledge that you want your own little fiefdom."

Like others, she remembers the relative ease in writing. For one thing, the producers "spent the whole day on the story conference; with some people, two days. When you went home you really knew what they wanted, and when you went back with the script they let you come to the table and help with the rewriting." Another aid was the distinctiveness of each character. "One thing that was so great about the show was that you knew what Rhoda sounded like, what Mary sounded like. In most shows everybody sounds the same if you're reading the script. But in *Mary* you really had distinct characters and you knew what each person was going to sound like."

Her picture of Mary is somewhat different from that of the other writers already quoted. Unlike the image of mediator, favored by Treva Silverman and some of the others, Silver thought of her as the center and everybody else turning around her, like a wheel with spokes. "She was the real, solid thing in the middle, and the others were more like 'characters.'" Silver thought of Mary, especially in retrospect, as too perfect and was happy to see, in later seasons, how the writers were able to have a sense of humor about this Goody Two-shoes nature. She is proud of a kind of breakthrough, seen in episode 50, "What Is Mary Richards Really Like?" that came partly in response to a letter from a critic in Chicago who felt that Mary was too virginal in this day and age of women. He even called her undersexed, a line Silver would employ as a question from Mary: "Rhoda, do you think I'm undersexed?"

Silver concludes, "So I got to write the show where she was going to sleep with somebody." Not that the point was rubbed in any viewer's face, but there is a strong hint that Mary's date with a reporter who is writing a story about her included their spending the night together.

And, like the spokes leading to the wheel's center, her conversation about Mary Richards leads back to her main theme, the significance of the show to the burgeoning feminist cause. "Women's Lib was just starting and so were we. There were just a few of us— Treva, Lila Garrett, Joanna Lee, Susan Harris, not a lot of others. We had a great opportunity."

THE SECOND GENERATION: ED. WEINBERGER

With an established hit on their hands and an abiding interest in continuing it, Allan Burns and Jim Brooks found it possible during the third season to share leadership with a second generation of writer/producers. Brooks and Burns turned partly to other endeavors and, during the 1972–73 season, Ed. Weinberger began his extraordinary career with MTM. He came to *The Mary Tyler Moore Show* from Bob Hope, for whom he had been writing monologues. He had just returned from Vietnam with Bob Hope when he was hired by Burns and Brooks, who had seen a screenplay that he had written about a young woman in her early thirties who was out trying to make a life for herself after her boyfriend left. "This was written before *The Mary Tyler Moore Show* went on the air," he said, "and it had some similarities to it and was written, I guess, well enough for Jim and Allan to hire me."

Unlike some of the other writers, Weinberger had had some experience in the sitcom format, as co-creator and executive story editor of the first *Bill Cosby Show*, which ran two years, 1969–71. He and Jay Sandrich had worked together on that show, and it was Jay who recommended that Burns and Brooks have a look at Ed.'s screenplay. Such is the small world of interconnections in Hollywood.

Although his title was writer/producer, his main job was to write. Between 1972 and the final show in 1977 he wrote twenty shows, twelve of them in collaboration with Stan Daniels. "I think the blend of people who were writing the show and the cast seemed a perfect mix, and it was so brilliantly cast that whoever came in and worked with them, the show just was so strong, such clearly defined characters, that a lot of people could have come in and just fit right in." Weinberger feels that his life with the show was very easy because of this remarkable congeniality of sentiment and effort. Even the people who came in later, like Betty White and Georgia Engel, seemed to fit in perfectly.

He never felt that the show broke new ground in the way that Norman Lear's shows were doing at that same time. "Our stories were not looking for anything radical, nothing that would alert the censor, nothing that got into any difficult areas." He does remember one of the few political issues ever dealt with, a few jokes about gun control, which elicited more letters of complaint than any other thing they ever did, but even this was minor. As a writer he felt that they were very original, but not in any sense groundbreakers in the social or political realms. Even the matter of treating women with intelligence "didn't seem like such a radical idea to me at any time," and so the promoting of secretaries like Pat Nardo and Gloria Banta to writers and the handling of "feminist" themes were normal ways to act, he believes.

Much of the male chauvinism, as we have suggested elsewhere, was weeded out or ridiculed. "But we never sat around and consciously deliberated these points. There were intelligent sensibilities at work about women and men and how people deal with each other."

Writers were made very aware of sitcom clichés of the time and the need to avoid them. Weinberger remembers especially the happy ending, where everybody hugs, as well as the " 'Screen Gems' ending, where everybody gets to chuckling over some little joke." The setting in Minneapolis was itself a break with the cliché of New York/Hollywood/American small town to which television had relegated its situation comedies. And using a Jewish character he feels was a major breakthrough. "Think about it, try introducing a Jewish character in a television show today and see how far you get. Networks are going to give you notes: Is that really necessary? I don't see any out-and-out Jewish characters today. Morgenstern from New York. That's definite."

In the pursuit of freshness the writer had constantly to find new ways to enliven the material. But the rule was to find it in the characters, not in some idea. "We really started with characters and what would be a good mix. If we could get Ted mad at Murray, then exploit that with Mary and Murray, who were always close, we'd get something started that would cause one of the characters to do something he or she had never done before."

Reality and the unexpected are often compatible and sometimes believable. A case in point concerns Ed. Weinberger's birthday party—a favorite MTM story.

"One funny experience that came out of my true life was the show about Lou Grant's surprise birthday party, in which he locked everybody out [#87, written by David Lloyd]. Well, that was written because I did that, about three weeks before that script was written.

A woman friend threw me a surprise birthday party and I don't like surprise birthday parties, and I had just been depressed and they were all knocking at the door and I opened and they all yelled, 'Surprise,' and I slammed the door shut and yelled at my friend, 'What did you *do*?' I was in my underwear; I wanted to watch the fight; I wanted to have a steak dinner, and I didn't want anybody there. I was mad as hell!

"Now, they couldn't get in. So they talked about just leaving the presents and going home. Finally my friend opened the door and they all flooded in. It was the worst birthday party anybody would ever want to attend.

"A couple of days later Jim talked about it. He had been invited, but didn't go. He said we should do it as a story. Everybody does a surprise-birthday-party kind of a show. That's a standard sitcom kind of a thing. But here we'd do Lou Grant, a surprise birthday party and he won't let anybody in. It was not too unusual for us to do a show that had some personal experience—that kind of reality—behind it. But we didn't tell anybody who didn't already know that this was a real experience.

"So while we were doing the show Mary took me aside. She was worried. She thought we were making Lou Grant too neurotic. She said, 'Nobody would ever do a thing like this. It's just not believable.' And I think I just smiled and said that I thought we could make it work! So we ended up dealing with the show on its own terms. We couldn't have a subtitle that told the viewers that this actually happened and therefore they should believe it." And so the fictional reality was born.

Like other creators, Weinberger claims that much of the success of this and other scripts derived from the extraordinary harmony that reigned among the writers. "It was one of those rare things. We all felt close and we all liked each other and we felt we were doing good work and there was no real undercurrent of dislike anywhere. There was no gossip about other people, no unpleasantness, no door-shutting and saying he's going to have to go, I can't work with him. Everybody had a clear place in the show and I think everybody felt well treated."

He spoke of other shows where personal animosities thrived. It is possible to begin a little argument by talking about whether an actor should sit or stand while delivering a line, and gradually the fight can descend to another level and become about something altogether different. "I always had the feeling on this show that the best idea would win, and I think we all felt that way, and whoever had the best idea, the best line, the best joke, the best solution to a problem would clearly win. The boss at that particular time was whoever had the best idea."

Weinberger also feels that the early seventies were an exciting time to be in television, a kind of second golden age. Norman Lear, MTM, and *M*A*S*H* constituted a Glorious Revolution, which lasted perhaps five or six years, before the ratings wars escalated to open warfare and formula/exploitation shows crowded the more imaginative ones into the background. "I don't remember a lot of ratings talk, not the study of ratings that we have today. We knew the kinds of ratings we were getting; we were not always in the top ten; we always had some fall-off from the show that we followed, but it was not an issue." They were also aware that *All in the Family* and *M*A*S*H* got far more press coverage than did *The Mary Tyler Moore Show*, but there was satisfaction with their audience and with the respect they commanded.

Echoing the sentiments of Burns and Brooks, Weinberger describes Tinker's special talent for delegation. "He left you alone creatively. He seemed to be just an affectionate bystander. He came to the shows and just enjoyed them. There was the whole sense of a quality gentleman running the show.

"In fact, it was like you were having fun as a child and there were no grownups around. Grant was the grownup, but he didn't bother you. Moreover, he protected us from the network."

Weinberger laments the change of atmosphere since the seventies. "I don't think that you can assemble the kind of writers that we had or that *M*A*S*H* or *All in the Family* had. In the eighties anybody who would then be a story editor on one of those shows would now be off doing his own show. We then had a strong sense of loyalty. I took the job. I said, 'This is my job.' And it never occurred to me at the end of a year that I would now go to my agent and say, 'Okay, I did that for a year, now let's go to the network and sell me off and get another show somewhere.' I liked what I was doing. And so I settled down for the run of the show. You rarely find that today. Anybody who's a successful part of a show is going to go on and do his own show. So you don't have the continuity of staff or the continuity of writers and producers."

The ogre in the business is money, which Weinberger believes has altered television in a detrimental way. "Interesting statistics on what *Mary Tyler Moore* sold for in syndication per half hour, something like $17,000. Take a show that might be comparable, like *Cheers*. That's over a million dollars. So having a hit show then and now, the numbers are totally different, so astronomical. The money has changed the business so much that everybody's a partner now or out doing his or her own show."

THE SECOND GENERATION: STAN DANIELS

A writing partner with Ed. Weinberger, Stan Daniels came to the show in its fourth season. The two Easterners had, a few years earlier, spent their first years in California writing for *The Dean Martin Show*, and there they had become good friends. Stan stayed with Dean Martin after Ed. left to join the *The Mary Tyler Moore Show* one season earlier. They still collaborated, on a pilot and a number of *The Mary Tyler Moore* scripts, several of which were produced while he was still with Martin. Then, in the fifth season, he joined Ed. as co-producer and remained until the end of the series. In all they are jointly credited with twelve scripts, including contributions to episode 168, "The Last Show," and the Emmy Award–winning season opener in 1974–75, "Will Mary Richards Go to Jail?"

"I came into the show during a very turbulent year, when Brooks and Burns were starting *Rhoda* and a show called *Paul Sand in Friends and Lovers*. So they were up to their necks getting these two new shows launched, trying to be everywhere at once. I remember they were always with us during final rewrite night, but by the fifth year they split—one would take one week and one the next."

Unlike many of the other writers, who tend to remember writing and even rewriting as the proverbial piece of cake, Daniels details a more difficult schedule. "There are stages you go through, from ideas, story lines, first draft to second draft, and then the staff starts working on it, getting it ready for the reading, and then the first reading of the cast around the table, and then the next version, which is what the cast actually rehearses, and then a final version, after the director and cast have put it together, and then the rewrite night—Wednesday for us—which could go on to three or four in the morning."

But Daniels agrees with his colleagues that the writing was easy, at least compared with the usual grueling task undergone for other shows. Even from the beginning the writing seemed to flourish in the atmosphere of congeniality and mutual respect already described. "The first script I wrote [the second of his that aired] was called 'Lou's First Date' [#80, November 3, 1973]. Lou needed a date for an awards banquet and asked Mary to find him one. By mistake he ended up with an eighty-year-old lady. I wrote it, with Ed., on my hiatus from Dean Martin duties. I'd play tennis all morning and go over to Ed.'s office in the afternoons. I first met Allan Burns there, I remember. I had a sweatband on my wrist, and when we shook hands he commented that I must play tennis real fast. Anyway, it was great fun writing that script. When we first blocked it out we didn't have the idea of the old lady; in fact, we had written the whole first act before we got that idea. At first it seemed too broad, but we checked it out with Jim and Allan, who told us to go ahead."

He insists that Brooks and Burns, now executive producers, somehow managed to maintain their schedule during this season for three shows simultaneously (the Sand show lasted only one season). There was, of course, some delegating of duties, but their imprint remained firmly on each show. By the sixth year the crucial rewrite night was handled by the six men who were delegated producers: Brooks, Burns, Daniels, Weinberger, Lloyd, and Ellison.

The continuity of actors and directors provided a momentum that made everyone's job easier and more pleasant, he believes. Even those, like himself, "who rebel at the thought of something funny happening to a bunch of people every week" found satisfaction in working together, even when the hours were arduous. There was an ease of assignments, he claims. For example, there was a division of responsibilities between Weinberger and himself, the former handling the executive duties, the latter on the line with the actors and the director for each show, but also rewriting and working with other writers on their scripts.

He echoes another much-quoted theme: Each character was so well defined and so clear in the actor's mind that the writers knew what wheels were turning in each head. Daniels writes aloud, as it were, "talking for each character, with a secretary handy to get it all down—as opposed to sitting with a paper and pencil." And much of that dialogue makes it right through to the final show, even though the actors or the director might put an original spin on the words unforeseen by the writer. "That's one reason why it's good for the writers and producers to go down to the stage when the actors are reading, rehearsing, or running through the show. If something is wrong, you have to be able to suggest what it is—script, performer, director—and you have to work with each of them to determine where the trouble lies. We'd be under a lot of pressure to get the trouble corrected in a hurry, and, with everybody right there, we could make decisions fast."

This kind of ensemble effort tends to inform the writers' memories about individual shows: they may be ones written by or at least involving others. For example, Stan remembers the Weinberger birthday show for a slightly different reason from the reluctant host's. "Ed. and I have the same birthday, and at the famous party when he didn't want to open the door, I was one of those guests waiting in the hall and just about to walk away from the door. My special memory was that I was going to get all the presents intended for him, since it was as much my birthday as his! But he opened the door just in time to collect them for himself."

Another show that is memorable because of its transfer from real life, again involving the group, was episode 113, "The System." One of the pastimes of many of the men on the show, no doubt inspired by the Damon Runyon part of Jim Brooks's personality, was the football pool. "A lot of the guys used to bet on football games. I watch football games a little bit, but really was innocent about how betting on them works, how a bookie gives odds, and what 'points' was all about. These people were reading each week about this quarterback and that defense and explaining how that worked with the betting, and suddenly I understood. A revelation. So for my own satisfaction I started just making paper bets with myself. And what happened? This was the year they moved the goalposts back in professional football, and for some reason all the underdogs started winning. I had a system! I calculated that if I had actually bet with a bookie, I would have had about $1,400 in three weeks." Obviously this was too good a piece of news to keep to himself, so he shared it with Jay Sandrich, Ed. Weinberger, and Jim Brooks. They began a mini-syndicate, each putting up $250. "By the end of the season, with me doing all the betting, the Syndicate had turned its $1,000 into $1,800. This was fact!"

One could almost predict the rest of the story. The next season everybody wanted into the sure thing. Eight people put up $250, and this time the Syndicate lost its whole $2,000 in two weeks.

But all was not lost. Out of the triumph and tragedy came a fine show in which Ted devises a similar foolproof scheme, and Lou, no admirer of Ted but a consummate gambler, gets taken. In a particularly perverse way all of the creators of the show got paid for their experience.

Daniels is more comfortable with this kind of reminiscence than with the issue of social significance. He denies any particular involvement with the Women's Movement until writing and producing the show increased his awareness. Letters would come in and suggest certain themes that might or might not have been in the minds of anybody connected with the show. At least not consciously. "Maybe the only reason we seemed political was that we were writing about a woman who had a job in the early seventies, and that kind of a woman would, herself, have had to be politically aware. So if you're going to write truthfully about her, you include her political awareness. It was only that, and not, repeat *not*, to get some point across."

He is, however, proud of an award from the Population Institute, delegates from which had come to the staffs of various series shows and offered a $5,000 award for an appropriate show on world population. Stan and Ed. gave it a shot, and the result was episode 108, "A Son for Murray," which aired November 30, 1974. "It was about Murray's wife not wanting another child, since they already had three girls, and their finally adopting a Vietnamese child." The episode won the Population Institute award and the plaque stands prominently in Daniels' living room.

Stan Daniels speaks of the sanctity (not his term) of the written word. Even though it is customary to speak of television as a visual medium, "nothing could have been more controlled on this show than the ultimate authority of the script and the producer. Actors were always free to try anything, make suggestions, try something different, say what they didn't like, suggest something better. And many times they would come up with something wonderful. But basically we stuck to the words, where it all started. We didn't ad

Stan Daniels holds the Population Institute Award received by him and Ed. Weinberger.

lib. We didn't delete. Nothing, without the authority of the executive producers. Even Mary, even though she was ultimately the
financial boss of that whole operation, was wonderful about this.
What happened, rarely, was that if Mary had a problem we couldn't
agree on how to fix, she went out and did it the producers' way and
gave it the best shot and made it work that way. Although she was
the boss of the entire operation, she acknowledged that creative
authority."

THE MOST, AND MANY OF THE BEST: DAVID LLOYD

The most prolific of all the writers on *The Mary Tyler Moore Show* was
David Lloyd. David had started out in television writing for Jack
Paar on the old *Tonight* show. In 1965, he began a five-year stint
writing for Johnny Carson, followed by three years with Dick Cavett.
Lloyd had been grimly determined not to move to the West Coast:
"Like most New York writers, I swore I would die before I'd come to
California. But, of course, most of us came."

Back in his days with Carson, one of Lloyd's co-monologue writers was Ed. Weinberger, who had begun to produce *The Mary Tyler
Moore Show* in 1972. At a chance meeting Ed. suggested to his old
colleague that he try his hand at script writing. After all, he had
written several plays and had even had one produced on the West
Coast. Ed. had seen it. Although MTM didn't usually commission
scripts by telephone, they made the exception, and the result was,
in Lloyd's words, "lousy, but apparently it showed enough promise
for them to ask me to try again, this time a specific idea, about Ted
running for city council." "We Want Baxter" became episode 84
(December 1, 1973).

Now it can be told. Lloyd was entirely unfamiliar with the show
when he was asked to write it. "I had never seen it. My oldest kids
watched it, and when I decided to do it I rushed home and watched
it, and my daughter, who was fourteen years old, said that she
would make me up some kind of a list of who the characters are,
what their relations are, because I didn't have a clue as to what I
was to be doing here. So she did. I still have it somewhere, a
fourteen-year-old's perspective on *The Mary Tyler Moore Show*. But at
least it told me a little bit about the attitudes of the characters toward
each other."

Another assignment followed, and then a call from Grant Tinker, whom David describes as "wonderful about acquiring people and making them happy. You get good people, and give them a good deal, and make them happy, and they'll do the job—simplistic, but it really paid off for him during the golden age of MTM."

Tinker authorized a move for the Lloyd clan—David, his wife, and their five children—to Los Angeles for the last three weeks of 1973, to come there "just to follow them around and see how it was done," preparatory to settling in as a staff writer. This was, for him, a totally different way of operating, nothing like the comic monologues for Carson, Paar, or Cavett, or the occasional sketches and bits for those shows.

During that three weeks he did indeed "follow them around" and also wrote a third script. Between then and March 1977—the last three years of the show—he wrote twenty-seven more, plus collaboration in the final episode.

He had joined the show at a crucial time. Valerie Harper had just left, for *Rhoda,* and Betty White's Sue Ann Nivens, although she had been introduced earlier, was becoming a more frequently seen character. Lloyd feels that the show would have been stronger during its final three years if Valerie had continued with it. But he felt a special affinity for the character of Sue Ann and was also a fervent admirer of Betty White. "The year I joined, Jim and Allan wanted to increase the influence of other female characters, and so Sue Ann was used more and I found myself writing a lot of her stuff." He goes so far as to say that Sue Ann took on some of his own personality. "I know that's a terrible thing to say. No man wants to be thought of as speaking like Sue Ann Nivens. But there it is. I said it." Although Sue Ann is often spoken of as a monster, or vixen, or bitch, her dimensions are indeed more complex, and in her complexity we can all recognize something of ourselves. But Lloyd's special kinship seems to go beyond this, the way Treva Silverman's did with the Rhoda character.

Like most of the others, he denies any particular involvement with feminism, despite his assertion about increasing the influence of other female characters. Perhaps Treva, "who was my predecessor there and very much a feminist, had a lot of ideological axes to grind, but I don't think the rest of us did at all. I don't think at the time it ever crossed our minds to ask whether a certain thing was what today's woman would do. We were just trying to write stories."

Despite this disclaimer, a close look at the content of Lloyd's thirty-one shows will reveal a constant awareness of the gender revolution of the seventies.

A few examples. In episode 95, Ted fires off one of his sexist editorials—"Why Stewardesses Should Wear Tighter Skirts." Through-out the series Ted is the typical male chauvinist, constantly asserting his superiority over females, referring to them as "broads" and "chicks." In episode 107, Lloyd lets us know that Ted's mother always referred to Georgette as his broad. Not all chauvinists are male, after all!

Lou is also a rich source of outmoded attitudes about women, although, like Ted, redeeming features always humanize him and allow us to laugh at some of his posturing. In episode 112, "Mary Richards, Producer," when Mary, in her hesitating way, demands more responsibility, Lou's first instinct is to ask her to fix his squeaky chair. He, the wily male, disarms the frightened female with com-pliments and double-talk, but she rallies and gains strength, with the resulting promotion to producer. Following the expected tribula-tions (Ted suggesting a change of name to "The Ted Baxter Show," a drunken sound engineer, a violent argument between two men on the staff), her show is fine. Lou pretends reluctance with "It didn't stink" and takes her for a celebratory drink.

A similar episode, "What's Wrong with Swimming?" (#148, Octo-ber 16, 1976), demonstrates how far Mary has come since the previ-ous season. Now producing the Six O'Clock News, she wrangles with Murray, Ted, and Lou over the innovation of putting a woman, in this case an Olympic swimming champion, in charge of sportscasting. Finally, using the firmness that she has over the years become capable of expressing, she prevails. Along the way are dozens of little sexist remarks, most of them put-downs of this particular woman as "cute" or "a pretty little ninny." Each remark exposes the insecurity of the man who expresses it. Lou's feeling that football, not swimming, is sports, would probably find agreement among many viewers, much as some of Archie Bunker's sexist and ethnic pronouncements did on *All in the Family*. But just as we think we have assessed the feminist direction of the show, we are surprised to learn that the Olympic heroine has never heard of Fran Tarkenton, disapproves of any contact sport as violent, and demonstrates an arrogance that translates as blindness toward her duties. Mary tries to defend her and wrests from Lou a chance to talk in a calm, logical, and friendly way with her new employee. Lou goes home, without dinner, and Mary discovers that B.J. chooses to see her position as a matter of conscience, which is really ego thinly dis-guised. This is a complex show, a forum for discussion, in a comic mode, of traditional gender roles in American society. Finally, in one of Lloyd's best scripts, B.J. explains that she prefers to cover swimming over football because swimming is nonviolent:

Mary: Mr. Grant and I feel that there are a lot of people who are interested in those other sports. You see, since we are the producers of the news, we have to decide on the content. So, B.J., I'm asking you, please, to try to make an attempt to do it our way.

B.J.:   Well, you may be the producers of this show, but nobody can make me do anything against my conscience. I'm going to do the sportscast the way I think it should be done, and if you don't like it, well, you're just going to have to fire me. [*She gets up and goes to the door*]

Mary: B.J., hey, B.J., hey, hey, hey, hey . . . come on, listen, sit down.

B.J.:   [*Seated again*] Yes, Mary.

Mary: You're fired!

Three episodes featuring the age-old battle of the sexes, with inevitable modern overtones, are Lloyd's "Mary's Aunt," "Mary's Aunt Returns," and "Lou Proposes," with Eileen Heckart guesting as Mary's Aunt Flo. All three episodes (#126, #141, and #153) feature Lou in a broad role, that of the embattled defender of men's prerogatives. Aunt Flo is an internationally celebrated reporter, a legend who casually drops almost every famous name in modern Western history, as well as a few from the more exotic traditions— anyone she can use to impress her listeners. But overbearing as she can be, her tales are known to be true. When she meets Lou he rises at once to adversary, and this modern Beatrice and Benedict tear at each other with all the relish of people who love the conflict and admire each other. The result is a struggle of the sexes located firmly within an evolving character, Lou, who becomes more lifelike under the assault. Yet, it is Lou who breaks away from the battle of words and establishes a good relationship with Flo. Mary is perplexed, since she thought her aunt had insulted Lou. Lou explains, "People like Flo Meredith broke the ground for people like Mary Richards." Mary rises to the occasion and, looking straight at Lou, says, "You're not what I'd call a liberated man, but sometimes Mr. Grant, wow!" It seems we are hearing Mary express her solid feminist views in this brief encounter. But we are not left with this serious thought: In one of the tags, Aunt Flo mentions casually that she is off to a beheading in Iraq. And Ted is left to pronounce solemnly upon large egos. Women, he feels, should be gentle and refined: "If God had meant them to be pushy and arrogant, he'd have made them men."

Lloyd's scripts are studded with such situations and references, demonstrating an openness to women's issues and a sensibility that he as an artist downplays. His success with character humor and his avoidance of preachiness are ample proof that his disclaimers are honest. But the theme is there.

The closest of Lloyd's shows to explicit gender study is episode 134, "One Boyfriend Too Many," which aired December 13, 1975. This is another show where Mary is the center, being pulled in two directions by strong forces—in this case a current boyfriend and a former one who suddenly attempts to come back into her life. The situation becomes the occasion for a great deal of examination of male and female roles, not only by Mary and her two suitors, but by the newsroom "advisers," who help to make the serious points comedically. Ted Bessell, as the "new" friend, Joe, gives a kind of apologia for hapless males who are taught not to cry when they are unhappy. "The male version of crying," he says, "is trying to act like it doesn't hurt." And he implies, to his own satisfaction at least, that this hurt is greater than the woman's, whose sorrow is some-how assuaged by tears. But that is not the message of the show. We see right through Joe, as well as the posturing of her "old flame," a smooth professor played by guest Michael Tolan. In the end the choice is, as it should be, Mary's. Along the way the script is fairly explicit about physical intimacy, words, and looks that corroborate

Scene from "Mary's Insomnia."

the earlier assertion that Mary has an active sex life. But all these points are incidental to the style and grace of the comedy.

The two scripts by Lloyd that received the most notice are episodes 127 ("Chuckles Bites the Dust," October 25, 1975) and 155 ("Mary's Insomnia," December 4, 1976). The former won an Emmy for Best Writing and the latter a Writers Club nomination. Each tackled a serious subject—death and sleeping-pill addiction, respectively—but managed them successfully within the comedy of character. "Chuckles" is regularly referred to as the masterpiece of the series, still providing hearty laughter by writers, critics, and audiences, who remember it vividly. For readers who don't, the situation concerns the death of Chuckles the Clown, who, while serving as grand marshal in a circus parade, is killed. He was dressed as Peter Peanut and "a rogue elephant tried to shell him." ("Shell" alone is worth the Emmy.) Led by Murray's wisecracks, the nervous laughter among the people in the newsroom who must report this absurd death outrages Mary, who alone seems abashed by the death of a fellow human being. The final act is the funeral itself, when Murray, Ted, Lou, and the others who had found death in this circumstance so funny are finally sober. It is Mary who cracks as the minister sanctimoniously drones on about Chuckles—his life and his make-believe television friends, including "Mr. Fee Fi Fo." Mary's gradual and unwilling descent into laughter is a perfect example of her comic abilities, truly a delight to be seen and not described.

The sleeping-pill episode likewise gives Mary some of her finest comic moments—first, as the spaced-out insomniac, then through permutations of relief when the pills work, to alarm at possible addiction, to guilt when she lies to Lou (a sort of guardian angel in this episode) about giving up the pills. A scene of broad hilarity takes place in Mary's bathroom when first Lou, then Murray, then Ted barge in during her bath to check on her. Throughout the long scene Lou sits quite naturally on the toilet, its lid conveniently down. Safe but distinctly uncomfortable beneath a mound of suds, Mary has to endure this invasion of her privacy by her concerned friends.

In addition to his role as writer, Lloyd acted for three years as the show's warm-up comedian. His wit is ready and spontaneous, and he is adept at the comedian's trade, no doubt honed with Paar, Carson, and Cavett. So it was natural that, following Lorenzo Music, he took over this arduous job. "I was always in great awe of Lorenzo, as I had watched him over the years. I don't mean just how he was quick-witted with his jokes and continued to be personable with the audience, but how he danced around the set and avoided getting hit by the moving cameras. I had been used to

David Lloyd in his warm-up role.

writing material like this, for Carson, but I turned it in and let him do it and maybe went home and watched him on television. I had no idea this albatross was going to be hung around my neck." As he now remembers it he did some little amusing monologue at a party for cast and crew, improvised something that was apparently successful. "So they came and asked me to guess what I was going to get to do this year. I was absolutely terrified. People in the audience were going to ask me all those questions that they ask the warm-up person, and I wouldn't know the answers to anything. They were going to ask what that man over there does, and I don't yet know the difference between a gaffer and a dolly grip. I didn't know how much the show cost, I didn't know how many feet of film are in a camera. And Jim and Allan just told me to make something up." After a crash course in facts and details, he discovered that he could occasionally make a joke to avoid an answer, but he was frequently embarrassed by intelligent questions and his ignorance about the identity of someone or his job, someone who had been on the show for years and was still unknown to him. He finally developed some running jokes, which were successful week after week, and grew more comfortable in the job. "One was a gig about Allan Burns being an alcoholic. Allan always looked more dignified than anybody, always better dressed. I found I could get a laugh by playing on his aura of elegance, by pointing him out to the audience as someone who was so crocked that he hadn't had a cogent thought since midmorning. The crew would laugh, too, so I embroidered it a little more each week. One day Allan came over with a pair of clippers and cut the microphone cord—just cut it and walked away. He had been suffering silently with all those drunk jokes for weeks and decided to do this. First—he's a prudent man—he asked an electrician whether he could get electrocuted if he cut that cord, and he found out it was safe. So he put the clippers in his pocket and just waited."

Another of his memories coming out of this warm-up phase is instructive about the way the show worked. "One day, for some reason, they forgot to turn the microphones on. And so we got a very silent show. Mary, Ted, and Ed came out for the first scene and did their lines, some very funny ones, and heard no response from the audience. They didn't know that the audience couldn't hear. So they began to get louder and to push and take the pace up, and the whole thing deteriorated. Within about three pages they had gone haywire." The problem was soon diagnosed and corrected, but Lloyd had been permanently impressed by the fact that, even after four successful years of The Mary Tyler Moore Show, these veteran actors were still so humanly fallible, not at all the machines they might have become. There was no going through the motions, as there is on so many long-running sitcoms. The freshness remained. "I thought these people would sail through any old episode, no matter what. But when that laugh didn't come, they started compensating, trying hard, then too hard." There is a famous story of the great conductor Toscanini, at the height of his legendary career, leading his orchestra into disaster during a performance of Ravel's "Bolero." Apparently the timing of this overly rhythmic piece was off just a little, then a little more, then gradually chaos. It can happen to the best of them.

FUN THEN AND FUN NOW: BOB ELLISON

The last major writer to enter the scene has a now-familiar background. Yet another New Yorker, Bob Ellison had been a publicity writer, then a writer for stand-up comedians in nightclubs. His most important client was Dom DeLuise, a classmate from the High School for the Performing Arts in Manhattan. He asked Bob's help for a television special; when that was a success, the team moved to *The Dean Martin Summer Show* with Rowan and Martin. There followed another special for DeLuise, *The Bar-Ump-Bump Show*. Ellison also wrote for a dizzying assortment of variety shows: *The Steve Allen Show*, *The Dean Martin Show*, *Kraft Music Hall*, *That's Life* (with regular Robert Morse, but with an assortment of guests such as Sid Caesar, Paul Lynde, Ethel Merman, Goldie Hawn, Alan King, and Tony Randall). Along the way he moved from writing to producing variety shows, including some Alan King specials. It was due to his success, at different times over the years, working with both Jack Klugman and Tony Randall, that he had been asked by producer Garry Marshall to come to Hollywood to write for *The Odd Couple*. "I resisted and resisted, to stay in New York and work for variety shows, but that market was dwindling. I found myself working more often in London, as variety slowly died on television." And so he was ready, at last, when *The Mary Tyler Moore Show* beckoned. "Somehow I think the invitation came from Klugman and Randall through Garry Marshall to Penny Marshall to Jim Brooks. At any rate, she was the one who recommended me to Jim. Ed. Weinberger had heard about me because he had also done *The Dean Martin Show*. He and Stan Daniels. We didn't know each other there— different years—but they knew of my work."

Like many other writers who became successful in the half-hour situation comedy format, Ellison was not really familiar with such shows. "I wasn't a big fan. I am one of those guys who can honestly say I didn't watch *Lucy, Beaver, Andy Griffith*, any of that stuff. But the old *Dick Van Dyke Show* and *The Mary Tyler Moore Show* for some reason I watched . . . and loved." At least part of the reason is clear to him now: At the time he was a musician but was really interested in comedy writing. "Here was this guy, Rob Petrie, who *was* a comedy writer. All day he worked in a room with Morey Amsterdam and Rose Marie. I thought this must be the greatest life in the world. All day long, somebody who is paid to think funny." He adds, with the sure instinct of the stand-up comic, New York accent and all, "Funny. Funny is good."

He took a major cut in salary, realizing that variety was a dwindling opportunity and that he was lucky to be invited into the only current show he really enjoyed watching. "I had had a crush on Laura Petrie. I really believed her, thought that she seemed more real than any of the other women in comedies. That show had a better quality than all the other shows around. And *The Mary Tyler Moore Show* seemed to me to be an extension of this, of that kind of reality, but updated." He joined at the beginning of the sixth season, as story editor, is credited with the first episode of that year (#121, "Edie Gets Married," September 13, 1975), and stayed for the duration of the series.

Without denigrating any of his earlier or later work, he still refers to 1975–77 as his halcyon days. "*Mary* was my first experience with situation comedy, and I had no idea that the other shows weren't like this until I found that on other shows the writers were going home at two or three in the morning, and we never had that. We used to do a lot of cutting up, that maybe was a part of working, but we still managed to get home at a decent hour. The show would be in good shape every step of the way. A good group. And it was a good time in television. I don't think we've seen it since, that kind of a lineup, with us and *M*A*S*H* and the Lear stuff. If you liked comedy, you had a lot to choose from." He agrees with Jim Brooks that the competition in those days was not so much between shows as within the show itself. "We were striving each week to be more real, more funny, more true to our developing characters, but this didn't at all keep us from being delighted with a great Norman Lear show."

It was this harmony and relative ease that allowed him, without too much strain, to contribute his own scripts as writer and also, as story editor, to participate in rewriting the work of others. "There was a lot of time for both on that show, because there were a lot of times when we weren't in major trouble. In fact, I don't ever recall being in major, major trouble on that show."

In all he is credited with fourteen episodes, plus an involvement in "The Last Show."

For him the key to *The Mary Tyler Moore Show* was realism. It was that quality that had led him, first, to the old *Dick Van Dyke Show* and then to what he saw as its successor. "But by realism I don't mean the disease-of-the-week show. I did admire *All in the Family, Maude,* shows like that. They managed to be funny, also. But that was always the parting of the ways—the Norman Lear camp and the MTM camp. We did things that were a little simpler, perhaps, and we left the abortions and diseases to Lear, who did them very well. Our realism was of a different sort."

Nor does he believe that the reality of the show involved a conscious attempt to speak for women. "We were just trying to do the most entertaining show possible and deal with subject matter that was fairly contemporary. There were many women working on the show and they may have made suggestions. Mary herself may have made suggestions. And probably Treva Silverman had set a tone very early on. But by the time I got there all the writers and producers happened to be men. That didn't seem to make a difference."

His work on *Rhoda*, however, was quite another matter. There the social and political messages were much more pronounced. "There were a lot of times we had conferences about a line or expression that we didn't want to say. I think it was because Valerie Harper was, and still is, more active in world affairs than Mary. And Valerie does a lot of analyzing."

He does remember a few crossovers from real life into art, however. One was a show in which Mary, the producer of the Six O'Clock News, discovers that Lou has promoted Murray to co-producer without her assent (#150). That idea came from Ellison's wife. She had worked in New York for Harry Reasoner and knew of a similar situation, although it happened to be a struggle between two men.

Generally the kind of reality admired in the show is threatened by fantasy shows. In fact, fantasy shows are a sort of shibboleth in the business, usually signaling desperation on the part of the writers and producers. And yet Ellison speaks of two very fondly. In the first, "Mary's Three Husbands" (#165, February 26, 1977), dream sequences were used to speculate on what life might have been like if Mary Richards had been the wife of Ted, of Murray, or of Lou. Because the fantasy was so thoroughly rooted in strong characters who had been developed over the seven years, the episode became less a standard fantasy than a continued analysis of character.

Another was a flashback show with a guest star, "two sure signs," as one critic has it, "that a sitcom is headed for the end of a long run on network TV." And yet one commentator adds, "It's a credit to the ambition of the creative staff of *The Mary Tyler Moore Show* that they dared to dust off *both* these old sitcom chestnuts in a single audacious episode" (Vince Waldron, *Classic Sitcoms*). Ellison remembers this show as, indeed, a desperate time for them. It was near the end of the series and nothing clicked, until suddenly he was touched by the most recent muse (not yet named, but assigned to the electronic media) and he wrote "Mary's Big Party" in less than three days (#166, March 5, 1977). "Mary is throwing one of her bad parties, the kind she was famous for. So that this one will be a success, she invites a big celebrity as guest of honor. Our problem became: Who? We needed somebody, but the script required that person to remain in the dark. All we needed was the voice. We were calling everybody. Someone mentioned Warren Beatty. We called him and he promised to consider it if Mary herself called him. She did, and they chatted, but he had some sort of commitment and we didn't get him."

The problem was finally resolved in a way that they had scarcely hoped for. Ed. Weinberger "called in some kind of a marker" and Johnny Carson came over, memorized his lines (necessary because you can't read cue cards in the dark), and even warmed up the audience. "He came out after the show and told everyone it was the second most fun he ever had in the dark."

Above all, Ellison remembers the fun. "The chemistry was just right. We had a lot of respect for each other. We appreciated each other's work. And had fights. Yes, fights. But never ugly ones, just stubborn fights, where you didn't give in. And always for the good of the show. It was never personalities. Amazing! We would fight over a single word and now, in syndication, they take that finely crafted work, cut and edit out a couple of minutes . . . and it still works."

5

MARY TYLER MOORE/
MARY RICHARDS

TURNING THE WORLD ON WITH A SMILE

MARY TYLER MOORE

The young actress Mary Tyler Moore found no easy road for her career when Laura Petrie left CBS in 1966. Dick Van Dyke's starring role and his successes in film, particularly *Mary Poppins* (1964) and *The Comic* (1969), were in marked contrast to Mary's three years of professional work at the close of the decade. And CBS seemed mired in a style of comedy that was a far cry from the genius of Carl Reiner and the classic *Dick Van Dyke Show*.

One looks back twenty years to a very different CBS. In 1969–70 the network had thirteen of the top twenty-five series on the air. The dominant comedies were bucolic, featuring *Mayberry R.F.D.* (#4 in the ratings), *The Jim Nabors Hour* (#12), *The Beverly Hillbillies* (#18), *Hee Haw* (#21), along with *Green Acres* and *Petticoat Junction*. There were no less than seven one-hour variety shows, a couple of dying Westerns (*Lancer* and *Gunsmoke* [#2]), and a few leftovers from the sitcom days (*Here's Lucy* [#6], *The Doris Day Show* [#10], *Family Affair* [#5], and *My Three Sons* [#15]). As new network president Bob Wood looked at the schedule in 1970, the single jewel seemed to be *The Carol Burnett Show* (#13). Wood determined to scrap a successful ratings lineup and redirect the network schedule for the seventies, an action that revolutionized television comedy. By October 1971 only five of the thirteen series of 1969 remained, but the network continued to dominate the Nielsens with eleven of the top twenty-five shows for the season 1971–72.

77

However, the first of the many new faces, Mary Tyler Moore's, did not appear by the mere waving of a wand. There was no automatic generating of an instantly recognized and heralded brilliant series. In fact, the creation of *The Mary Tyler Moore Show* may best be described—as we have—as an accident of time and place involving the emergence of new and unestablished talent wedded to the gifts of Mary, who was starring for the first time in her own series.

In 1975 writer/producer Jim Brooks, reflecting on the comparison between the *Van Dyke* and *Mary* series, made it clear that Mary was untested as a television "star" in 1969. She had come from "a brilliant, yet trouble-free environment on *The Dick Van Dyke Show*. We couldn't use her that way again, any more than we could have used *Father Knows Best*." So they had to find a new situation for her, something for the seventies but something that would be congenial with the talents she had demonstrated a decade earlier with Van Dyke. With her less-than-spectacular films and a stage disaster, Mary Tyler Moore was facing the cynical notion that she "had merely ridden to her Emmys on the coattails of Van Dyke."

It was then something of an irony that the Dick Van Dyke special, *How to Succeed in the 70's Without Really Trying* (aired on CBS, April 13, 1969), featuring Mary Tyler Moore, should rekindle network interest in her. This variety hour was written and produced by Bill Persky and Sam Denoff, who had done the *Van Dyke* show. It was heralded on the cover of *TV Guide* with a brief article entitled "They're Together Again!" closing with the sentence, "The two stars and the two producers hope to produce again the chemistry that once resulted in television success for them." Mary translated her several spots on the show into special moments. As one critic put it at the time, "Mary was hot again."

We have previously cited Grant Tinker's assessment of the reunion and its importance in affording this chance with the network for a new series. As it began there were the requisite interviews, in which Moore was guarded in her appraisal of her own ability. She is quoted with typical modesty in one: "I never went the Actors Studio route. I'm not an actress who can create a character. I play me." This statement, often repeated by her and others, coupled with her apparent ease in creating the character of Mary Richards, seems to have resulted in the unfortunate identification of the two Marys that continues to plague her.

We might also note that time has contradicted this assessment, by herself and others, that Mary Tyler Moore is Mary Richards, as her career in film has exposed a fine range, from *First You Cry* to

Ordinary People to *Vidal's Lincoln.* Her stage successes have added further luster to her career, demonstrating versatility not only in comedy but also in drama.

Of course there almost certainly is a reflection of the talented comedienne in her creation of the sensitive, decent, caring Mary Richards. Her associates from those years confirm this judgment, saccharine though it may sound. Ed. Weinberger, for example, feels that "Mary Richards's brand of Midwestern all-American sort of perfection" was very much like that of the person playing the part—even though she was born in Brooklyn.

Susan Silver wishes that she had gotten to know Mary better. Looking back, she believes the reason Moore was so quick to master her part was explained by the fact that the character was very close to her. "She just knew. And Mary went right on with the character, knew what it was. Of course if something new came in, she'd adapt, but there wasn't a lot of searching because she really was on top of the character."

On a more personal note, Mary Tyler Moore met Grant Tinker in connection with *The Dick Van Dyke Show* pilot in 1961. They started dating some months later and were married in 1962. "My image of her from the beginning," he says, "was Laura Petrie. We were married for eighteen years, and I must tell you there was something restorative about rediscovering a woman I really admired named Mary Richards who was sort of a relative of Laura Petrie even though the situations were terribly different." Obviously, the warm glow of affection still lingers. They remain friends.

Was Mary Tyler Moore really Mary Richards? It appears that most dedicated fans of the series want to think so. But we believe this does her an injustice, a typecasting born of affection. Certainly, Moore, the actor, mother, divorced, remarried, now a stunning success, at the very same age as Mary Richards when she asked for her first job from Lou Grant, was hardly typecast in the new series.

Marge Mullen, script supervisor for the entire run of the series, director of four episodes, and close friend of Mary, has locked on to the best reading. "She has wonderful instincts. I don't know that she gives herself credit for this. And she's extremely bright. If Mary had decided to be a top corporation or trial lawyer, she could have done it. The only reason she didn't become a terrific dancer, I mean a prima ballerina, is that she had so many other interests, and maybe she didn't start young enough and she didn't eat, breathe, and sleep ballet. But as a dancer, when she crossed over to acting, she was extremely disciplined. She was ready to rehearse all the time and she enjoyed rehearsal.

"She took classes constantly. In that special she did with Dick Van Dyke that got such wonderful ratings, if you look at the film, you can always cut to Mary. Something is always happening. She reacts to everything. She doesn't just act, she reacts.

"From the beginning of the *Mary* show in 1970 she was always extremely generous with focusing on somebody else in a scene. She wasn't the kind of star who said, 'Well, this show is not about me this week, I'm not going to do it.' There was no ego that way at all. She wanted the show to be terrific and she knew the strength of the characters she had. If it meant switching lines or giving someone else a laugh, she'd say, 'Go ahead and do it, it will be better for the show.' "

In late October 1988, Mary Tyler Moore provided a rare look back as she talked about her new show, *Annie McGuire:* "I want to try something different. Win or lose, I want it to be about something different, something that I really trust and am interested in myself." But *USA Today* did not allow this plea to prevail. It closed the interview with her by almost predicting another failure, commenting, ". . . if Moore can't make it after all in a TV series again, you silently understand that she probably won't have another second chance, that the shining, smiling ghost of Mary Richards looms too large— even if the good girl is a woman now."

We demur. This ghost does not "loom." In the first place, over ten years have passed since Mary Richards graced American homes in originally run episodes. Second, the syndication of the series has not produced nearly the exposure MTM had hoped. Today the series is comfortably settled into perhaps 25 percent of the TV market at any given time. Third, there are vast numbers of new viewers who are prepared, with no clear past images, to accept the kind of quality comedy of which Mary Tyler Moore is capable. Indeed, that quality is largely the cement for this entire volume.

The Mary Tyler Moore Show was a special moment in television history. Brooks and Weinberger with *Taxi,* Sandrich with *SOAP* and *Cosby,* Lloyd and Ellison with *Cheers,* all look back to those exceptional relationships in the seventies. Mary Tyler Moore has no ghost to dispel, only a talent to display, the talent that gave life and vitality to a dozen associates, all of whom know she possesses the chemistry to enliven the screens of the future with her smile and grace.

The fragility of a television comedic series is ultimately the reason why ensemble is so essential, something unsurpassed in *The Mary Tyler Moore Show.* But such rare collections of talent require time and network commitment while seeking an audience. One need only be reminded of the previously quoted assessments of *Mary* by *Time* and *The New York Times*. That luxury did not exist for *Molly Dodd*, it does not exist for *Annie McGuire*. Further, the emergence in the eighties of cable and the disastrous coalition of television networks with corporate ignorance has caused a catastrophic decline in network concern over quality and content. The broadcast-wise network executives of the past—William Paley, David Sarnoff, Robert Wood, Pat Weaver, Grant Tinker—have been replaced by a mentality that comprehends little of what may be at stake in the most popular art. Certainly the public taste that elevated Geraldo Rivera's NBC special "Devil Worship: Exposing Satan's Underground" to a Nielsen rating of 21.9 and a share of 33, in the very week when the new offerings by Van Dyke and Moore premiered to disappointing numbers, reminds us that quality is no guarantor of success. Yet there was a time when series experiencing initial hard going in the ratings were allowed to mature and seek an audience. We repeat: No such attitude prevails in today's market.

The early demise of *Annie McGuire* in that market is a sad reminder that another talented actor wasn't given a fair chance. We would like to suggest three remarkable talents that Mary Tyler Moore combines: a convincing acting style; a treasury of facial, voice, and body responses; and a controlled ego. Cloris Leachman was, in many ways, the opposite of Mary as an actor. For that reason she knew whereof she spoke when she remarked of Mary, "She was so patient with us. We fooled around and changed the pace. She said, 'Well, I just wait until you carve a little path and then I just dance down it.' She couldn't have been more honoring of us and of our right to work the way we knew how to work." Weinberger believes she was able to cope with the differing acting styles of Leachman and Harper because "Mary locked in immediately. She always knew what she had to do and did it that way from the moment that she picked up the script. She honed in on it, locked it, and had it perfect." Sandrich concurs: "Mary's the only person I've ever worked with who can take a totally rewritten page of dialogue, look at it, in effect stare at it once, and go do it. That's a gift."

On this subject Grant Tinker probably puts it best. "Mary had some wonderful abilities to mix that spunk with uncertainty. That was the Everywoman about Mary Richards." He continues, "She set such a great example for everybody else in terms of being on time, knowing her lines, hitting her marks, never missing a beat, never playing the star. We all know that there are stars . . . and stars. Some of them are a giant pain in the ass and do indeed think of themselves as something loftier than their fellow actors. Mary wasn't that way. It didn't mean that we all socialized together a lot, in fact that didn't happen. That's one of the things I appreciated about Mary—her professionalism. The fact that when she came to work, she came to work. And her genius. People miss a lot of what Mary did because she was surrounded by such a wonderful group, getting better all the time. Everyone really grew as actors, including Mary. I would be in the booth during the filming and become very emotional about the quality of work. I was so proud of the way those people were doing their jobs, beginning with Mary. I used to be so proud of her, even when Mary and I were having problems of our own at home. That part of my feeling about her never wavered at all and doesn't to this day."

If all these comments by associates on the show, in retrospect, help in understanding the person who worked at Sound Stage 2 at

Knight, MacLeod, and Asner warm up the audience with new lyrics to an old tune, "More."

"Moore plays the meddler who is full of mirth,
Moore is part Lucy and part Mary Worth.

Moore has a boss who's tough,
Yes Moore likes that hackneyed stuff,
'Cause Moore knows what viewers go for,
Else what would they watch her show for?

Moore gets the close-up shots galore,
Is the one that fans adore,
'Cause that show is owned by Moore!"

Mary Tyler Moore, along with Steve Allen (right) and Dr. Frank Stanton (former president of CBS), is inducted into the Television Academy Hall of Fame in 1986.

CBS in Studio City, the millions of dedicated viewers who waited for Mary every Saturday evening knew only those twenty-three minutes a week in which she provided the focus of what, in 1985, a select group of television critics identified as the "top TV sitcom of all times."

It is a fact that her millions of loyal followers "believed" Moore was Richards, but this identity, we say again, derived from her remarkable acting gifts. And there is little doubt that Moore had a genuine sympathy for the character of Richards. Is there some magical link between Moore and popular culture's heroine of the seventies, the girl from Minnesota, reared in a traditional environment, at the age of thirty, trying "to make it on her own"? Certainly their backgrounds were dissimilar. We believe that the catalyst for the near-instant acceptance of this decent woman, the daughter many viewers imagined as the ideal, the young woman other viewers came to consider as a model for their own struggles in the early seventies, was the credibility of Moore, something already established in *The Dick Van Dyke Show*.

MARY RICHARDS

Moore's role as Mary Richards evolved as writers and producers polished the gem so carefully crafted in 1970. And always as the subtle changes were effected we were reminded that from the moment, in the first episode, when Mary says to Rhoda, "Because if you push me, then I might just have to push back," and Rhoda responds, "You can't carry that off!" Mary's character is defined. She replies, with quavering voice and facial expression to match, "I know."

In those early episodes Mary seemed most at home in her associations with Rhoda and Phyllis. We recall that Burns and Brooks had expected the Harper character to be one of two major figures around whom Mary's life would revolve. The other was Lou Grant. Thinking back to 1961, it is easy to see how Mary is in one important way a continuation of Rob Petrie. He had his home environment with its center in Laura, and his work world with Sally and Buddy. That format was unique for its time, offering two distinct worlds, with the lead performer providing the center for both groups, bringing all the characters together. Mary did precisely the same thing, but with her own particular genius.

To even the casual viewer of *The Mary Tyler Moore Show* the central significance of Mary Richards never diminished from September 1970 through March 1977. Yet Mary changed, grew, progressed even as she remained for Lou that "same naive girl" who came into his office seeking her first job. Rooted though she was in traditional Midwestern values, Mary was nevertheless a modern woman, indeed a career woman seeking to "cope," to achieve independence. She was a pioneer for vast numbers of women of the same age who struggled every day for identity against male dominance and conventionality. Hers was a breath of reasonableness in a time when little rationality attached to questions of females in society. Mary was every bit a person and every bit a woman. Lou may have been wiser, but Mary was smarter, the most intelligently alert person in the newsroom. She conveyed the ability to deal with the rising new world that was shattering her sheltered existence and that of her colleagues. She neither accepted without question past values nor rejected them out of hand. She was able to crack conventions because people believed her to be genuine. In Brooks's words, "Mary believed that people should be open and loving toward one another."

The images of Mary Richards etched in the mind of the frequent viewer began with her driving to Minneapolis while the credits rolled and the theme song urged, "Love is all around, why don't you take it?" The first year the writers experimented with ways to give substance to this new person on the television screen. Seven years later she would be so real that one newspaper columnist wrote

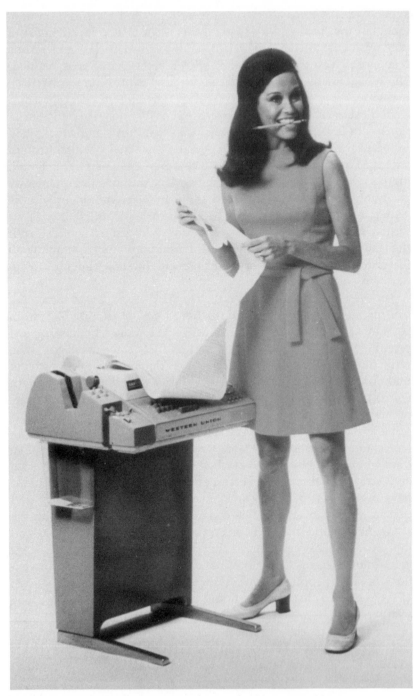

America's first look at Mary Richards. *TV Guide*'s preview issue, September 12, 1970.

that he could not watch the show in syndication because the reruns reminded him that Mary Richards was not the real person he had come to accept as a friend.

The early image continued with Mary in a wig that Grant Tinker remembers as silly, and a miniskirt. It is an image that now haunts or amuses many women who were young during that period. In a recent interview with the authors of this book, Marlo Thomas remembers how she and Gloria Steinem set about preaching women's rights dressed in tiny little skirts and enormous hairdos. Images of women in those years seem especially sexist now. In episode 2 this early version of Mary is worried about being addressed as "ma'am," a title that in 1970 was deadly in the minds of millions of "thirtyish" single women. The next week Mary was off on a shopping excursion with Bess, Phyllis's young daughter. It was the exuberance of the day, the carefree relationship established, that informed us early about Mary's "real" self, in contrast to some of the excesses of wardrobe.

One of the delights of the first season was the comic romance Mary developed with her IRS auditor, played brilliantly by Paul Sand. The final show of the season found Mary pleading with the station owner, played to his absurd hilt by Slim Pickens, to give back Lou's job, a casualty of ratings.

By the second season Lou's office became the launching pad for a large percentage of the plots to follow. Burns believes you can catch the essence of each episode by viewing those few minutes Mary spent in Mr. Grant's office each week. Perched precariously on the edge of the chair facing Lou's desk, Mary was uneasy, if spunky, in the early going. Slowly she relaxed, moved back in the chair, and exchanged conversation with her boss. It was the location in which Lou would lecture Mary about the business, and she would lecture him about human relations and fairness. It was, in a peculiar way, a networking experience that reminds one of those exchanges between *Cagney and Lacey*'s detectives in the station-house rest room. It was there that Mary was "fired," cared for Lou in his anguish over divorce, challenged his unfair pay scale for women, received love-life advice from Lou, faced the specter of going to jail rather than reveal a source, tricked Lou into a date with Sue Ann, and asked him for a date herself.

Essential to our image of Mary Richards were her quick changes—not of costume, but of facial expression. The illustrations in this section give some clue to the amazing mobility of her face, which could express uncertainty and resolve simultaneously, and then move like lightning into a special blend of apprehension and relief.

In one episode Mary came to Lou with the idea of her singing during the annual Teddy Award dinner, a program she was to plan. Stunned, Lou asked for an audition and Mary obliged with perhaps the worst singing performance recorded outside the *Gong Show*. Her mannerisms and movements and expressions were a comic master-piece. Mustering all his skill, Lou listened, paused, and then laughed, telling Mary how funny it was that she was "putting him on." She fumbled a moment and then agreed that it had all been a joke and left crestfallen. She had been serious. Lou, caught by the camera alone in his office, uttered a huge sigh of relief. He had stopped her without offending and without sending her out to make a complete fool of herself. In repeated similar scenes we come to understand her co-workers when they insist that Mary Tyler Moore's comic range made every other performer excel.

Mary, a part of her generation, was sophisticated concerning sexual relationships. She might on occasion worry about being sin-gle and thirty, but her behavior made it clear that there was no desperation for marriage in this woman. As she became involved with more than a dozen companions over the run of the series, we knew she would demonstrate maturity and graciousness in her relationships. Mary never had an affair, but most certainly she was physically involved with some of her male friends. The birth-control-pill incident referred to in the previous chapter is evidence of this

Mary matches gestures to the words of "One More for the Road."

fact, and we have seen the acknowledgment among writers (announced in the format of 1970) that hers was not a cloistered virtue.

Usually Mary dated men who were her intellectual match, but on
a single occasion she had a relationship with an empty-headed,
muscular ski instructor to whom Mary could have been attracted
only, as Jay Sandrich observed, "because he must have been good in
bed." Watching that episode (#98), we are struck by the turn of the
tables. How often have we watched men respond to "just another
pretty face" without any serious question about intellect? The difference is one of expectations in a male society. As the writers explored
this theme they were turning the tables on an old and accepted
custom—men placing a premium on physical attractiveness. It is a
theme touched once and then abandoned, because in fact it did not
make sense for Mary to become involved with someone only for

physical reasons. In the final season Mary articulated this directly when she was taken home by a date who began to disrobe upon closing the door. She threw him out, kindly let him return after he apologized, and then, when he repeated the action, in a rage threw him out for good. From this experience she reflected on all those men we have met with her and she pointedly described most as a waste. From that musing came her decision to "date" Lou Grant.

And it was as a liberated woman that Mary asked Lou to go out. But that was no recent development for her. She had exercised courage and fortitude born of a commitment to equality virtually from the beginning. She had posed the question of equal pay for women. She had faced the taunts of Ted and others over hiring a female sportscaster and had stood firm. She had stood up to Lou and told him she would handle a hiring decision because it was her job. It was Mary who had educated the newsroom to the meaning of Women's Liberation, clearly seen in the numerous allusions to the subject over the years. It was Mary who had stood up for journalistic integrity in the question of revealing her source, a decision that sent her to jail. It was Rhoda who had told Mary she had a "Ms. kind of job."

So Mary was a woman comfortable with the fresh ideas of the seventies, something we must presume was true of the producers as well. As part of that revolution Mary reminds us that being feminine unapologetically is part of it. She was consistently kind, never wanting to hurt feelings. One remembers her extravagant efforts to buttress the ego of a forlorn and washed-up football player in episode 5, her regular zealous efforts to reinflate Ted's ego so that he could function, well presented in episode 12. And of course there was the elaborate effort to befriend a prostitute she met in jail, becoming her "guardian" and friend in episode 117.

Mary's friendship was unquestioned. If you were her friend, then she cared enough to nurture the relationship. Some friends, like Phyllis, put a strain on her, but she was loyal. Sometimes her concern for friends interfered with her work, but she always found a way to put people first. And the friendships allowed space for anger. She could show it in relation to Ted when he acted insensitively toward Georgette, or even toward Rhoda when a betrayal of confidence was involved. But her definition of friendship compelled her to restore communication.

Whereas each of the other major figures in the cast had shows centering on them, this series was about Mary. As the mediator earlier described by Treva Silverman, or as the center of a wheel as suggested by Susan Silver, Mary Richards was the focus of the series.

In Mary Richards we saw lightness and gentleness that spoke eloquently to an American society torn by political strife. Mary—Richards and Moore—was not about politics or power or patriotism or position so much as about people. The producers/writers speak of all the shows, in one way or another, being love relationships. Yet the Mary Richards concerned about people was a particular kind of person who had political and social views that made her recoil at anti-Semitism, stand firm for a free press, believe in racial equality, respect gay rights, believe in equal pay for women, favor gun control, and endorse the new freedom in sexual mores. As we have suggested in the previous chapter, such a person was created by writers who shared those sentiments. She was the creation of very bright, humane, and genuinely liberal minds.

THE PLAYERS

RHODA: FROM ZAFTIG TO GLAMOUR

Valerie Harper played Mary's best friend and confidante, and sometimes foil, for the first ninety-four episodes, until almost the end of the fourth season. During that time the character evolved from what *Ms.* magazine described as a "rather frumpy, overweight, wisecracking man-chaser" to "the very attractive, wisecracking Rhoda who now makes jokes about the men who are chasing her instead of those who got away." The common denominator of those two descriptions, "wisecracking," is perhaps not quite fair to the character or to the actress, who gave her smart-aleckness innumerable nuances, but it will serve as a beginning. More accurately, and more important in the long run, Gail Rock, who wrote that article (December 1973), made the point that Rhoda was just as funny after she became an attractive woman.

From the beginning Rhoda Morgenstern was designed to be a crucial character: the 1970 format anticipates that the relationship between the two women will be a major emphasis in the series. Rhoda was to provide a degree of the sex on the show. In fact this 32-year-old independent Jewish woman from New York was cast as having had numerous relationships.

She is confrontational by nature. Her first words to Mary are "Hello. Get out of my apartment." This hard edge is easily associated with her New York background and in direct contrast with Mary. As a character foil to Mary, she would grudgingly start to like this trusting, Protestant native of Elm Street. And Rhoda would learn that pushing Mary too hard would reveal a rare militant Presbyterian.

In the first episode the confrontation noted in the format is fleshed out into several scenes, including elaboration of hostility between her and Phyllis but also with the crucial information that Bess, Phyllis's daughter, likes her. As we noted earlier, the creators of the show believe that Bess's approval was an important factor in helping make the audience accept Rhoda as a friend. Toward the end of the first episode, when the argument is winding down over whether Mary or Rhoda gets the apartment, the two accept that there's some agreeable chemistry between them that will probably prevent their disliking each other. Or, as Rhoda puts it, if they are going to be enemies, "We're both going to have to work on it."

Thereafter, for ninety-three more episodes, the relationship develops, "composed of love and conflict," as Brooks and Burns recall. Because the show was so well conceived and written, it does not develop as conflict one week, love the next, but every week as a blend of the two. There is always a little vitriol associated with Rhoda, which as we have seen usually gets described as "wisecracking." Like Murray, she demonstrates some hostility through her witty one-liners, although Valerie Harper rings enormous changes on the tone. She can, among other turns, register anger, self-deprecation, rue, playfulness, or defensiveness. Mary once describes her as competitive. When we meet her father, as played by Harold Gould in episode 52, we find that she is something of a chip off the old block. He, too, will have his little jokes at others' expense, usually ending with a smile, a pointed finger, and "Gotcha." Typical of her humor is the blend of subjects and tones in this remark to Mary: "You've got the kind of job Gloria Steinem would applaud. Mine, on the other hand, Gidget would have passed up to go hang ten" (#91).

Much of her humor seems to derive from her image of herself. From the beginning Rhoda has a self-image problem. Her most lasting job is not a prestigious one, as the world judges such things: She is a window dresser at Hempel's Department Store, a job that she accepts after being fired from another store (#36). Mary and her other friends rally and bring her back to enough self-esteem to be employable again. Her talent at decorating is seen in her own apartment and in several episodes where she becomes embroiled in decorating or designing for others in the cast (Mary, Ted, and Lou, for example). But she is not really *proud* of her job.

Neither does she, in contrast to Mary, have the satisfaction of independence. Her mother's apron strings are still tied securely

Mary is the center of attention as she moves into her new apartment.

around her daughter's neck. Ida Morgenstern, played in several
episodes by Nancy Walker, makes her first appearance very early in
the series, in "Support Your Local Mother," written by Brooks and
Burns, who won the Emmy for Outstanding Writing Achievement
in Comedy for this episode (#6). Ida specializes in guilt, which
Rhoda is smart enough to diagnose but powerless to struggle successfully against. All during this episode she refuses to see her
mother, who consequently descends on Mary to try her hand at
guilt-dispensing there (and with some success). Mary, as usual, is
the blessed peacemaker, understanding the mutual love between
mother and daughter that eventually resolves the issue, with Rhoda
and Ida reconciling. But along the way Rhoda points out that Mary
knows only about Midwestern love. Bronx love is a different sort of
a thing, chiefly because it is encumbered with a "certain amount of
guilt."

This Freudian relationship with her past includes an episode with
her sister in "Rhoda's Sister Gets Married" (#75). Her family pro-
vides some of Rhoda's funniest but also some of her most poignant
moments. And Valerie Harper makes the most of them, assisting the
writers and producers in moving far beyond the stereotypical Jewish-
mother situation and jokes. Rhoda's feelings of inadequacy actually
help to provide one of the overall themes of the show: her quiet

desperation, linking with Ted Knight's and Phyllis's, even Mary's and Lou's at times. Guilt thus becomes part of the human dimension that we can all relate to and not simply a caricature.

Further, like Mary, Rhoda is single and always made to be aware that her status in society is that of "spinster." She confesses that she has felt like an old maid since she was twenty-one years old, and Mary understands. She is more predatory than Mary, however, more inclined to lament the absence of men in her life and more frantic to do something about it. Her dates usually turn out badly, none more so than in episode 2, "Today I Am a Ma'am," the first by Treva Silverman. In this one she goads Mary into a double date, only to find that her man—whom she has met under her car when she ran over him!—is married. Her laconic introduction of him and his wife as "my date" is a gloriously funny moment, as is her introduction of herself to Mary's date, who is too entranced with Mary to notice her: "Allow me to introduce myself. I'm another person in the room." And she is given the tag line at the end of the show. After a truly terrible evening, and the first of Mary's dull, misfiring parties, the two women agree never, never again to get themselves into such a position. Rhoda adds, "Not unless my date is a couple I really like."

But if her job, her mother, and her spinsterhood are problems, the major contributor to Rhoda's low self-esteem is her weight. It is a subject that is probably overdone in the series itself and certainly in the magazine and newspaper commentary on the show. We hear and see from the first episode that she is overweight and that her problem is a compulsive subject with her. In episode 2, for example, we watch her stuff food by the handful in response to her nervousness and disappointment over her married date(s). In episode 4, another Treva Silverman script ("Divorce Isn't Everything"), she is again the plump single woman, this time pretending she is divorced. In this same episode, exercising with Mary, she is cheating on every movement while Mary demonstrates real agility and strength of purpose.

And so it goes throughout the first several seasons, augmented both on the show and in the public mind by numerous articles that stress the subject. The *Ms.* magazine article already quoted is a case in point, as is an earlier one in *TV Guide* that begins with a reference to "plumpish," a problem that the real-life actress is said to share with her fictional character—although the article does have the grace to mention that it is the unflattering wardrobe on television "that gives the illusion of girth." But the most insistently one-note article was a *Time* cover story on October 28, 1974, that, from beginning to

Emmy Awards, 1973.

end, dwells on "the fat girl who grew too big for her bitches [*sic*]," the "zaftig 150-pounder who made everybody grin," the "chunky, shiny-eyed" actress whose weight soared when she contracted hepatitis early in her career. She is quoted as being relegated in her private life to "dear homosexual friends or guys who were like brothers," groups who presumably overlook fatness or somehow thrive on it. The article cannot forbear noting her advancement in her career as gaining "some polish and a few more ounces." As late as June 1988, *Redbook* is still harping on her weight problems, which, they note, reappeared in earnest with the cancellation of *Rhoda*.

One retreats to episode 54, "Rhoda the Beautiful," again by Treva Silverman, for the definitive treatment of the weight loss. By now Valerie Harper has lost weight and the show's creators have possibly lost patience with the fat jokes (some of which have been transferred to Lou Grant). This episode meets the subject directly: She and Murray, both dealing with a weight problem, are conscientious members of a diet club, Murray having risen to the post of group leader, or "Grand Zaftig." The weight loss complete, Rhoda must now deal with the low self-esteem that it has helped to engender. Mary helps, struggling throughout the episode to make Rhoda see herself as attractive as she in fact is, but resistance is high. Others help: Lou compliments her on her new look, even Phyllis bluntly comments that she has "dropped a ton." When none of this seems to be working, Mary toughens her stance by accusing Rhoda of refusing to allow herself one moment of pleasure. We are reminded of Ida Morgenstern, who worries and self-denies and cajoles everyone out of compliments in her rush toward egocentric self-abnegation. Mary's job is finally done, however, when the new, stunning Rhoda wins first place in Hempel's beauty contest, looking glamorous in a formal black dress. "I won," she finally says with pride, "after thirty-two years." Treading close to endorsing such contests, Silverman inserts a needed satire on beauty queens. In this light Rhoda's triumph may be seen as a human rather than sexist one.

The dynamics of Rhoda's presence on the show are many and varied. She is a foil to Mary in ways just discussed. In addition, her chief antagonist is Phyllis, who begins the series by referring to her as "that dumb awful girl" upstairs and never misses the opportunity to be snide. Phyllis is even delighted to learn that her brother is gay—a confession that might otherwise have horrified her—because it dissolves her fear that he might marry Rhoda. Because "love is so much all around" on this show, the antagonism is part of a larger feeling in which affection and even support play a role in the

Rhoda-Phyllis relationship, so we can freely enjoy ourselves when each puts the other down.

Rhoda and Mary are generally in agreement, but an obvious way to generate some tension is through arguments between the two friends. These are frequent, although usually short-lived, as just a part of a show. More sustained is episode 91, "Best of Enemies," in which a serious breach has to be healed. Rhoda thoughtlessly reveals that Mary has lied on her job application, claiming a college degree that she does not have. Rhoda is right to say that the little lie is no longer important, but she is wrong to reveal a confidence. When Mary blows up at her and calls her "insensitive," Rhoda gets her dander up, and the friends part with very angry words. Georgette tries to act as peacemaker, breathlessly carrying a "Hello" from one apartment to the other. "You two belong together. . . . You, Rhoda and Mary, are a lot like Pittsburgh," a strange vision that she explains in terms of two little rivers meeting and forming one great big one. Then Lou tries to cheer her up with several moments that are useful here and also beyond this episode as commentaries on the show as a whole. First he tells a joke about Billie Jean King and Bobby Riggs, an unfunny joke that both he and Mary can enjoy, he says, because it has "Women's Lib in it for you and sports for me." He follows this with an insightful comment about people who make light of things "because it's a way of covering up their feelings. People can make jokes and really care, Mary." This is true not only of Rhoda, but of the whole series, in which most laugh lines simultaneously reveal the sensitivity that is a part of each character. It is essentially this benign spirit, rather than the little plot device, that eventually resolves the argument. We knew all along that the misunderstanding would clear up, and so it does. By the end Rhoda and Mary are embracing in the hall, over their garbage bags. It remains only for Ted to come in and demand their reconciliation, for Georgette's peace of mind. Thus he accomplishes, with much self-congratulation, what has already taken place: "I feel like Kissinger."

There are other shows that chronicle tension between friends: "Bob and Rhoda and Teddy and Mary" (#9) deals with Rhoda's boyfriend becoming attracted to Mary; "Where There's Smoke There's Rhoda" (#45) puts the two friends into too-close proximity after a fire in Rhoda's apartment; "Some of My Best Friends Are Rhoda" (#47) in which Mary seems to be weaned away from her best friend by a new one—the last is the foray into anti-Semitism already commented upon by its author, Steve Pritzker.

A different class of shows centers on the madcap adventures of the two girlfriends, who get into the sort of scrapes that might sound in outline like those of *Laverne and Shirley* later, but a definitely sophisticated variety. They include the double-date caper and the divorce club in the second and fourth episodes, respectively, as well as a Mexican adventure in "He's No Heavy, He's My Brother" (#27) written by Allan Burns. One of the funniest scenes in the series is Ted's reading over the air a joke obituary written at 4 A.M. by the two girls in a silly mood.

The total of so many individual moments is the establishment of Rhoda as so important to Mary that it might seem her departure would wreck the series. It is a tribute to the writers, producers, and cast that it did not. Of course her loss did not erase her memory from the show. In a much later episode, when Mary is feeling depressed, she confides to Georgette that she wishes so much for Rhoda, who would have known how to lighten the sad moment with her special brand of joking. When Georgette tries to fill in, hilariously, the comedy is uppermost, but another important note is sounded: Rhoda has been irreplaceable and unforgotten. Her appearance on the last show is entirely natural and easy, picking right up with her struggle with Phyllis, her friendship with the people at WJM, and the richness of her bond with Mary.

LOU: PAPA BEAR

Burns and Brooks recall that Lou was an old-fashioned, able newsman who had dropped out of high school. He thinks electronic journalism has destroyed traditions such as reporters wearing hats.

From that somewhat terse description, Lou Grant, as embodied by Ed Asner, took his place as one of the most important presences on *The Mary Tyler Moore Show* and one of the most complex, evolving during the seven years probably to a greater extent than any other character in the series.

Any adequate description would have to include some seeming contradictions: Lou is a gruff bear, often impatient, loud, a very physical person whether he is being aggressive or not, but he is also a father confessor, capable of great patience and understanding, even gentleness. He is at times blunt and straightforward, but at times tentative, even delicate, capable of choosing his words with compassionate understanding. He is not young and does not sport the all-American tapered figure, but he is attractive to women, whom he knows how to treat in positive ways. He is a man's man in the traditional sense, but a woman's, too, in the sense emerging in the 1970s.

He is the boss, the symbol of male authority, whom Mary Richards always addresses formally as "Mr. Grant." Such is the nature of life reflected on the show that the other men in the office address him familiarly as "Lou." Commentators during the life of the show sometimes criticized this dichotomy, claiming that the show fostered chauvinism, but such statements do not look comprehensively enough at the total picture of the men and women presented.

Mr. Grant's office was one of the sets used virtually every week. From his pragmatic point of view, director Jay Sandrich remembers it chiefly as small and cramped, a space in which it was devilishly hard to manipulate a camera. In at least one episode several of the characters themselves complained about its small size. Audiences saw it, consciously or not, as the habitation of all those contradictions mentioned earlier: the den of the bear, the cave of the guru, the seat of authority, a place where the wounded could repair for strengthening, a dreaded tyrant's seat. Prompted by a remark from Allan Burns about the office itself, the authors of this book have recently extracted the office scenes from most of the episodes and examined them back to back. The result is interesting. We see just how multifaceted is the character, and consequently something of the extraordinary range of the actor. We also see how Mary Richards becomes more authoritative, more capable of ease, in his presence, even in his gruff moods. As the series progresses she moves from her perch on the edge of the chair farther back, although she never lounges there or seems supremely comfortable. But as the years move on she meets his eye more and more successfully and protests some of his decisions and pronouncements with increasing vigor— even to the point of reopening the door after one angry exit and slamming it again after her.

There is one small curiosity that is interesting in the light of recent attempts by television's creative and business communities to avoid trivializing alcohol or other substance abuse—Lou frequently repaired to a handy bottle of whiskey, which he kept in his right-hand drawer. In the first episode he offered some to Mary, and during times of stress we would see that bottle and sometimes its contents. The context was always a joke, and perhaps the joke soured a little in the light of alcohol abuse in the real world. Indeed, Jim Brooks commented in 1976 that "somebody will say, 'You've been doing a lot of stuff about Lou drinking and getting laughs off it, it's a little irresponsible.' We'll tend to listen to that because it makes sense to us." In the eighties the Caucus for Producers, Writers and Directors finally undertook a campaign to stop glamorizing alcohol or treating it as a joke. Perhaps resulting from the comment Brooks cited, Lou

Lou explains the cause of his indiscretion with Sue Ann.

reached for the bottle less frequently, although he continued to be quite at home in the neighborhood bar.

We have already told the story of the casting of Asner as Lou, against type and against the skepticism of the network. The combined forces of Ethel Winant and Grant Tinker prevailed over an apparently abysmal reading at the original casting session to the decision point, where Asner's own assertiveness and the celebrated wisdom of Brooks and Burns took over. It is hard now to imagine more perfect casting, but testimony proves it was not difficult then.

His success with the part was immediate—discounting the Tuesday fiasco described in Chapter 3—but Ed Asner had more to develop over the years, feeling that he found powers of revelation in the comic mode, powers that he had previously associated only with drama. "When you can find the way to do it, humor can reveal important truths in a refined, slow way, as Charlie Chaplin did in *The Great Dictator.*" It may be that his choice of Chaplin's most political film to demonstrate this point is suggested by Asner's own highly publicized interests in contemporary political events. *The Lou Grant Show* (the final MTM spin-off from *The Mary Tyler Moore Show*, succeeding it in the fall of 1977) continued his story, but this time with tougher journalistic content, augmented by Asner's own pronouncements in the press about domestic and foreign politics. These dramatic events belong to another volume, but there is a pertinence here in his feeling that he became more politicized during the seventies as Lou Grant in Mary's show. "I can't tell to what extent I was an ERA supporter before *The Mary Tyler Moore Show*, but I certainly was one by the end of it, to such a point that my agent brilliantly instituted a contract concerning equal opportunity and progressive hiring practices for *Lou Grant*. I can remember being enormously influenced by an adoring mother and two sisters. They taught me a lot, and as a result I don't think I was about to shortchange women. I maintain and carry macho habits with me always, probably will die with them, but I have constantly tried to get rid of some and modify some others."

This sensibility is the actor's, but the feeling and the reality of it might equally apply to his Lou Grant persona. Lou is certainly macho, one of the boys. Like Asner, he likes football, horse racing, drinking, roughhousing, male bonding in its traditional aspects. Asner resorts to this sort of traditional maleness in describing his concept of the role: "To me Lou was primarily a typical American Midwestern good old boy. He believed what he read, expected his elders to dispense good advice, and I suppose through attrition of war and profession became slowly more and more aware of the subtleties of life, or the subtleties of print. He became wise, slowly but surely, and at the same time he always operated with what I think is a great common core of honor, an honorable center, beginning with a straight shoot. I think life had given him the opportunity to make the right choices and the right selections about what was important and what wasn't, what was news and what wasn't, who were good people and who were not. I think he was a creature of, even a captive of, his profession." Jim Brooks saw Lou in similar terms, but puts it another way. "Conservative/liberal arguments are not ever an issue with our show. My guess would be that Lou is a pretty conservative guy, but it doesn't come up."

And so Asner adds to our earlier list of capabilities and traits another that he considers essential: Lou was a practitioner of journalistic integrity, and perhaps we can say that he wanted his office to run according to the highest principles. But instead of PBS he got a little low-rated station in Minneapolis, WJM, with crack anchorman Ted Knight! What a delicious comic setup. In episode 66 there is a wild celebration in the newsroom when Lou brings the news that they have moved from bottom to next to bottom in the ratings!

To get further into the character of Lou Grant it may be practical to follow a suggestion by Treva Silverman, who speaks of the evolution of the Lou and Edie story as perhaps the most ambitious continuity line in the series. Edie was Mrs. Grant, whom we saw on roughly a score of shows, but whose presence was felt far more often because Lou and others mentioned her regularly. As intimacy among the characters grew, Edie, like other wives, sweethearts, and friends, became part of the family. In this context, we remember the theme song and the name of the first episode, "Love Is All Around."

Toward the end of the opening season there occurred the first shock in the long-term and presumably stable Grant family. In episode 21, "The Boss Isn't Coming to Dinner," writers Dave Davis and Lorenzo Music began the long-range story of which Treva Silverman spoke earlier, when we learn that Edie and Lou have separated. The divorce would not come about until two seasons later, signaled by Silverman's Emmy Award–winning "The Lou and Edie Story" (#76). Edie was played consummately by the well-known character actress Priscilla Morrill.

The scene in which Lou and Edie separate, pathos modulated as always by comedy, is one of the most poignant of the entire series, outside of the last show itself. After the requisite attempts by the office family to comfort Lou, he must go home, where Edie has promised to wait before her departure so he will not have to come into an empty house. True to her word, she is there, and their conversation turns on little irrelevancies. And then Lou indulges in an absurd monologue about the nuisance of the pits in oranges, watermelons, tangerines, cherries—"they can all go to hell." His anger and frustration erupt into violent words while his face betrays confusion and hurt. Finally, during his paean to pits, he simply stops. There is a long silence, and very quietly he asks, "How can you leave me, Edie?"

Her answer, delivered with infinite caring and tenderness, is a remarkable piece of drama:

Edie: Lou, it's not you. It's me. I'm forty-five years old, Lou. You only go around once, and I want more.
Lou: You only go around once! That's a beer commercial, Edie.
Edie: [Pleading] Lou . . .
Lou: Edie, you're walking out that door and I still haven't figured out why.
Edie: When I married you I was nineteen years old, and I thought you were the most wonderful man I ever met. I still think so. But I want to learn more about the rest of me. Not just the part that's your wife. I may hate it, and I may screw it up, but I want to have time to get to know Edie Mackenzie Grant.

Friends and almost lovers.

The big scene takes only four and a half minutes, but it condenses all their past life together and crystallizes a moment that we know they will never put behind them. In 1976, Brooks reflected upon the Lou and Edie relationship. "We had Lou separate from his wife. He moved out. He's the last person who should do a thing like that. Then we had a show where she didn't come home, where she wanted to step out, where she reflected what was happening in society then. I thought it was good because we didn't concentrate on her. In the other shows we're doing that, you know, women's rights. But here we concentrated on this guy left behind, sort of an old-fashioned guy hit by this."

Lou's sexuality is an important part of his character and is kept alive for us by a series of dates, beginning absurdly with an octogenarian woman (#80, "Lou's First Date"), one with Rhoda (#94, "Lou's Second Date"), one with a rather loose lounge singer (#100, "Lou and That Woman," played wonderfully by Sheree North), one with an old flame who comes back briefly into his life (#130, "Lou Douses an Old Flame," played by Beverly Garland). In episode 139, "Ménage à Lou," he has to confront his feelings when another old flame shows up at one of Mary's parties with someone new. Bob Ellison wrote this script and Janis Paige was the guest star. And of course there are the encounters with Mary's Aunt Flo.

But of all Lou's affairs with women, the most sustained, the most fun, the most serious, and the most complex is his relationship with Mary. It is a love affair that occurs practically from the first interview in episode one, with an epic scope ranging from light banter to anger, through broken confidences and wounded feelings to comfort and support, involving communication that is sometimes easy and sometimes hesitant, even to misunderstandings. But always these two major characters—whether seen alone in his office or her apartment or in the company of others of the ensemble or guests—are growing together. Toward the end of the series the writer/producers decided to come a little more out into the open with this relationship. In episode 165, "Mary's Three Husbands," Bob Ellison has fun with a fantasy show. In three dream sequences he shows us life as it might have been for Mary if she had married Lou, or Ted, or Murray. Two weeks later, in the next-to-last episode (#167, "Lou Dates Mary"), the long-standing date finally occurs. It was time for all of us to know: Would Lou and Mary make it together after all? We have spoken earlier of the inspired resolution to this seven-year line of suspense. Their game attempt to forge a mere love affair, maybe even a marriage, out of a precious friendship yields a mighty case of the giggles. It is a brilliant conception, hilarious and true. And it is a fine comment on the sexuality that Treva Silverman calls the special appeal of the older, heavy man. For people who lament the stereotypes that flourish almost out of control on television, Ed Asner's Lou Grant remains a cause for celebration.

The women in Lou's life—some of them.

PHYLLIS: "SPARKLE, CLORIS"

In the opening scene of the first episode Phyllis the landlady begins to establish her character by proclaiming that she has already signed a year's lease for Mary, to keep "that dumb Rhoda" from getting the apartment. Poor Mary. While she is still in mild shock over this effrontery Phyllis exits and Rhoda comes in to claim the apartment. Right away Mary finds herself in a baffling position between two argumentative friends—a design that was to occur again and again on the show.

A little later in the show Phyllis is subtly demanding that Mary get married to Bill, her ex-boyfriend, who is coming to visit (and whose visit supplies the major drama of the opening episode, the break with her past and the beginning of Mary the independent woman who will try to make it on her own). Phyllis describes the "realism" of marriage: "Face the fact that it means a certain amount of sacrifice. Denying your own ego, sublimating, accommodating, surrendering."

Anyone who has seen this consummate actress work can see with an inward eye her particular grimace, her smug tone, and the hesitant phrasing of these words—all combining to let us know how powerful are the restraints on this strong-willed woman. A nice little satire on marriage too.

The concept was pretty well fixed at the beginning, in the original Brooks and Burns format. She was *Marna* Lindstrom then, but her tendency to boss Mary around was firmly in place (the precipitous lease signing was there), as was her difficulty with Rhoda and the major configurations of this important character. Phyllis, Burns recalls, was designed as an organizer of other's lives. She controlled her daughter through "progressive" child rearing.

Cloris Leachman had trained with the Actors Studio in New York, and her work was well known by Ethel Winant, whose casting for the show we have already detailed. "I had no idea that Ethel was casting this show. I had known her since I first came to New York, right after I had been in the Miss America contest as Miss Chicago. I had used my thousand dollars from that to come to New York and launch my career and had met Ethel during that period. I adore her."

It is dangerous to identify the actress with the role, but impractical not to try, especially with such strong personalities as Leachman and the Phyllis that she created. Her *Mary Tyler Moore* colleagues unanimously describe both her acting mode and the character of Phyllis as "brilliantly eccentric."

Phyllis has earlier been described by Treva Silverman as attempting the strong nourishing role of mother, but as too eccentric to fulfill it. "I feel that as an actress I helped to develop that character. As conceived, I think the word 'neurotic' was always used. I don't find fun in that. I think it's abrasive in a way that's unattractive and uncomfortable for people. I got a fix on it, though. I think I can best describe it as *a sure firm touch on the wrong note.* I metamorphosed from neurotic, which I think is a negative, into perfect."

Her thoughtful description of Phyllis points to dimensions that she brought to the character through responsible analysis. Perhaps this is the method actor at work; perhaps it is just the conscientious and introspective person reflecting on a major role. "Phyllis is simply perfect. She is everything that the *Ladies' Home Journal* said we were supposed to be—chauffeur, psychologist, chef, hostess, whore in the bedroom. That might have been very boring if it had come from yawning and sitting around idly. But with Phyllis all that wild combination came from an active wish to be those things."

She sees her typical entrance into a scene as highly descriptive of the part: "I'd say Hiiiiiiiiiiii—and bound into the room as if I'd been shot from a cannon." She was, according to Brooks, supposed to sweep into a room and fidget nervously with the household props. Leachman theorizes about the prodigious energy that she projected, that it might have derived in part from television's time-is-money syndrome: "Talk fast, they told me, because everything costs so much."

But she feels that a more likely source for this fiercely projected energy is a childhood lesson. "My mother, every now and then, used to say, 'Sparkle, Cloris!' And I'd just bat my eyes and sparkle. Just a silly family joke. At the Rose Lorenz dance recital every year, when Andy Williams and his brothers would sing—they had a quartet and they would sing at the recital—that's when I first learned that you were supposed to smile when you danced. They always said to smile, smile, smile. And out of that I think came 'Sparkle, Cloris.' And out of that came a command to bring energy and life to the stage. Just before I went down the runway as Miss Chicago, my mother said, 'Sparkle, Cloris.' "

Leachman the dancer/pianist/painter sees analogies among the arts that help to explain her craft. In music the pianist "stretches out the feeling and makes it almost agony, and in modern dancing there is an alternation between contraction and release" that helps define her energy as an actress. She chooses a favorite example from *The Mary Tyler Moore Show*. "Mary is about to go out and Phyllis has a pair of earrings that she describes to Mary as the most beautiful pair that anybody has ever seen. It's the way I say it, just *yearning into it.*" Leachman the actor punctuates these descriptions by leaping from her chair to act out the agony of music, the contraction/release of dancing, and the "yearning into" of the earring story. "Phyllis is desperate for perfection. She feels a difference between being perfect and being where she is at the moment, and I think that is very different from being neurotic. It comes from wanting to be all things to all people."

Phyllis seems equally desperate for attention and for approval, but in a general and plausible way, one that we all recognize within ourselves. For example, when she and Rhoda return as guests on the last show, they are ushered into Mary's apartment by Lou, who commands Mary to close her eyes for a surprise. She obeys and he brings in the two old friends, Rhoda slightly ahead of Phyllis. Just as Mary is told to open her eyes, Phyllis tries to push ahead of Rhoda to be the first embraced. It is a magically comic moment, an inspired bit of acting.

Phyllis's desire to be central is part of her eagerness to please, comic yet with a real edge of pathos. In episode 3, for example, "Bess, You Is My Daughter Now," she reveals to Mary that she is raising her daughter, Bess, by the books. She names the process "creative child-rearing" and is directed by an armload of books, which she brings to Mary as guidance for a baby-sitting weekend. When Bess arrives at Mary's apartment, in her mother's wig and makeup and calling her mother "Phyllis," we see the consequence of love misdirected by the manuals. The little girl is a travesty of childhood, pushed unsuccessfully toward premature adulthood, willful, spoiled, and confused, a victim of parents who are insecure and therefore trying too hard.

When Mary spends the day treating her as a child, Bess responds by becoming "a nice little girl." More problematical, she becomes fixated on Mary, who has treated her as child, preferring her to mother Phyllis. We see Phyllis's unexpressed hurt as she capitulates ("by the book") to Bess's wish that she stay with Mary and not return home.

The two "mothers" in this crazy arrangement finally have a confrontation in which Mary agrees sympathetically with Phyllis's description of herself as a "lousy mother." Mary finally blurts out to her friend that her problem is that "you come on so strong all the time" and she likes her better "when you come on weak." Phyllis, crying now, revealing the vulnerability that always lies behind her aggression, is overseen by Bess, who recognizes her at last as a loving mother who needs her daughter.

Phyllis takes charge.

If this summary seems too treacly, one must remember that this serious plot is punctuated by highly comic moments: Ted confusing "vegetarian" with "veterinarian" in his nightly newscast, Rhoda being ticketed for feeding a buffalo in the park, and the biggest laugh of the show, when the distraught Phyllis asks Mary whether she should keep on crying until Bess comes back into the room and notices her real distress. The audacity of the writers is shown when they dare to call attention to the sentimentality of Phyllis's big moment, when her true motherly feelings for Bess erupt in tears, which she then devises a strategy for using.

The Phyllis who comes on too strong is a constant component of the series, from the first episode, when she prematurely signs Mary's lease, through the last, when she attempts to push ahead of Rhoda at their reunion with their old friend. But what of the actor behind the role?

It became one of Jay Sandrich's major challenges to integrate Leachman's method actor's style into the very differing ones of Valerie Harper, Mary Tyler Moore, Ed Asner, and the others. Sandrich and Leachman sometimes clashed, but in a productive way. He says, "Cloris is very smart. I remember saying to her after the second show, after she had gone somewhere she had never gone and the cameras didn't follow her, that she had just accomplished a sensational bit of business but it was a shame that it wasn't on film."

Leachman had begun in live television, when "I worked right up to air time. We had one man and one camera and it was like a pas de deux. We breathed together. I could do anything and this guy would follow me. I was used to that and I think that's terrific. You really got attuned to each other, you had to." But in filmed television, with three cameras and an elaborate blocking procedure, the actors had to find their marks on the floor every time or the scene would almost certainly be ruined. Sandrich remembers that Leachman soon learned this and never lurched about the stage uncontrolled. She, however, still prefers another description: "I would always try to find some different way to do a thing and I suppose that Jay would then have to try to figure out how to get it on camera. I don't yet know the three-camera technique very well, and I almost don't want to know it. I don't want to get into a pattern because patterns deaden. I see some actors go dutifully to their spots, cameras on them, being a good girl or boy, and that's not the stuff of greatness."

This is an interesting description of her method by an actor who was, despite her acknowledged eccentricity, an integral part of the ensemble. "She did it a different way during each rehearsal," says Sandrich. "I would sometimes get notes that asked why I was letting Cloris do what she was doing. Well, I wasn't. Cloris would do what Cloris wanted to do. She would do wonderful, brilliant things. Some of them would work and some wouldn't. It was my job to help keep the good ones and work somehow with the others." And Marge Mullen adds, "Cloris would give the most amazing readings, a brilliant surprise to all of us. And she kept working on things right up until the moment she went onstage. Part of my job was running lines with the cast the night of the show. I'd go backstage when they were in makeup and getting their hair done, and I'd run through the upcoming scene with Cloris, who very often had trouble learning her lines because we had lots of changes going on, even up to the last minute. So I'd be running lines with her right outside the front door that she was going to enter through. It would be typical that she would say, poised right there at the door, 'Now what if I did this or that?' and I'd say, 'Cloris, three cameras are going to run into each other and the other actors are going to be standing there not knowing what the hell is going on.' "

She learned early not to follow directions as such but to be clear about what the directions are. "At Actors Studio they always said to cross out any directions that writers give to actors. I always read them first because it seemed that the author was giving the actor permission to do something. You should be clear about the author's intent but try to illuminate that and fulfill it, and then the excitement will affect the audience. The only way to do that is to bring your own translation of the author. So I always saw that permission as an opportunity to do something wonderful."

Somehow, the ensemble of cast and crew integrated into the show this obsession of hers with self-expression, and it fed the mode of unexpectedness that we have earlier described as the show's special signature. "I think my body is all in separate parts anyway. I look like one of those books that's in three small horizontal strips, that lets you put a different head with a different body and so on. That's why I can play so many different parts. When I was doing live shows in New York, my hair would be blond one week, black another week, brown, red. I was English, Chinese, all kinds of American. In mood I can be cute and I can be silly. In sixth grade we had a sort of little notebook where they wrote a little blurb by each child's name. Mine was 'cute but silly.' That was prophetic for me. It's too boring just to be cute, so I had to find a way to have the fun that comes with being silly."

But cute, silly, and fun were not descriptions of Cloris Leachman's life during the 1970s. "I felt so guilty much of the time. I was usually late and I usually didn't know my lines as well as everyone else. I felt I was wasting everyone's time. My marriage was breaking up, my five children were young, I had to be on the phone all the time. I also had eighteen workmen at my house, a large contemporary place being changed into a modern farmhouse. Every time I'd leave they would cement something in upside down or put a thermostat in the middle of a beautiful wall. I didn't know that Ethel Winant all this time was over at CBS telling everyone not to worry, that it was much more important for me to be home right now than anywhere else. I called up my husband many years later, after we were divorced, and told him, 'Oh, George, I understand what a hard life you must have had!' " "George" is George Englund, one of television's most prolific producers.

One can see a lot of Cloris Leachman in Phyllis, trying to be the perfect all-around woman, all things to all people, brilliantly eccentric, tough and yet vulnerable. "When I was up in Oregon working once, I was in a café one morning and I heard some guys talking about Mary Tyler Moore and sniggering. 'She thinks she can go out on her own. Isn't that a crock?' I didn't say anything, but I thought, 'We'll just see about that.' And of course she did. But I was very aware then of how wives are perceived by others—you're a role, you're not a person with possibilities. And I think Mary's show did a great deal to subtly but profoundly address that. It wasn't addressed consciously perhaps, and certainly not head-on, but it was certainly in the air, the whole sensibility about women and wives and their place. I had not been affected myself—I had had a career before I was married and knew who I was in that regard, but I can certainly see how in marriage once you're the support member, you perfect that skill, and the better support you are, the more you can

push. If you and your spouse are both trying to climb up the hill together and if one is doing the pushing, then you settle into that mode and you become a certain version of the dutiful wife. You deal with things from a certain point of view, which is that a wife's part is not to make money or to be out there in the world. We had three little children one right after the other. To put thirty little toes in socks is a big thing. By the time you stand up from that your back is—you know. By the time I had straightened up from that task I realized that I hadn't worked very much for fifteen years because of the family. I certainly did sublimate myself, in my own way, but what saved me was that I did have this other part of me that survived."

And survive she has. In her galaxy of brilliantly executed roles, both in television and feature films, she has proven a breadth and dexterity matched by only a few actors. Phyllis was perhaps her most successful, the actor's strength augmented by the power of the writing, by the director's skill with her eccentricities, and by the others in the acting ensemble.

TED: THE ANCHOR AROUND EVERYONE'S NECK

Like Phyllis, Ted is an audacious concept, a character type that could have annoyed the audience as much as he did the other fictional characters and so distanced viewers from the show. Instead, like his contemporary pain in the neck, Archie Bunker, he became a beloved figure, affording America some of its richest laughter of the decade. Besides Mary and Lou, his is the most constant and the strongest presence in the series.

Our first introduction to Ted comes in the first show when Murray presents him to Mary, on her first day at work.

> Mary: I'm Mary Richards. I'm the new . . . ah . . .
> Ted: Wonderful. I've been telling Lou we needed a new one. Welcome to my Six O'Clock News team.

Already we have the sublime sense of self-importance and its consequent obliviousness to everyone and everything around him. This is a distinct advance over the presentation of Ted in the 1970 format, where he was only an off-camera voice, unwittingly making a joke, set up by Murray, about the drama of making Phillips Avenue one-way.

Ethel Winant has already spoken of the casting of Ted Knight, whose visibility as an actor was not high in 1970. He was a bit player and often out of work, although his talent was known to people who really knew how to assess such things. Given his chance, the actor turned the part into the essential one that we all watched as it evolved into greater heights of complexity and nuance.

But let it be said right away that, no matter how Ted Knight and the writers worked with the character and no matter how sympathetic he became, Ted Baxter was wisely never allowed to outgrow the characteristic that most delighted the audience—his fundamental boorishness, the fated capacity to say the wrong thing at the wrong time, to plant his foot firmly in his mouth on all occasions. He always represented something of the buffoon, even after he became a husband and father and revealed a vulnerability that humanized him beyond his early appearances. Knight experienced intermittent despair over this image of the egocentric idiot that all America knew as Ted Baxter and, to some extent at least, as Ted Knight. He was plagued in much the same way as was Mary Tyler Moore, who *was* Mary Richards in the public mind.

Ted Knight became quite concerned about this problem at one point in the third year. Disturbed, he went to see Allan Burns about it. Burns recalls that Knight said to him, "I can't do this, I can't play this character, this stupid, arrogant, ignorant man who is a laughingstock. It's just gotten into my soul, and I can't, it's just so difficult for me. I'm identified with this person. And I just don't want to do it anymore." Burns continues, "I thought, 'Oh boy, we've got problems here. A lot of our biggest laughs come from him. If Ted leaves the show, what are we going to do?' I was in the middle of trying to hold him off and Ed. Weinberger walked in and asked what was going on. I explained to him very carefully. Ted at this point was literally on the verge of tears about how humiliating it was for him to play the part. I said, 'Ted, you're the only person in America who feels that way. This is a beloved character, we feel, like Jack Benny, who was cheap and difficult and conceited. I doubt that Benny ever felt that way about himself.' Ed. got real eloquent talking about the history of the great clowns. I didn't know where he was pulling this stuff from. Ted seemed to be feeling better. The sobs didn't come, and he felt like life was worth living after all. We were relieved, and just then Jim [Brooks] walked in and said, 'What's going on?' We told him that Ted was feeling funny about playing Ted Baxter, and Jim said, 'Wait a minute. That character is one of the great schmucks of all time.' Ed. and I groaned as we saw Ted crumbling again, his face starting to go. Jim always had great timing!"

Fortunately the out-of-sync producers managed to mollify Ted, in spite of Brooks's contribution to the discussion. Nevertheless, "we did work with the writers to find the humanity in the character," Burns says. "We tried to get a little deeper, understand Ted Baxter's fears. Some of that is evident in the shows with Georgette where Ted had trouble saying 'I love you.' All of this occurred as a result of our anxiety to make Knight feel more comfortable with the role. He would have his problems from time to time, but I think he got more comfortable after we started that process. Gradually, I think, he realized that people really loved the character."

One of the special dimensions of the Ted Baxter character was its satire on broadcasters and broadcasting, a part of the show given extra resonance because viewers were seeing it on the very medium that was being targeted for fun. Many of the episodes highlighted this appeal, including several dealing with the Teddy Awards, a coveted local equivalent of the Emmys. It was Ted who was especially driven to win, although everyone, including Mary, felt the pressure. In addition to winning, Ted childishly wanted to snatch the award away from competitors and savor their loss.

Perhaps Jim Brooks's background at CBS News in New York, where he began his career in 1964, has some pertinency here, but certainly any thoughtful viewer of television in the 1970s would also have some opinions concerning the low quality of local news shows. Episode 90, "The Co-Producers," features the small-bore egos of both Ted and Sue Ann as Mary and Rhoda try to produce a new Sunday afternoon talk show. *Newhart* would later have a fine old time with a similar television show-within-a-show in which Bob Newhart is an interview host with a succession of guests who run the gamut from insignificant to outlandish. "The Outsider" (episode 101 of *The Mary Tyler Moore Show*) features the constant preoccupation with ratings at the local level. An outside consultant, played by Richard Masur, is hired by management to bolster WJM's low Arbitrons, and the result is pandemonium among the staff. *WKRP* would later give us the radio version of a group of barely competents always on the defensive about their small listening audience. Yet another episode, "The Good-Time News" (#49), deals with the concept of "happy news" among the news team. It was an idea whose time had seemed to come in the early seventies and there was much supercilious discussion in the print media about the idiocy of hundreds of grinning and joking anchor men and women all over America.

One episode in particular brought the satire straight out of the fictional *Mary Tyler Moore* world into the real one of the daily CBS News. "Ted Baxter Meets Walter Cronkite" (#93) was written by Ed. Weinberger and features a surprise guest appearance by the oracle himself. It had become a cliché to describe the genial host of CBS's nightly news as "avuncular," and Cronkite was regularly listed in polls as one of America's most admired and trusted individuals. *His* ratings were secure enough, and he projected a kind of authority that perhaps no newsman has had before or since. He ended each broadcast with a somewhat pontifical "That's the way it is," perhaps thus claiming an objectivity and inclusiveness that mere mortals do not usually possess. He might have said, more modestly, "That's the way it looks from here," or "That's the way it seems." Further, the stentorian quality of his voice and deep projection seemed an idealized version of Ted Baxter's attempts. Or, more accurately, perhaps Ted Baxter seemed a parody of Walter Cronkite.

Whatever the relationship with Cronkite (and the foregoing remarks are not intended as a swipe at a national institution), there is no other character in the series who can be classified comfortably as a parody. This is Ted's strength as well as his limitation.

This special mixture of traits evolved toward greater complexity as the show ran its course, although everything was provided for from the beginning. In the first episodes we got to know WJM's anchorman as a combination of pomposity and incompetence. There was, for example, the matter of his malapropisms. In his blithe mangling of the language he continued a rich tradition that included Shakespeare's Dogberry and Verges in *Much Ado About Nothing* ("Dost thou not suspect my years? Dost thou not suspect my rank?"), Sheridan's Mrs. Malaprop herself ("allegories on the banks of the Nile"), Gracie Allen ("Don't burn your bridges before they hatch"), Jackie Gleason ("a mere bag-o-shells"), and Archie Bunker (choose your favorite, from any show). Ted could stop us cold with such Orwellian muddledthink as "You gotta be nice to the people on the way up before they do it to you," or "A final item, after this further message." He would sometimes realize his mistake ("In reply to that question, a White House souse said today . . .") and correct it (to "source," in that case), but more often he was blithely unaware of his gaffe: "my comprehensive analysis" of the local city election "will begin at 7:30, right after *The Three Stooges*." Mary's joke obituary, referred to earlier by Treva Silverman, announcing the death of Wee Willy Williams could not have been read by anyone who had the slightest comprehension of the copy in front of him.

It was this nightly copy that accounted for the running conflicts in the show: Murray versus Ted. Murray, of course, wrote the copy and each night lived to see Ted do something awful with it . . . or in spite of it. This frustration keeps Murray at all times alive to the possibility of putting Ted down with a series of remarks at his expense. When Ted objects to Rhoda's repeated use of the word "dumb" to describe some of his ideas for the new Sunday afternoon show, Murray supplies the reason: "Maybe you don't like it for the same reason I don't like 'bald.' " This is a double joke, referring also to Sue Ann's constant attention to Murray's shiny head. A theme often repeated is Ted's desire to write, a talent for which he has absolutely no aptitude. The darkest episode occurs near the end of the series in "Murray Ghosts for Ted" (#164) in which Ted takes both credit and money for an article that Murray mercifully wrote for him. The treachery requires explanation, public airing, and forgiveness—all of which are supplied in the clever David Lloyd script. The ending reveals some real affection between the two men, who will nevertheless revert to the confrontation mode for most of the brief time remaining in the series.

But if Murray found ways to compensate for his annoyance at Ted, Lou never did. Ted was his nemesis. With high standards of journalistic integrity, Lou was constantly infuriated by Ted's incompetence. The boss's withering looks are completely ineffectual, although Ted does respond to Lou's physical attacks. When Ted prays on the air, as part of his campaign to win the Teddy Award for best newscaster (#93), Lou is frantic, repeatedly threatening murder and restrained only by Mary. In "You Sometimes Hurt the One You Hate" (#99) he actually throws Ted out of the newsroom and so frightens himself with this display of temper that he spends the rest of the show treating Ted with unctuous politeness. But usually the banter is lighter: "Ted, don't say 'scoop.' 'Scoop' is what Lois Lane says to Clark Kent. If you want to say 'scoop,' go get a job on *The Daily Planet*."

But Ted never does, although a slightly unconvincing offer to host a game show in New York (#125, "Ted's Moment of Glory") almost takes him away.

Ted's incompetence is played off not only against Lou but against other characters on the show also. As they realize his shortcomings and generally forgive him for them, he seems not to notice but forges ahead in a vacuum of selfhood. But there is another dimension usually at work: his insecurity, which must be based partly on his knowledge of what others think of him. He begs and pleads like a child when he wants something: "Please, Lou, pretty please." He often mentions his lack of a college education, although usually in comedic terms like this one: "You know, it's always been one of the big regrets of my life that I didn't have a chance to go to college. College. Flirtation walk, fraternity handshakes, panty raids, election of the homecoming queen, kissing rock. Yeah, higher education must be a wonderful thing."

And there are his constant schemes for self-improvement, proof of his desire to be something better, or at least something else. Like the rest of America, he once takes up jogging, reducing himself in several days from a functioning physical being to a mass of interconnected stiffness and pain. Once he tries to make his mark via a creative writing class, as homework rewriting Murray's story of a bank robbery from the bank's point of view: "In the cold, gray chill of dusk, the bank felt the robbers enter—and violated" (#91). Soon after he tries again, this time crashing a creative writing class that Mary is taking and plagiarizing her work after trying fruitlessly to write something of his own. In "Ted Baxter's Famous Broadcasters School" (#119) he gets hoodwinked into endorsing a school that has only one student. He tries opening a bar with Lou and with no luck. And he is constantly trying to improve his vocabulary, with hilarious results: he calls Mary "lascivious" when he means "lethargic." His explanation: "They're on the same page."

If he couldn't write, he couldn't speak either. In an early episode by Lorenzo Music, "Anchorman Overboard" (#12), he's stumped when Phyllis asks him to speak at her Women's Club to give his views on the world situation. Murray dutifully writes his speech to fill in the vacuum supplied by Ted's total lack of ideas, and we fade to the next scene. Phyllis reports that Ted read Murray's words well. But the first question, "Are you for or against Women's Liberation?" caused a disaster.

Mary: Oh. Was he for it or against it?
Phyllis: Well, we don't know. He just stood there, with his mouth open, like he was going to say something, and then a sort of glaze came over his eyes. He giggled a couple of times, said something nobody understood, and then he asked if there were any more questions.

Like the bloody murders depicted offstage in Greek tragedy, the audience knows Ted well enough to picture the details of this scene, as well as those that follow, when Phyllis describes an hour's worth of questions and two minutes of answers. Of course Mary's role then becomes that of talking Ted back into some vestige of self-respect after this humiliating experience. From abject humiliation the climb back to boorish ego is an easy step.

His self-centeredness is amusing when presented as childishness, a little darker when it borders on callousness or even deliberate cruelty. However modulated, the core is pure, unvarnished ego. As often as possible he lapses into his autobiography, which always begins the same: "It all started in a small 5,000-watt radio station in Fresno, California. . . ." He is never allowed to get any further by his friends, although he can occasionally con a new acquaintance into some elaboration, as when he explains to a reporter that he got into television because God told him he was too handsome for radio (#156).

The Teddy Awards, a rich source of many jokes involving virtually all of the characters, became a hallmark of Ted's narcissistic desire for approval. In one episode (#93) he even employs Rhoda to manage his ad campaign, at eight dollars an hour. This is the one he wins, and his acceptance speech is an elaborate pastiche of elation, wild gratitude, braggadocio, and general incoherence. The satire on Emmys and Academy Awards is not lost on the viewer, although never specifically mentioned.

The walls in Ted's dressing room are covered with improbable testimonials, among them one from Pope John XXIII (which Ted would probably pronounce "ex, ex, eye eye eye"). His non sequitur, when questioned about this one: "Popes watch the news."

One interesting variation on the ego theme occurs with the introduction of his brother, Hal, played by Jack Cassidy ("Cover Boy," #30, written by Treva Silverman). Cassidy specialized in arrogance and ego (as when he played the actor Oscar North on *He and She*, a series that had just concluded on CBS and that had involved Allan Burns, Treva Silverman, Jay Sandrich, and Dave Davis). In this episode Hal is a two-bit actor most familiar as the "clear bag" man in television commercials. He establishes himself right away:

Mary: You must be Ted's brother.
Hal: No, no, no [*With a broad smile*]. Ted is *my* brother.

There follows a struggle similar to Sue Ann's with her sister in a later episode. "He's always coming on like he's better than me, like I'm nothing," Ted complains to Mary, who helps him out by letting him show her off as his girlfriend during a memorable evening. The brothers explain that the "natural" competitiveness of young boys was fostered by their parents, who used to toss a toy up into the air and make them jump for it. When they decide to come clean with each other at the end, the exercise becomes one of competitive self-abuse.

Not so memorable but worthy of mention are two other "Freudian" episodes in which we are introduced to Ted's father (#78, "Father's Day") and his mother (#107, "A Boy's Best Friend") and in which his notions of the old-fashioned family are jolted.

With this sort of story we come closer to more tolerance for Ted's grosser qualities. The problems with this understanding are many. He is, after all, too old to get away with childishness as an excuse for his lack of thoughtfulness. His male chauvinism is always there, causing him regularly to refer to women, even Georgette, with such denigrating terms as "chicks" and "broads." He ad-libs an editorial on why stewardesses should wear shorter skirts. In affording us a view of this foolishness the series is unquestionably making a feminist statement. And yet in this attitude Ted is not some monster out of step with his times. He is much closer to typical.

It became the series' task to humanize him so that his character might expand enough to continue to interest audiences. The chief method by which this was accomplished was the introduction of Georgette Franklin. This milestone occurred in an episode featuring Rhoda ("Rhoda Morgenstern: Minneapolis to New York," #62), where she is little more than an incidental character, but it begins the love interest for Ted. Soon afterward, in "The Georgette Story" (#66), the romance continues, although not with much stability,

Wedding, anyone?

proceeding to "Marriage: Minneapolis Style" (#116) when Ted proposes to her on the air.

The memorable wedding occurs in episode 129, "Ted's Wedding," with John Ritter playing a minister interrupted from his tennis game to perform the impromptu ceremony in Mary's apartment. This impulsiveness was reprised later, in the opening episode of the final season ("Mary Midwife," #145), when their baby is born without professional help (a doctor's or an anchorman's), once again in Mary's apartment. It is a scene in which Ted excoriates himself as useless, less than a man, until the others help him back to the insufferable braggart that they all seem comfortable with. Alternating with this marriage-birth sequence are episodes 144 ("Ted and the Kid") and 151 ("My Son, the Genius") in which Ted and Georgette adopt a child and discover he has the IQ of a genius.

The love affair and the marriage are punctuated by several episodes in which the marriage is tested, during which Georgette also grows in stature as a character. A pair of balancing episodes deal with her suspicion that he is having an affair (#86, "Almost a Nun's Story") and with his successful struggle against the wiles of an attractive reporter at a convention in Los Angeles ("Ted's Temptation," #156). In this sensitive and very funny script by Bob Ellison, Trisha Noble plays a temptress who is physically and aggressively attracted to the handsome anchorman. We, like Murray and Mary, who accompany him on this trip, are shocked to be reminded that he is really a distinguished-looking person. He, on the other hand, has frequently pointed us in this direction, once complaining that "when you're really good-looking, no one takes you seriously." By the time he has the stamina to reject the woman, she is naked in his hotel bed, but, remembering that Mary has enjoined him to "be a man and do what's right," he dredges down very, very deep within himself and tells the reporter of his happy marriage and of his determination never to break his marriage vow. It is all accomplished with the customary comic dexterity, but, nevertheless, in Ted's favor as a believable human being.

In sum, then, his life with Georgette is a mixed affair but in the aggregate honorable and faithful. She generally seems to thrive on it, and he certainly does.

MURRAY: THE BROWN BAGGER

He was first introduced to CBS as Richard Slaughter in the 1970 format, one of two harassed newswriters amid a stereotypical newsroom clutter—stacks of paper, ashtrays filled with cigarette butts and gum wrappers. Obviously, during the year of preparation for the show, the producers sanitized this setting. There was never any real attempt to make it look like *The Front Page*, or *The Daily*

Planet, or those dozens of Hollywood films—comedy or drama—where hard-boiled reporters typed and talked and never removed their cigarettes from their cynical lips. Burns says, "We never tried to provide a realistic setting for the newsroom. We were as spare as possible."

So Richard became Murray, the clutter became order, and no fierce clacking of typewriters and whir of rushing reporters ever intruded into the WJM newsroom.

But there remains in Murray one stereotypical characteristic inherited from newspaper dramas of stage and screen—the attraction to one-liners, smart remarks that find a target quickly, strike, and then skim away. In the design of the comedy he supplies the clever, self-conscious laugh line in response to the other characters, who often set him up unwittingly. In the casting process Gavin MacLeod said that he was drawn to Murray and the possibilities of that character by one such line. "The rhythm of that line was so magical, Murray introducing Ted with mock exaggeration and an imaginary drumroll, 'And here he is—the Mastroianni of Minneapolis.' I just loved that line." While we doubt that MacLeod settled on seeking the part solely upon that piece of dialogue, it is clear that something made him turn away from the Lou Grant character, for which he was reading, in favor of the newswriter.

The chief objects of Murray's put-down wit are Ted and Sue Ann, and there are several hilarious examples from almost every show. Like Lou, Murray is enough of a newspaperman to find Ted insufferable as part of the team. Unlike Lou, Murray has a fine old time putting down the pompous anchorman, although without explosiveness.

The net effect of these laughs at the expense of Ted is an interesting one. We are led to laugh at Ted's excesses, but at the same time we cultivate a need for this object of our attentions, just as Murray obviously has. Gavin MacLeod was very good at projecting comic vitriol. We never believe there is any hatred toward Ted, but instead always an element of enjoyment in the frustration of having to work with this clod. Like Rhoda, Murray is never cruel or mean-spirited. And there is never the hard edge that would have worked for the Norman Lear comedies of the time. MacLeod's reading of his put-down lines is always a little rueful and self-amused, perfectly suited to the atmosphere created for the show.

With the arrival of Sue Ann he has a more formidable combatant than Ted. The formula for their typical encounter runs something like this: (1) she enters with a provocative remark; (2) he interrupts her with a remark, usually about her sexual promiscuity; (3) she

pauses while we anticipate her retort, usually a sweet sarcasm about his baldness.

The audience would need only the presence of Murray onstage to activate the wit combat when either Ted or Sue Ann entered the door. And they were never disappointed. MacLeod says, "The running gag with Sue Ann established a relationship and the audience began to anticipate the line."

Stacked end to end, these one-liners might seem too formulaic, too obvious, but of course they were never abstracted from the rest of the show. Thus they serve as part of the peculiarly successful integration of comic modes that blended into *The Mary Tyler Moore Show* as a whole.

Murray smiles through another sweet sarcasm.

Just in case the audience should begin to doubt that the wisecracking Murray was part of the general theme of "love is all around," there are episodes that point out his real fondness for his colleagues. In "Murray Can't Lose" (#154), after a serious argument with Ted, there is a serious reconciliation, during which Murray says, "Ted, you're filled with joy, love, and wonder, and I like you." Ten episodes later, in "Murray Ghosts for Ted," another reconciliation is necessary. Here his line is "You're a fine man, Ted Baxter. It's an honor to know you." There is no trace of irony; he absolutely means this.

Similarly, with Sue Ann, Murray gets serious in an episode where she needs him to express his genuine feelings, even though hers are not 100 percent pure. It is "Sue Ann's Sister" (#147), when the Happy Homemaker has taken to her luxurious bed in the latest chapter of her lifelong sibling rivalry. True, it takes the urging of Mary to get Murray (as well as the other men) to visit Sue Ann to comfort her, but when he consoles her and tries to restore her confidence he expresses a friendship we have suspected all along.

But none of this is intended to blur the enjoyment of Murray's one-liners. This is the classic part of his character, the one best remembered. Perhaps the purest example is in the lamented death of Chuckles the Clown, when Murray is the infectious source of the gallows humor about an elephant's "shelling" of their colleague and friend at the circus parade. Gavin MacLeod recalls some nervousness about the audience's possible reactions to this episode. "I remember that we were expecting the first laugh to be in Lou's office when Murray goes in and explains to him about what happened to Chuckles. Murray says, 'You know how hard it is to stop after just one peanut.' We felt if we got that laugh, we'd be home free. Well, the laugh lasted so long, we just relaxed after that and knew the audience was really with us in picking up on that kind of humor."

Gavin MacLeod muses on "that kind of humor" as gentle and kind. "Even when we were making statements, which we almost constantly were—about free press, adoption, divorce, marital

Murray and his son.

fidelity—we always made them in terms that allowed you to smile. We avoided, for the most part, what Mary called 'turkey-bladder time' in our comedy—slapstick."

Murray's humor was a constant ingredient during the entire series, but it was never central. MacLeod speaks of the character he embodied as "the behind-the-scenes guy who doesn't get the credit for what he does." The thoughtful actor sees an evolution of the role: "In the beginning of the series Murray was broader, wilder, but as Ted's character became so full and rich and expansive, if you had another expansive character against him, the relationship would not have worked." Although this "unexpansiveness" would not be the most significant aspect of a memorable character, it might be a key ingredient. "He's the brown bagger," says MacLeod, "the domesticated guy who would bring his lunch." Murray came complete with a devoted wife, Marie, to whom he tells us he has been married for ten years in episode 41 and eighteen years in episode 102—such was the fictional passage of time between January 15, 1972, and October 19, 1974. (He would probably say, "How time flies when you're having fun!") He has two daughters as the series begins and Marie gives birth to a third during the first season. Later they adopt a Vietnamese son (#108). Marie, played by Joyce Bulifant, appears in several episodes, as does one of his daughters. But usually this family, including Marie, is a presence offstage and not really a part of the action. They seem to exist primarily to flesh out, if ever so slightly, this essentially "behind the scenes" character.

In several episodes, however, he becomes central to the story. Allan Burns remembers that "Murray was one of the harder parts to write. He was so good at doing the one-liners. But on those occasions, once or twice a year, when we felt obligated to give him a show where he was front and center, it was always harder to write than the others. I never was quite sure why."

The first of these "front and center" shows was "We Closed in Minneapolis" (#19), featuring Murray Slaughter, would-be playwright. We rejoice with the writer whose rejections are so numerous that he can hardly believe his good fortune when the Twin Cities Playhouse agrees to produce his play. Then we agonize with him as he learns that Ted, who describes himself as the company's "resident star," will play the lead. Mary lands a minor role, as the "cute and perky" girl in the fictional newsroom of the play.

Premonitions of disaster abound and the worst of them come true. At one of Mary's ill-fated parties they gather to await the review, everyone but Ted realizing that the evening has lived down to all expectations. Murray, Marie, Rhoda, Mary, and Ted make leaden conversation until Lou arrives with the notice, which is entitled "Bomb Hits Minneapolis." This concludes the festivities in Mary's apartment.

The next morning Mary arrives at the office with a book of notices, and we are treated to a little piece of satire that no doubt sprang from some deep feelings on the part of the writers (Kenny Solms and Gail Parent are credited, but the passage also seems to have the imprimatur of Brooks and Burns). To cheer up Murray, Mary brings a book of reviews by John Simon, whom she identifies as the theater and film critic who "hates everything." She reads Simon's devastating attacks against two plays that he has found abominations: *Death of a Salesman* and *My Fair Lady*. Murray seems a little cheered, and before we have time to think too hard about this comparison, the episode ends.

In the second season "The Slaughter Affair" (#41) brings Murray's marriage to a point of tension. Marie has been a presence on the show since her introduction the season before in #17, "Just a Lunch." Now she is wracked by suspicion that Murray is having an affair with Mary. The plot is something of a tangled web, and part of the fun is the convolution itself. We begin when Murray, like Homer, nods and writes mistaken copy that Ted reads in his usual mindless fashion, urging the drivers of Minneapolis to "Drive carelessly." We learn that Murray's error is caused by exhaustion, which is caused by sleeplessness, which is caused by a moonlighting job, which is caused by his desire to buy Marie a compact car for their tenth anniversary. He has told her, as he had told Mary, that he is teaching writing in night school—a plausible and acceptable occupation —when in reality he is driving a cab. When, through a series of events, Marie checks with the night school, she finds that Murray is not teaching and leaps to the conclusion that he is having an affair. She chooses Mary as the object of his attention because she has a pretty good idea of what passions are barely leashed at the WJM newsroom, where attractive men and women work day after day in close proximity. Of course everything is all explained in the end, and she is delighted with her anniversary present, the very same compact car that she had wanted. It is the very same compact car, now ten years old, that they had been unable to afford when they were married.

An interesting premise for this episode is Marie's absolute conviction about Murray's charismatic attraction to all females. Her naiveté about him—it is a sort of idolatry—and about the steamy crowd at WJM has the slightly unfortunate effect of making us laugh at the notion of Murray's attractiveness. It's almost as if the writers had sided with the later baldness jokes and with all of television's attitude about middle age. Perhaps Murray is no Adonis, but he is not physically unattractive and this sacrifice of his character is a little akin to that aspect of Rhoda's during her "fat stage." Anyway, Marie finds him devastatingly attractive, as a wife should a husband and vice versa.

We get the same attitude again in "I Was a Single for WJM" (#96, Treva Silverman's script that ended the fourth season). Here Marie weeps at the prospect of Murray doing a story on location from a singles bar, certain that he will be snapped up by the hungry predators there. Such is not the case.

Several episodes in later seasons compensate for the notion of his unattractiveness in the earlier ones, although we have no evidence that such compensation is by design or was felt necessary by actor or writers. In "I Love a Piano," also written by Treva Silverman, Murray almost has an affair with an attractive divorcée, principal of an elementary school and friend of Georgette and (perhaps) Ted. As played by Barbara Barrie in décolletage and silk, Judy is a marvelously believable vamp from the unlikely field of childhood education. Everything is very civilized and low-key between her and Murray, but we sense her loneliness and we see his identity crisis as he seeks help in his struggle from Mary and Lou. This is Murray's big episode, his bad angel whispering in one ear urging him to reassert his youth and manhood and seize the day, his good angel at the other ear calling him back to faithfulness and Marie. There is no doubt, of course, of the outcome, but the scene when he tells Judy good-bye is very effective in its understatement. It achieves some of the delicacy of scenes with other principal characters but not so often afforded to Murray. And along the way there are some of his finest comic moments, including a delightfully believable tipsy scene, when he floats back to the office after lunch with Judy on a wave of pouilly-fuissé (Lou is disgusted at Murray's choice of beverages to overindulge with; he doesn't know whether to sober him up with coffee or cheese). Murray is also very fine in a duet with Judy at her grand piano, singing "Strangers in the Night," just those words over and over again because he doesn't know the lyrics. Never has that fatuous song been so put in its place.

Climactically, his love life is tested most severely in "Murray in Love" (#124), one of David Lloyd's scripts, in which the love expressed is for Mary. Unlike the Lou-Mary love affair in "Lou Dates Mary," there is very little in the relationship between Murray and Mary up to this time to suggest this development. Nevertheless, the episode is handled with the kind of tenderness that helps to round

out the character and more fully humanize him. The first half of the show is a comic masterpiece of suspense, with Murray's attempts to express his love constantly thwarted by every manner of interruption. Ted is particularly fine, with his determination to be confided in when he knows there is a problem. For 123 episodes he has been Murray's bête noir, and so his prominence in this episode gives the situation a brilliant comic edge. MacLeod says that he got the heaviest mail of the seven years from this story. "Guys who were sitting next to women in offices empathized completely with Murray. Many who wrote said they were still infatuated."

There had to be some significance that Murray was a writer on a show dominated by writers, where the writers were also the producers, and where the writing process was continuous and painstaking. Every week we saw Murray the writer at his desk, often working with the words that were to be credited by listeners to Ted Baxter. Murray knew, and we knew, that Ted was incapable of putting words together on paper. In our chapter on Ted we have already looked at several episodes where the anchorman tries, so to speak, to "make it on his own." There and elsewhere Murray helps to remind us that writing is the heart of both news and entertainment and is a difficult matter to perform. But this difficulty is not part of the common perception: Like writers in film and television, Murray suffers from a lack of recognition for his craft. He consistently fails to receive a Teddy Award, even suffering the embarrassment of being promised that he is going to win and then failing (#154). In another episode (#164) he writes an article for Ted on freedom of the press, which gets national attention for Ted. It will be reprinted in *The Reader's Digest*—no doubt this is a glancing blow at that homey all-American publication out of Pleasantville, New York. This is a sort of celebration of writing talent, especially when Ted "comes clean" at the end, leaving Murray to receive credit from family and friends. Under the resolution, however, there is still the theme about writing being relegated to a low place in the public mind.

Since we all feel, at least sometimes, unappreciated, it was easy to identify with Murray. His native shyness, his struggle for recognition, and his defensive wit combine to make this Everyman-of-the-newsroom an appealing member of the ensemble.

GEORGETTE: THE BETTER HALF

One of the methods of sustaining the freshness that makes a television series successful in the first place is to add and drop characters, to force a change in the mix. This procedure does not guarantee a long run, but it does help to keep staff, crew, and cast on their toes. It was certainly one of the key ingredients in *The Mary Tyler Moore Show*. The introduction of Georgette midway into the third season is a good example.

The episode "Rhoda Morgenstern: Minneapolis to New York" (#62) was written, like so many of those featuring her favorite character, by Treva Silverman. In it Rhoda announces her move back to New York, Mary gives a surprise farewell party, and Rhoda is so moved that she decides to stay in Minneapolis. One of the guests at Mary's party is Georgette Franklin.

We first see her talking with Lou Grant. The immediate impression is both visual and aural. We see and then hear a wide-eyed, fragile little blond woman projecting innocence and naiveté, talking with the hard-boiled Lou Grant, who seems nonplussed and, for once, incapable of handling his end of the dialogue. Here's a little of it:

> Georgette: I'm so sorry Rhoda's leaving Hempel's. I've been going crazy worrying about it. See, I'm the other window dresser there. There are six windows, so

now instead of decorating three, I'll have to do . . .
[*Pause, while she calculates, carefully and eventually with
success*] six.

It's not just what she says but the way she says it that convulses
the audience. Here was another original to add to the cast of
nonpareils.

The introduction of Ted to Georgette comes, in the real/absurd
manner associated with this show, when both are crouched down
behind a chair waiting to jump up and yell "Surprise" as Mary
brings Rhoda into the apartment. Ted, who has spotted this attractive girl and staked out his claim, introduces himself pompously,
though on his knees, as a face no doubt familiar to her, Ted Baxter,
anchorman of the Six O'Clock News. "Terrific," she says in the
little-girl voice and with the questioning eyes that always seem to be
trying to focus on a subject. "Are you covering this?"

Like a child, she is the first to jump up and delightedly cry
"Surprise," and, in a roomful of extras, the director has seen to it
that she is prominently featured for the camera during the crowd
scenes.

The new friendship between these children/adults forges ahead
when Georgette asks Ted to read Rhoda's farewell cards because "I
just love his voice." After the party Ted announces self-importantly
to Mary and Rhoda that he will be squiring the new girl home
and—with a leer—will no doubt be late to work tomorrow. While
he's talking Georgette gets in her car and drives off. Okay, Ted will
see Mary bright and early tomorrow morning.

It is a delightful but definitely low-key introduction. It could have
been the last appearance, just a girl whom Ted loved and lost in his
customary fashion. But the producers and the director saw something special. Sandrich reconstructs their reactions. "It wasn't planned.
There was a show with a surprise party for Lou at Mary's and Ted
needed a date. Georgia Engel was due here to do a play and I had
seen her in the play. She had two lines in our show, just one shot.
She was just so wonderful that I remember right after the show we
all said, 'We've got to find something for her to do.' So, she was
brought back as Ted's girlfriend."

And four episodes later she did return in Ed. Weinberger's "The
Georgette Story," in which she established herself as an equal part-
ner in the burgeoning relationship with Ted. She is now a "Golden
Girl" (no reference to the show of later fame), going from door-to-
door selling cosmetics (brightly announcing "Ding Dong, Golden
Girl"). We learn that she is being mistreated by Ted, who allows her

to do his shopping and his laundry but who frequently doesn't have time for socializing with her. In short, he's taking her for granted. Mary and Rhoda decide to do something about this situation by talking this frail little person into a greater respect for herself. She comes along slowly but she does come along ("I'm nice . . . very nice . . . *damned* nice").

The big scene with Ted is now set up. She demurely but very firmly breaks off the affair, and when he pleads with her not to send him packing, she makes a few conditions. She doesn't want to do his laundry anymore. Okay. She doesn't want him to patronize her by calling her "baby." Well, not so easy for him to understand, but he tries, suggesting "cookie, honey, lambkins, angelpuss, ducky—or something that Murray can come up with." She opts for "Georgette," and he agrees. He is truly delighted when she takes him back, and she is pleased to do so.

In the tag to this episode Ted tells Mary that Georgette is now the new woman and everything is equal between them. Last night they cooked dinner together and then she selected the movie. Ted seems pleased and, of course, Mary is delighted. But Ted's final line brings us back from near-politics to good character comedy: "As long as I live, I'll never forgive you!"

Now the character is set. Without oversimplifying egregiously, one may describe Georgette as a mixture of the wide-eyed innocent (never the dumb blonde, *never* that) and the increasingly aware woman. Critics rushed to the challenge. A *TV Guide* article (December 8, 1973) dredged from others such descriptions as "a cross between Stan Laurel and Marilyn Monroe," "a new ZaSu Pitts" (the wide-eyed comedienne of the thirties), a "female Gomer Pyle." All strained. Alice Ghostley, herself a comedienne without analogy, describes Georgia Engel as "one of a kind, a true original, a remarkably sweet girl and a dazzling actress." Engel's own description is the more modest "pipey-voiced."

The innocence is suggested by the appropriateness of her decision to join a convent ("Almost a Nun's Story," #86) when she suspects Ted of an interest in another woman. But more regularly that little-girl quality is seen in her dialogue. These pearls, for example:

"I love the wine. It's one of my favorite kinds. [*Pause*] White."

She returns from one of many memorable meals at one of Ted's stable of cheap restaurants suffused with a glow over the service. It seems that they even make special orders by saying, over the microphone, " 'Hold the pickle'—and they do!" Another time she reports dropping her tray at one of his gourmet restaurants.

Or another time: "Excuse me. I hate to interrupt and I don't mean

Georgette belts out "Steam Heat" at the annual Teddy Awards banquet.

to spoil your fun, and it's certainly no comment on the dinner, because it's delicious and you'll have to give me your recipe sometime, but right now I think I'm going to have a baby." And she does.

The wide-of-eye approach to life that she so charmingly embodies is frequently a source of non sequiturs, which Mary is particularly adept at reacting to. From the Chuckles the Clown funeral: "Well, I mean we take people for granted while they're with us. Then when they're gone, we wish we'd been nicer to them. So we dress in black and cry our eyes out. [*Pause*] Why don't we ever think to do that while they're still with us?"

Because she is so conscientiously good-hearted, Georgette sets herself up for Ted to take advantage of her. Given his character, he will always do this, but the writers (and the actors) are not going to present the viewer with the painful situation of abuse, no matter how gentle. This dimension of her character began in episode 66, with the frank talk already partly quoted, in which she defends her rights.

It continues with a much more serious dressing-down of the irresponsible Ted in episode 129, "Ted's Wedding," when she firmly calls a halt to his joke proposals of marriage. At brunch with Mary, Ted asks Georgette to marry him, his mouth full of onion roll. This to him is obviously just cute banter, but to her it signals the time for an understanding. She asks Mary to leave the room and reminds Ted of earlier offenses: a marriage proposal in a car wash, another in a revolving door, spelling one out with socks on laundry day. Enough. It is time. "So what do you say, Buster, do you still want to get married?" Yes, "Buster" does, and they do so right away, in David Lloyd's unforgettable wedding script. She can never really be hard-boiled, as the expression goes. But she can be firm. When the decision is made to adopt a child—a decision made because of Georgette's patience with Ted and her ability to impart some wisdom to him—she turns on the lady from the agency who is in the process of vetoing their suitability to adopt:

"Suitable. You don't think we're suitable? Let me tell you about suitable. That man has papered an entire room with the three bears for his new child. So it's the kitchen. So he made a mistake. But he cares so much. And you say he's not suitable." She points to the electric sockets, all of which Ted has moved to a height of six feet for safety. He has spent twelve dollars for toys, a sum that she puts in perspective by contrasting it with the smaller cost of her engagement ring. The lady is impressed and we know that Georgette has turned the interview around. Ted is impressed too: "My lord, I'm a beautiful human being."

Georgette has gone into her marriage with eyes wide open. Before her impromptu wedding she responds to Mary's half-spoken question about impetuosity: "Mary, I know what you're getting at, and believe me, I know how Ted can be. Nobody knows that better than I do. But I know how I feel." Of course she loves him, she declares in a very soft and poignant moment, and then ends the scene with "Somebody has to."

One final example of the depth of her character is one of her best. In Bob Ellison's "My Son, the Genius" (#161), Georgette prevails over Ted to take their adopted son to a child psychologist to find the cause for his slow performance in school. She is very much in control, even when they learn that David's IQ is 160 and that boredom is his problem. She is delighted when she returns with the boy the next day, after enrolling him in a school for bright students, where a nine-year-old girl has given her directions to the ladies' room in Latin. All their pride is crushed, however, when the prodigy reminds them, by throwing a tantrum, that he is a normal child. He *will* go to the museum, regardless of his parents' other plans. "Ted, if you won't handle this, I'll have to." But she is reduced to tears when her son says he "abhors" her. The moment is set up for Ted, and the scene is really his, but Georgette has claimed an equal share of our sympathy—and admiration.

Lest all of this sound too much like a movie of the week, we should close by enjoying a few of Georgette's remarks that delight through their surprise. That tiny little voice with the quizzical phrasing is capable of such gems as:

"Here's mud in your eye, for trading in your freedom for a ball and chain. Keep her pregnant in the summer and barefoot in the winter. . . . I got that out of a book of party toasts. It's pretty dumb, but it's what [Ted] wants." So runs her version of a good old boy's toast at a bachelor party.

Another, this one to Mary when she's dressing for the wedding: "I always dreamed of being married in something old, something new, something borrowed, something blue. [*Pause*] But what the hell, we're in a hurry."

Telling Ted that she's pregnant, after the doctors told him he was infertile and just after the adoption: "Well, you know those little guys you said you didn't have enough of? Well, you may not have as many as the doctors said you should have, but one of the little buggers did the job."

This, by the way, was the *Mary Tyler Moore* cliff-hanger at the end of the sixth season, their version of "Who Shot J.R." to keep the audience in a frenzy of suspense all summer long. Ted and Georgette have adopted David and are showing him off to the newsroom staff when Georgette whispers the news of her pregnancy to the astonished father-to-be. The opening show of the seventh season,

"Mary Midwife," centers on the birth of their child at what turns out to be one of Mary's more memorable parties.

At the wedding, the earlier impromptu event in Mary's apartment, Georgette had extemporized a brief speech in which she had promised always to make Ted happy because he always made her happy. Within the limits of the reality imposed on the characters, especially by Ted's ego, we feel that the promise was mutually fulfilled.

SUE ANN: THE HAPPY HOMEWRECKER

Betty White describes "the Betty White type" as "icky sweet, and sickening, my image since 1949 in television. I would say the bawdiest of things on Jack Paar or talk shows or game shows [including *What's My Line, To Tell the Truth, Match Game, Password,* and *I've Got a Secret*], and the audience would think, of course, poor sweet Betty doesn't know what she's saying. If she only knew what that really means."

Well, poor sweet Betty is one of the shrewdest and most subtle actresses on the sitcom scene. Jay Sandrich is quoted in a *TV Guide* article in 1974 (July 20) describing her as a "witty, inventive, *brilliant* lady." She was a true original then, on *The Mary Tyler Moore Show,* and remains so now, on *The Golden Girls,* where her Rose constitutes another variation on the White persona, the irony of complete naiveté. "Rose is a long way from Sue Ann, the neighborhood nymphomaniac," Betty White says. "She's completely naive, not stupid, although Rose as the village idiot gives me a handle on the thing. She just takes every word at face value and never looks for a second meaning to the word." Indeed, there seems to be something of Georgia Engel's Georgette in Rose, especially the non sequiturs and the little absurdist anecdotes from her past. But as Sue Ann she was consistently dealing in second meanings in a way that the audience immediately "got" . . . and loved.

We have earlier told the story of Ethel Winant's casting for the first season. When it came time to cast for episode 73, the first show of the fourth season, Winant was still assisting the producers in that task. She recounts the story of how Betty White was selected for the part of Sue Ann, a part originally designed for a single episode.

"Betty and Allen Ludden and Grant and Mary were the best of friends and they spent a lot of time together; they would always meet socially, they had been friends for years. Perhaps because of this relationship, every few months someone would say, 'Well, we really ought to find a part for Betty.' So one day this script [#73] came in and I loved it. I thought they had written a part for Betty. So I did something I never do—I called and set her for the part. Tuesday or Wednesday I got a call from Jim—'Ethel, aren't we ever going to see any actors for the Happy Homemaker?' I said, 'Oh, I thought you wrote the part for Betty White.' He said, 'No, Betty's so sweet, and she's Mary's best friend.' I said, 'Well, there's this slightly embarrassing thing here. I've never done this before, but I actually just set her for the part.' There was a little crisis now, because they just thought she was wrong for it. I had called the agent and made the deal. I would never have done that except for those conversations about writing a part for her. As I say, when I read the part it was, in my mind, so clearly written for Betty that I thought, okay, they did it. We all know each other so well.

"Allan and Jim called a meeting and said, 'We can't. What if she's terrible? That'll be worse for Mary. We have to read her.' I said, 'That's going to be a little hard to do, since she thinks she's already set for the part. The only thing to do is to tell the truth.' So I called the agent, and the agent of course screamed. I said, 'I didn't say I wouldn't pay, that's not the point. I said, all I want to do is call Betty. It's all my fault. Mary doesn't know anything about this. Jim and Allan didn't know anything about it. I just did a stupid thing.' I called Betty, and she said, 'I'll go in and read. It's such a wonderful part, I would kill for this part. If reading for it is the only way to get it, I'll go in and get it.' And she did and she got it and she was wonderful. But I'll never forget it. Oh my God, how could I have done such a dumb thing? After that, if it was a one-line part, I'd call and set it up the usual way."

White's version of this event includes some self-deprecation: "I think Ethel assured everybody that if I failed to get the part after reading for it, it really would be awkward for Mary. And then they all said, 'Oh, give it to her, she's been around the Horn often enough that she's not going to hurt anything.' " She also tells of a cherished moment when she surprised Mary with the news. "As soon as I accepted I called Mary and asked her to guess who was going to do her show next week? 'Who?' she asked. I said, 'Me.' A short pause and she said, with a smile in her voice, 'Wait a minute. I didn't have anything to do with that. I don't know what's going on but I have veto power and you're certainly not going to get near that show.' "

But she did. And the chemistry that apparently worked well in the private lives of the Luddens (Betty White's husband was the game-show host Allen Ludden) and the Tinkers carried over into the show. The *TV Guide* article puts it accurately: "The part was small. Betty had one brief scene at the beginning and one bruising confrontation with Mary and the irate Phyllis at the end. It was enough. As Phyllis slammed the oven door, decimating Sue Ann's precious chocolate soufflé—'Oh, my poor *baby*,' wailed Sue Ann—a bright new star of the Mary Tyler Moore stock company emerged."

In fact, White feels that the key to audience response to Sue Ann lies with Mary. "Mary was the only reason Sue Ann worked. I'm convinced that if Mary Tyler Moore had taken another choice as an actress, had she resented Sue Ann or been annoyed by her, the audience would have followed her assessment and the character wouldn't have been accepted. The option that Mary took was that this poor foolish lady believes all these things that she's saying about herself and, my, isn't that funny!"

Funny it is. Sue Ann, known privately as the bitch and predator, is publicly acclaimed as "The Happy Homemaker," whose television show on WJM is an exercise in self-promotion and hypocrisy. She offers to do the tribute to the recently deceased Chuckles the Clown on her show because her recipe features onions and her eyes will already be appropriately red. The arch sweetness that she projects is 100 percent fraud, a cover for the most mercenary remarks and actions.

Her entrances into the newsroom are typically suffused with smiles, her head tilted in an idiosyncratic way that fairly beams mock joy. The dialogue that accompanies all this sweetness and light is like Halloween apples with razor blades.

Here is a typical one. Sue Ann enters with a press clipping that refers to Mary's recent promotion saying she's now the most important woman at WJM. Sue Ann accuses Mary of hiring a press agent.

Mary: Sue Ann, I didn't give them this story. Although, I must say, it certainly is accurate!

Sue Ann: [*Smiling really hard now, voice dripping with sugar*] Oh, Mary, you sweet, innocent, naive, albeit ruthless child.

Professor Diana Meehan, whose *Ladies of the Evening* is a recent examination of the stereotypes of women on television, categorizes Sue Ann as the "harpy," the polar opposite of a "good wife." The harpy is "an aggressive single woman more predator than preyed upon, and never taken for granted. The harpy was strong, even overpowering, and she marshalled force and energy in pursuit of her objective, the capture of the man of her affections." With Sue

Ann we should substitute "men" for "man," but the rest seems accurate enough.

"She just got worse," says White. "She started out bad and then just got absolutely worse. She started the first show with the Lars Lindstrom affair, where Phyllis's husband took her home and somehow they didn't show up until 5 A.M. and thank God he called finally and explained that in avoiding hitting a dog on the road they had run into a tree and thank goodness they were able to find an all-night body shop. Isn't that nice! So she started from that premise and went downhill from there until she stopped just short of murder. She poisoned the whole company with rolls that she had left after the custard went bad. Her 'friends' had displeased her, so she saw to it that they got the custard. It wasn't her fault they didn't die; it was only luck that she didn't wipe out the newsroom staff."

But usually her murderous impulses took a more metaphoric form: "Well," she says to Mary, whose recent promotion to producer is so galling, "the inmates really *are* running the asylum." She follows this zinger closely with "Mary, believe me, I'm proud that you haven't been disheartened by those who murmur that you've sacrificed your femininity to your ambition."

The word that used to be used for this sort of scratching and clawing is "catty," but this term is perhaps unfair in stereotyping females, both human and feline. Still, there *is* a sort of purr in Sue Ann's harshest words.

She stalks all men, a delightfully flirtatious menace in their presence. (Murray once asks, "What kind of birthday present do you get for the woman who's had everyone?") But her special target is Lou Grant, whom she apparently finds irresistible:

Lou: Mary thinks I should lose weight.
Sue Ann: Nonsense, Lou. Your body's perfect, I wouldn't touch it. [*She pauses a beat while devouring that body with her eyes*] If I did, I wouldn't stop.

There is no mistaking Sue Ann's purpose—she is going to bed down with Lou Grant, somehow, somewhere, sometime. The two episodes that deal most explicitly with this are #133, David Lloyd's "The Happy Homemaker Takes Lou Home," and #138, "Once I Had a Secret Love," by Pat Nardo and Gloria Banta.

The former begins when Sue Ann brings a man by at 2 A.M. to meet Mary to show her the lengths to which she will go to get a date. This one is colossally dull and no more entranced with Sue Ann than she with him. It seems that, on a double date, their

Sue Ann's choice of a birthday present to herself from Lou.

partners "eloped" with each other, leaving the two losers to spend a long, long evening together. This klutz has a job just as fascinating as he is—he makes those little plastic tabs that fit over the ends of shoelaces so that they will go through the holes. This visit is Sue Ann's way of pleading with Mary to get her a date with Lou so that she might have a chance at true happiness. As absurd as this all is, there is a longing in her loneliness that makes Sue Ann a more believable, more interesting, and more appealing character.

Mary's sympathy for Sue Ann's predicament is based on her realization of this loneliness and this helps to elicit the audience's sympathy (we remember Betty White's feeling that it was Mary who made the Sue Ann character work). And so Mary undertakes, through trickery, to bring her boss together with her friend. It works in a highly comic scene where Lou agrees to date Mary's unidentified acquaintance, ending with Sue Ann swooping in upon him to claim her prize.

The big scene is in Sue Ann's apartment, where Lou has tried to make the meal last forever. Finally, it is time. Sue Ann leads him to the couch and quotes the old expression "A great meal is the prelude to a symphony of love," an old expression that she has just thought up. There follows a battle between his reluctance and her aggressiveness ("Go on, Lou, you're stronger than I am. Press your advantage"). Some high comic moments on the couch include a sort of arm wrestle that ends with Lou's escape and Sue Ann's despair. For once she drops the mask and asks him to be frank about what's wrong with her. In response he is gentle, although he's playing something of a part, gauging her reaction as he tries to get the hell out of there without doing her any real damage.

He tells her she's too good to throw herself at a man this way. Lou urges her to let the man pursue her. "The treasure shouldn't do the hunting, Sue Ann. You're a treasure. You should act like it."

After those sobering, if sexist, words she is quiet for once . . . and honest. "Isn't life funny? I've been accepted by lots of men and felt rotten. You've just rejected me and I feel like a million dollars. Thanks, Lou." But the scene ends with a laugh:

Lou: Maybe we'll do this again sometime.
Sue Ann: [*Eager, bright*] When?

The story of Lou and Sue Ann continues, after four intervening episodes, with Lou's crazed entrance into the newsroom, tie askew, unshaven, wild of eye, eager to throw away all the liquor (still in his drawer) so that he will never again get drunk enough to do what he did last night. Betty White claims that she remembers as the funniest moment in any show Lou giving Mary that bottle. He confesses that he has spent the night with Sue Ann (the "confession" is actually a fluke—Mary recognizes the handwriting on a love note, the "i's" dotted with little hearts, Sue Ann's special signature). Her enjoyment breaks through all her defenses, and she laughs and laughs at the joke. But she swears herself to secrecy.

The secret is too delicious, however, and in the very next scene she betrays the confidence to Murray in childish exchange for *his* secret. Soon the whole newsroom knows, abetted by Sue Ann's flamboyant returning of Lou's socks, washed with lemon juice and delivered with syrupy love right in front of Ted, Murray, and Mary. When Murray tries to make everything right by telling Lou that it's okay, he already knows, the joke is over and the show turns darker.

Now the subject is not sniggering over Sue Ann's sexual proclivities and Lou's intoxicated indiscretion. Now we are dealing with a violation of confidence. Lou admits Mary to his office and declares, "Mary, I'm not mad. I still respect you as a producer. I want you to stay here. I want you to work here. We're still in business. [*Long pause*] We're just not friends anymore."

At this point a new set of jokes is needed to get us all out of this very poignant moment. We know we can count on deft touches and they come. Mary cries, Lou reaches for his handkerchief—which is one of the socks Sue Ann has just returned, and it becomes a hilarious prop for the rest of the scene. Ted is also his usual magnificent self, intruding, saying and doing all the wrong things.

Two necessary scenes are coming. The first is the meeting between Sue Ann and Lou in which a dozen moods quickly succeed each other, resulting in Lou's promise that this can never happen again but that he can at least take her to dinner. She acts mortally wounded at this bribe but brightens up when he offers two dinners and a lunch. Wreathed in smiles, she says, "You got yourself a deal." So the game continues and in subsequent shows she still cozies outrageously up to Lou.

The next plot line that needs to be resolved is the rift between Mary and Mr. Grant. It is as graceful as we could want. Mary is in his inner sanctum when Lou arrives. She sees only one way to make it right—tell him her deepest, darkest secret and give him permission to spread it around the world. Her confession is delightfully absurd. It is her secret affair—with Walter Cronkite! Lou is unconvinced. She tries again. Roger Mudd? A few minutes of cajoling a smile from the downturned corners of his mouth result in success and a warm hug. This is enough in the sunny world of situation comedy, where we know all along that everyone is well intentioned and that all misunderstandings are mere aberrations in a world where love is all around.

Betty White appends a note to this episode: "All along I had been expecting objections to Sue Ann the nympho; actually I was expect-

The vibrating bed.

ing some mail on both sides. But I don't think I got any critical letters, even on the episode when I trapped him into spending the night at my house. Everybody took it in the spirit in which it was given and loved it."

In both these episodes with Lou, Sue Ann reveals a side of her character that deepens it far past the predatory harpy. She is alone (this is different from being single) and afraid, vulnerable beneath the stiletto that is itself often beneath the sunny smile. How can we not respond with sympathy toward her? She needs us.

This formula continues with episode 147, with David Lloyd's "Sue Ann's Sister," in which Pat Priest guests as sister Lila. Here Sue Ann's fear of failure takes another form—rivalry with her sister. Theirs is a long-standing history of struggling in which the result has been that Lila has systematically and regularly taken everything away from her older sister. Now she makes a play for Lou and—the crowning blow—auditions for a job as homemaker on a rival Minneapolis station, which will put her into direct competition with Sue Ann, WJM's Happy Homemaker. Lila gets the job, of course, and Sue Ann goes home "in a state of deep emotional depression."

In support Mary organizes a home visitation team of friends—Lou, Murray, and Ted—who one by one, orchestrated by Mary, enter perhaps the most magnificently crafted set of the entire series,

Sue Ann's bedroom. It is Erosville, U.S.A., a cacophony of frills, flowers, dim lights, feathers, softness in every available form, centering on a huge round bed, with Hollywood quilted headboard and countless fluffed pillows. Mary's double take when she enters intensifies our own enjoyment at the rich visual joke. The studio audi-

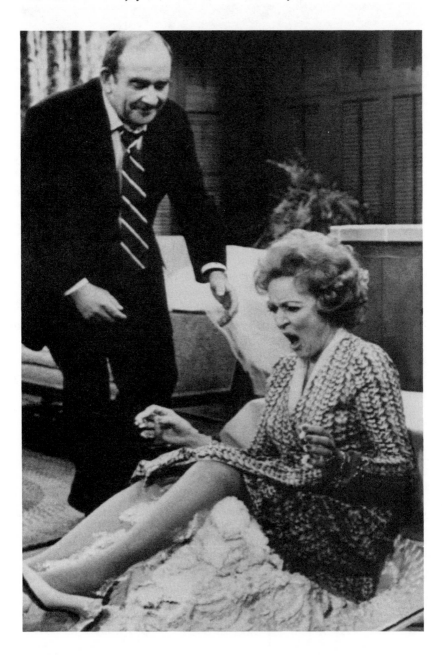

ence that night had the same surprise as the later viewing audience. The bedroom set was hidden from view until the scene began.

And then, one by one, the men enter, each responding in his own way to the excesses of interior design by Jung. "Did you decorate it yourself?" asks Murray. "Or did you have a sex maniac come in?" Ted has one of his—or anyone else's—finest moments as he looks up toward the ceiling, and, without any questioning look, arranges his hat in the mirror there. Betty White assures us that this was an ad-lib they decided to leave in. Next he triggers the bed vibrator, then the stereo system, which blasts forth Tchaikovsky at his most symphonically florid. The scene is set now for Lou, whom she summons to sit by her on the bed, where she plays Camille, then to his consternation turns on the stereo and the vibrator.

The final visitor to the playroom is Lila, who dutifully and perhaps lovingly turns down the competing homemaker job. At the tag Mary sneaks back into the bedroom, lies down, looks up into the mirror, cuts on the vibrator and the stereo for one glorious moment. Then, a little reluctantly and probably feeling a little foolish, she joins the others. Another wonderful ending that suits the elaborate joke but also derives with integrity from the characters as we have come to know them.

Not surprisingly, Betty White remembers this as one of her favorite shows, especially Ted's reaction to the mirror and Mary's "tippy-toeing back into the room to try out the vibrating bed."

It may come as a surprise to most of us to learn that Betty White did not make her first appearance in *The Mary Tyler Moore Show* until its fourth season and then never appeared in more than twelve episodes in any year. "Most of the time it was six or maybe eight times per season, but when I do interviews people seem to think I was there every week. That's because the part was so strongly written and also because of the generous way the company treated you." It is a mark of her own generosity as a performer and as a person that she credits most of her favorite moments in the show to others (Lou's proffer of the liquor bottle to Mary, Ted's gesture in the mirror, several of Mary's scenes). She also applauds the ensemble of writers and actors. "When I went on the show for the first day's rehearsal, to do this guest role for the one week, it was like walking into a house I was familiar with and seeing old friends there." She was thrilled when Allan Burns told her they had an idea for another script that would include her.

Fifteen years later she agrees that *The Mary Tyler Moore Show* is something to celebrate. "I'm just so proud and gratified to have been a part of this history-making show."

John Amos.

THE SUPPORTING CAST

For a series that appeared to live a charmed life with its casting of major roles, both in 1970 and in succeeding years, it probably comes as no surprise to discover that the choice of the actors to play occasional roles, whether single or multiple episode, was equally on the mark.

The most regular of the irregulars was Joyce Bulifant, who played Murray's faithful wife, Marie. She provided just the right blend of commitment to and concern for her family. She was the single snapshot of the traditional housewife supplied by this series. If she had thoughts of greater freedom of self-expression, like Edie, the news never reached the viewer's ears. We know more about her from Murray's references at the office than by a character analysis of her limited appearances. From the combination we know she worked patiently and lovingly to provide a warm and comfortable home environment.

John Amos gave a memorable reading of Gordy the Weatherman in his some dozen stints over the years, culminating in "Hail the Conquering Gordy" (#162) in 1977 when he returned to visit WJM after having risen to national prominence as a talk-show host. Amos remembers his relationship with Burns and Brooks and Tinker with appreciation. "It was a great company to work for." He recalls the way in which Phyllis reacted to Gordy, assuming, because of his color and size, that he was the sportscaster. It was a stereotyping that added humor to his role and was acceptable because of the sense of family solidarity existing among all the characters. Phyllis's attitudes were accepted by the rest as flawed, but she was still a part of that family.

Amos, who would become a victim of severe typecasting after his sterling performance in *Roots*, feels the role of Gordy was good for him. His lines always allowed him to appear to be the brightest of the WJM staff. Gordy's wry humor and raised eyebrow when dealing with Ted were a balance to Murray's sharp barbs. He likely would have been included on a more regular basis had not *Good Times* beckoned in 1973.

Lisa Gerritsen, who played Bess, gave a remarkably consistent picture of a growing girl. She was believable as Phyllis's daughter—no small accomplishment. As we noted in Chapter 3, it may have been her single line "I like Aunt Rhoda" that altered the future of MTM. History has turned on smaller things. In any event her interpretation of Bess earned her the same role on the new series, *Phyllis*, in 1975.

Priscilla Morrill's portrayal of Edie Grant was pivotal in the scheme of things for the show. Lou seldom let a week go by without referring to Edie, but she was seen far less frequently. Our first real encounter with Edie was in "The Boss Isn't Coming to Dinner" (#21) when she decides to go back to school. It was a harbinger of a plot sequence that would culminate in divorce and Edie's remarriage. Skilled writing, directing, and acting created a relationship in which the viewer could feel close to both Lou and Edie. Perhaps most of all in the character of Edie the writers and producers determined to address the impact of the Women's Movement on traditional marriages. Neither Edie nor Lou understood the why of their breakup. The viewer was left to ponder the causes and the consequences.

The role of Ida Morgenstern belonged to Nancy Walker. Looking back, we cannot imagine anyone else in that part. She took the lines and made them come alive in a character that was a caricature of the Jewish mother. The choice exchanges between Rhoda and her mother were usually high comedy. The network became disturbed about the first appearance, when Rhoda refuses to see Ida. Grant Tinker took charge and saw to it that the episode was made as written. It was the first of many battles Tinker would win with CBS, battles he kept at a considerable distance from his creative team. Brooks was so removed from those struggles, he was unable to recount them, a tribute to Tinker's extraordinary skill.

Finally, there was Eileen Heckart, who made three appearances on the series as Mary's Aunt Flo, beginning in the fall of 1975 (#126). In the hackneyed prose of decades of film critics, "she ate up the scenery." She painted a character so outrageous as to boggle the mind and then made it believable that Flo Meredith, the toughest and roughest of reporters, liberal to the bone, could become involved with Lou. We have addressed this encounter in the section devoted to David Lloyd in Chapter 4. She made a brief appearance on the *Lou Grant* series some years later.

7

THE LAST SHOW

It was time for a graceful exit.

All good shows, like all bad ones, must someday come to an end, and the *Mary Tyler Moore* ensemble decided to finish on a high note. In 1976 everyone was still writing, producing, directing, and acting on the highest plane, and the ratings were secure, but six years was a long time and no one wanted to look forward to a series that had begun to show its age. The way of the sitcom is inevitably toward staleness, actors moving through their now-familiar lines by rote, audiences still laughing because of some Pavlovian response, but more and more uncertainly.

Besides, these people were professionals, with careers that needed to develop. In the inimitable words of Hollywood, people needed "to stretch." And everybody connected with the show was eminently marketable at this point. There was no hint of anticlimax; everyone was in top form. Offers of film, television, and stage work would come like a deluge when the surprise word got around that the show was going to put itself out of business.

And so the decision was made toward the end of the sixth season, and the countdown began as the seventh season got under way. There was regret. As Betty White expresses it, "I don't think I was smart enough at the time to recognize what a great show, a breakthrough show, it was. I think when you're standing at the foot of the tree, you don't know how tall it is. But, by the last year, when we began pulling away from it, Mary came to work the first day saying that this is the first day of the first week of the last year. And that feeling went on every day all year long. Everybody knew that something magic was drawing to a close. It was in our pores."

The tension was terrific during the last season: Could they maintain the integrity of the show, along with its energy and spontaneity? Stan Daniels remembers that everyone was keenly aware of all the Emmys the show had won and how ghastly it would be to let down during the final year. By the time of the last episode that feeling was heightened almost unbearably.

Discussions of the story line for that episode followed the usual procedure, with work apportioned out among the six men who by that time were chiefly responsible for the writing: Brooks, Burns, Weinberger, Daniels, Lloyd, and Ellison. The plot, as usual, would be relatively simple, befitting the half-hour format. But the emotional burden would be huge—daunting, in fact. Once the story line was set, each writer was assigned a scene, but during the week the customary merging of ideas and inspirations occurred, so that the final script was really a group effort. David Lloyd recalls that he had one of the early scenes, but not one that he considered the best. "I think Jim Brooks did the last one, or shepherded us through it, or maybe he and Allan together. I don't know. But during the week it was the usual give-and-take, all six of us in a row, making suggestions, adding or taking out. In retrospect it is amazing that you can have six different people write something and they can merge."

The immediate reward for the writers occurred on Wednesday, the final rewrite night. Stan Daniels remembers the group working very hard "to get the script in shape so that we would have a big party. We finished about ten or eleven o'clock and went to a terrific restaurant. Ed. Weinberger bought four or five vintage wines to celebrate. I had the worst cold of my life and couldn't taste a thing, but I drank those wines, whatever they were, because they were about two hundred dollars a bottle."

What was this plot that deserved such a reward? It began with the premise that the owner of Station WJM has hired a new station manager to find out why ratings are so low. First impressions among the employees (and, of course, the audience) lead to Ted as the culprit. After all, for six years we have known him as colossally inept, a bloated ego matched to a minuscule talent. His insecurity is appropriate to his reputation, and the first scenes of the last show exploit this fertile strain of fun. Ted is frantic when he hears that he is being evaluated, begging on his knees before Lou for everyone to stand by him in his hour of trial. No matter that it is everybody else's hour of trial too. When they are summoned to the office of the new boss, played by Vincent Gardenia, Ted arrives with his wife, two children, and dog, dependents testifying to his vast responsibilities.

But, as usual, we are surprised by the twist: Ted will remain; everyone else is fired. Briefly, and with an almost painful struggle, Ted stands by his colleagues, then in a fine comedic moment turns away from them with relief. In the next scene, back in the newsroom, he is worried because he doesn't feel sorrier! Thus the writers stay true to this character who has always been mired deep within himself.

Mary has decided to grasp at straws—after all, the boss had referred to those he was firing as "guys." And she isn't a "guy." Right? Wrong. A telephone call dashes the silly hope. Guy or not, she's fired.

The comedy to this point has featured the shock of firing as it reverberates among the five principal characters: Ted and Mary have been given prominence, but Lou, Murray, and Sue Ann have suffi-cient lines and reactions. In the next scene a new element—nostalgia—makes its appearance. From here the real-life tension mounts because the actors' composure began to be threatened. Lou drops by Mary's apartment to comfort her with surprise guests Rhoda and Phyllis.

Each had left the show (Rhoda in 1974, Phyllis in 1975) for successful spin-offs, so both were still prominent in the minds of the loyal audience. The scene in which Lou springs his surprise, insisting that Mary close her eyes and count to ten, is nostalgic and heartwarming but also a fine one comedically. Rhoda and Phyllis struggle to claim the title of "Mary's Best Friend," even jockeying physically for position to be closer to her. Cloris Leachman remembers this ploy as her contribution, and perhaps it was, though the skilled hand of Sandrich is quite clearly at work as well. "It would have been typical of her," says David Lloyd. "She would always find wonderful stuff to do. When they're vying to comfort Mary, to hug her, Phyllis pushes in for a bigger hug." Whatever the source it was inspired, resulting in a scene as notable for its hilarity as its emotional tug. Here appears the unabashed "love is all around" theme that has accounted for much of the power of The Mary Tyler Moore Show.

As the plot continues we learn how these treasured friends from the last seven years will cope with their loss. Already Mary has received offers to go with Phyllis to San Francisco or Rhoda to New York. She needn't do either. We know that a bright, committed, attractive, resilient young career woman will do just fine in her next job. At the opposite end of the spectrum from Mary, Sue Ann already has a job, traveling on a cruise to the Mediterranean with an elderly gentleman as a "sort of practical nurse." Murray and Lou are left without plans, probably because it would be too tidy to provide for everyone. But Ted, of course, having risen to the level of his incompetence, remains.

So people are picking up the pieces and turning toward a new life, with genuine sadness but still a sense of hope. The story is working diligently on the audience's emotions. But it is also straining the actors in a way that none could remember previously. How would they get through the rehearsals? The run-throughs? And, most difficult of all, the actual filming before the audience? It would have been virtually impossible to go back and retake any significant amount from these scenes. They simply had to be played out as continuously as possible, both for the actors' and the audience's equilibrium.

Betty White remembers vividly, "We didn't know how the show was going to end. I don't think even Mary did. But we knew that the last week was going to be tough. The writers couldn't even write the last scene until Wednesday, and we didn't even see a script until blocking day, Thursday. Just reading through it was rough."

Amid all this emotion and the comic antics described below, the director, Jay Sandrich, encounters a cast welling with tears, anticipating a final audience composed entirely of family and friends. It was he who would guide the final show to its Emmy-winning quality. Sandrich knew that rehearsals were going to be nearly unbearable, so he told the actors to read their lines without feeling and to hold all the emotion for the Friday performance. He knew their performances would be on the mark, and he was correct.

Betty White adds her memories. "By the last week we were doing everything but hanging on to each other's legs as we'd walk down the hall. We'd go to lunch together and we'd come home together and we'd go over and sit down together and we'd always drag Vincent [Vincent Gardenia, who was guesting as the new station boss] along with us. And long afterwards he said, 'I didn't know where to look, I didn't know what to say—all those people. I felt like a pork chop in a synagogue. I really didn't know what to do with myself.' It was such a highly charged, emotional week. We knew by that time we were saying good-bye to something that had been more than special."

From David Lloyd's perspective, "the whole week of the last show and particularly the day of the last show there was such danger of bogging down in emotionalism and it was a time fraught with so much emotion that Ed. Weinberger was casting about trying to find some way to get through the final run-through without it becoming weepy and losing the energy that would be needed that night with the audience. Well, some company was shooting a Western on the MTM lot. So Ed. went out and found several American Indians in full regalia and brought them in, unknown to Mary, and put them at the desks in the back of the newsroom in place of the extras that usually sat there. So Mary came out and started her scene, and suddenly she found that she was getting laughs from the forty or so people who were there—not the audience yet, just people who worked on the show, plus whoever wanders in from the lot to those things. The laughs were coming in the wrong places and she couldn't figure it out. You know that sense that actors have that something isn't quite clicking, that the people out front are enjoying something that they're missing. So Mary turned around and saw all those Indians, all those cheekbones and unsmiling faces. And it just blew her away. She was fine for the rest of the run-through, no danger of her suddenly becoming too emotional."

Lloyd also remembers a flare-up on the set sometime prior to the last show, one of the rare times when Grant Tinker called a meeting in his office to calm everyone down. Both sides had their say and the incident passed. But what Lloyd chiefly remembers about the incident was Ted Knight's evaluation: "We're getting too near the end," he said. "We're experiencing separation anxiety!"

The final scene in episode 168 takes place in the newsroom. Bob Ellison remembers, "The speech about being a family was written by Jim pretty much as it was finally heard. That's the big speech. We knew we had to have one, but we had put it off, afraid of it. I think he didn't write it until final rewrite night. In it Mary turns to her companions and says,

> Well, I just wanted you to know that sometimes I get concerned about being a career woman. I get to thinking my job is too important to me, and I tell myself that the people I work with are just the people I work with. And not my family. And last night, I thought what is a family anyway? They're just people who make you feel less alone and really loved. And that's what you've done for me. Thank you for being my family.

To cut the treacle (an old Danny Thomas phrase revealing a method for savoring sentiment but avoiding weak sentimentality) there are inspired moments of comedy. The whole group has joined together in one mighty clinch, quietly holding each other in a last farewell embrace, a moment of real pathos but in its sheer physical clumsiness just on the edge of absurdity. Someone calls for a Kleenex, and, without breaking rank, the whole mass shuffles awkwardly to the table to pick up the box. That hilarious bit of business came up in a run-through, right on the stage. It was adopted, incorporated by Marge Mullen into the next script, and it became part of the final product.

Another classic comic concept has been mentioned earlier in this book—the totally unexpected and spontaneous singing of "It's a Long Way to Tipperary," the familiar song from World War I. Bob Ellison says that Jim Brooks was the author of that wonderfully logical piece of illogicality. "He just came up with that right on the stage."

With this last scene the emotional fervor of the actors was reaching the point where there was danger of breaking out of the roles and revealing real pain—which would have been fatal to the show. Betty White recalls that "when we got to that last scene, we were basket cases. Blocking day was a mess. It was just as damp behind the cameras as it was in front of them. When we got to shooting day we cried at dress rehearsal, we cried during the show, we cried later at pickups." Sandrich adds, "That Friday night there was not a dry eye in the studio."

To avoid a disaster people devised ways to break the mood. "To show you how much we cared for each other and to what lengths we would go to do a good turn, let me tell you about Bob Ellison and the Nazi uniform." So speaks David Lloyd, and then, when prompted, Bob Ellison. Mary Tyler Moore had once mentioned to Ellison that there was something impressive, even appealing, about men in military uniforms. In the group quandary about how to avoid emotionalism, Ellison remembered this casual remark. He vaguely recalls that something Ted Knight said prompted him to take charge of tension-breaking. And so he went out and secured a Nazi uniform. "I went to the wardrobe guy for a uniform, and I borrowed a monocle from an actor friend. I looked like something out of *Hogan's Heroes*. Everything was fine with the hat, the shirt, the coat, the boots—until I got to the pants. I looked at those pants and thought to myself, 'Wait a minute. Some Nazi might have worn those once.' It was the real thing. I couldn't do it. So I went back to wardrobe and asked for a pair of funny-looking shorts, boxer shorts. I drew the line at getting into a Nazi's pants. Call me crazy. Nothing happened to me in the war. Also, boxer shorts are funnier than uniform pants." We hear the comic writer at work.

It is easy to imagine the memorable moment that occurred as the unsuspecting Mary came backstage. She had just been introduced to the audience, a tradition that preceded filming on each show. "It was so difficult for her. She took her bow and coming back offstage she was in tears." But Ellison, ridiculous in formal Nazi attire and boxer shorts, was there to change the mood. In relief she jumped up into his arms and the problems were over for a few more minutes.

David Lloyd had the unenviable job of warming up the audience for the final show. He remembers it as a nightmare. There were virtually no strangers in the bleachers; everyone who had ever been a part of the show was there (Treva Silverman, for example, happened to be in town), as well as friends and family. "It was the darkest night of my soul as a warm-up guy," Lloyd says. "The audience was all specially invited, entirely made up of people who had worked on the show before and staff and family and friends. It was not the public. It was entirely MTM people and I had to waltz out there with effectively two hours to kill around the twenty minutes of shooting. Nobody had any questions that night. They just all sat and stared at me. They all worked there. Not only did they know everything they needed to know, but they had heard everything I had to say." This situation can seem funny only to someone who doesn't have to endure it, but it is perhaps significant that no one else interviewed remembers the inimitable David Lloyd as an embarrassment that evening. No doubt his comic flair embellished this scene, too, as when he ended his reminiscence with the one question that

someone finally called out: "Can you explain the syndication deal?"
No, he couldn't!

Somehow, they all made it through. There was a minimum of work to be done after the audience, also in tears, left.

There are three postscripts to this love letter.

P.S. I

There was a party that night. Every table was supplied with a box of Kleenex. And they were used.

Love,
David Lloyd

P.S. II

Six weeks later, when the film finally got put together in post-production, Mary gave a TV dinner at Chasen's, just for the people on the set and others directly involved. We had dinner and we watched the show. We didn't realize until we got that perspective how funny the episode was. But when we got to the last scene, and Ed Asner said, "I treasure you people," there was a sob through Chasen's that shook Beverly Hills. And then the waterworks. I have yet to see that last episode except under water.

Love,
Betty White

P.S. III

Emmy Awards, 1976–77

Outstanding Comedy Series: *The Mary Tyler Moore Show*

Outstanding Writing in a Comedy Series: Allan Burns, James L. Brooks, Ed. Weinberger, Stan Daniels, David Lloyd, Bob Ellison, "The Last Show," *The Mary Tyler Moore Show*

Love,
The Academy
of Television
Arts &
Sciences

8

A CHRONICLE OF
THE MARY TYLER MOORE SHOW

1970–77

1. WEEKLY GUIDE TO THE SERIES

The descriptions of the 168 episodes that aired from September 19, 1970, to March 19, 1977, have been carefully constructed from scripts, reviewing of all the shows as they have appeared in syndication or through the kind cooperation of the writers, references to *TV Guide* entries, and attention to the limited number of reviews that appeared during the original run. In addition we wish to acknowledge Vince Waldron's "A Critical Guide" to the series in his *Classic Sitcoms*.

We have included the name assigned by the writer, the number of the episode, its date of first airing, the writer(s), the director, and guest cast. (The listings of the roles played by the guest cast of each episode repeat the format of credits that followed the show each week.) It should be noted that the shows did not necessarily appear in the order in which they were filmed. Cloris Leachman was always billed as "Special Guest Star." A collection of photographs accompanies this section and the caption under each includes the number of the episode from which it was taken. The Saturday night time is listed once and then again only when the time changed.

First Season

1. LOVE IS ALL AROUND—SEPTEMBER 19, 1970—9:30 P.M.
WRITTEN BY JAMES L. BROOKS AND ALLAN BURNS
DIRECTED BY JAY SANDRICH
GUESTS: ANGUS DUNCAN, DAVE MORICH

161

This first episode, described in detail in Chapter 1, received the following notice in *TV Guide*: "Rebounding from a broken romance, Mary Richards takes a job in a Minneapolis TV newsroom. For better or worse, her office mates will be a caustic boss who drinks, a self-enamored news anchorman, an unflappable writer."

2. TODAY I AM A MA'AM—SEPTEMBER 26, 1970
WRITTEN BY TREVA SILVERMAN
DIRECTED BY JAY SANDRICH
GUESTS: RICHARD SCHAAL, JACK deMAVE, SHEILAH WELLS, DAVID HAYWARD

The attention directed to being single faded in later shows. Here Mary and Rhoda are self-consciously discussing the fact that "This kid comes over to me, he's about twenty-one or twenty-two, and he calls me 'ma'am.' " With snow falling outside their apartment building at 119 N. Weatherly, Mary remarks, "If there's one thing worse than being single, it's sitting around talking about being single." Desperate, the two women invite two men they have met over for the evening. Rhoda's "date" brings his wife, and all three guests are under the mistaken impression they were invited for dinner.

3. BESS, YOU IS MY DAUGHTER NOW—OCTOBER 3, 1970
WRITTEN BY JOHN D. F. BLACK
DIRECTED BY JAY SANDRICH
GUEST: LISA GERRITSEN AS BESS

Another show shot almost entirely in the apartment. Mary becomes a baby-sitter for Phyllis's daughter, Bess. Phyllis offers Mary a large number of books on child care to see her through the task. When Mary abandons books for personal relationship, Bess responds and the two have a wonderful time. The result is that Bess wants to stay with Mary, something Phyllis accepts, as a nondirective parent. Finally Phyllis shows emotion overseen by Bess, who runs from the room and goes to her own apartment. Mary explains, "I'm trying to figure out a nice way to say I think you're a lousy mother. . . . I like you so much better when you come on weak. And if I feel this way, imagine how Bess felt when she saw you just now." Phyllis tells Mary, "You're going to make a wonderful mother." "I know," she replies.

4. DIVORCE ISN'T EVERYTHING—OCTOBER 10, 1970
WRITTEN BY TREVA SILVERMAN
DIRECTED BY ALAN RAFKIN

The final curtain call.

GUESTS: DAVE KETCHUM, PATTE FINLEY, GINO CONFORTI, JANE CONNELL, VERNON WEDDLE
GUEST: SHELLEY BERMAN AS DR. WALTER UDALL

Another episode centered on the apartment and the relationship between Mary and Rhoda. They want to take a trip. Rhoda discovers a club with low rates to Europe, and talks Mary into attending in spite of the fact that it is a club for divorced people. Of course Mary becomes a victim of circumstances, her teeth so admired by a dentist, played superbly by Shelley Berman, that she is elected vice president of the club. Somewhere in all this mix-up there is time for Mary to comment on the state of being single and over thirty. "You know, Rhoda, sometimes I think I could discover the secret of immortality and people would still say, 'Look at that single girl discovering the secret of immortality.' "

5. KEEP YOUR GUARD UP—OCTOBER 17, 1970
WRITTEN BY STEVE PRITZKER
DIRECTED BY ALAN RAFKIN
GUESTS: JOHN SCHUCK, TIM BROWN

Mary meets Frank Carelli at the office when he comes to sell Lou insurance. Frank was a pro football player who was cut, quickly, from every team he joined. Lou knew him when he played for the

Vikings. Mary decides Frank would be a fine choice for sportscaster. Needless to say, he is thoroughly incompetent and fails to get the job. Sensitively played by John Schuck, Frank decides to take all his money and go to Florida, where he gets a job working with children at a municipal playground. It is one in a long list of episodes seeking to treat people as individuals and to encourage caring for others. A contrasting subplot centers on Phyllis, who darts in several times trying to raise funds to oppose capital punishment. Each contributor receives a miniature gallows.

6. SUPPORT YOUR LOCAL MOTHER—OCTOBER 24, 1970
WRITTEN BY ALLAN BURNS AND JAMES BROOKS
DIRECTED BY ALAN RAFKIN
GUEST: NANCY WALKER

TV Guide described the show by noting that Rhoda's "mother, charter member of the keep-em-feeling-guilty school of child rearing . . . had descended upon a bewildered Mary." She is bewildered when Rhoda refuses to see her mother, visiting from New York, because she uses money Rhoda sends her to purchase gifts for her daughter and then brings them to her. Finally the mother is leaving and Mary takes her by the department-store window where Rhoda is decorating. Some excellent sight humor serves as a backdrop for a meeting of daughter and mother, a resolution achieved by Mary. Allan Burns noted that CBS refused to approve the script initially because of Rhoda's treatment of her mother. Grant Tinker, in one of his earliest actions to run interference for his producers, endorsed the script. It was shot and won an Emmy for Brooks and Burns.

7. TOULOUSE-LAUTREC IS ONE OF MY FAVORITE ARTISTS—OCTOBER 31, 1970
WRITTEN BY LLOYD TURNER AND GORDON MITCHELL
DIRECTED BY JAY SANDRICH
GUESTS: HAMID HAMILTON CAMP, ROBERT ROTHWELL

The humor of this episode is multifaceted. Mary meets an attractive man seated at an interview table at the station. He asks her to dinner, she agrees, and then, upon standing, realizes he is at least a foot shorter than she. She likes him but, as she says, she is self-conscious about "her" height. The inevitable jokes are made, but the conclusion offers something special. The man is a writer and he has written a book about being short. He dedicates it to Mary. As the two enter into conversation with Rhoda it becomes obvious that the book is about dealing with being different. The writer and Rhoda discover that as "losers" they have much in common while Mary has always succeeded, being head cheerleader and dating the captain of the football team. In mock humor they abandon her when she admits that her high school graduation present was a car. She returns to their good graces when she insists it was an old car, a Hudson.

One of the earliest references to the Women's Movement occurs when Mary says about their first evening together, "Well, I think building a snowman in front of the Women's Liberation Headquarters is pretty different." He replies, "I thought they'd get a kick out of watching him melt."

8. THE SNOW MUST GO ON—NOVEMBER 7, 1970
WRITTEN BY DAVID DAVIS AND LORENZO MUSIC
DIRECTED BY JAY SANDRICH
GUESTS: RICHARD SCHAAL, IVOR FRANCIS, ROBERT ROTHWELL

Snow, a constant theme in the show, becomes the focus of the plot in a telecast of election returns during a blizzard. WJM is on the air but can receive no election news. Rhoda handles the tally board with no tally, Ted ad-libs throughout the evening while Mary assumes producing chores. Brooks, Burns, and Music all explain the Minneapolis setting, with its harsh winters, as a device for confining the characters from time to time.

9. BOB AND RHODA AND TEDDY AND MARY—NOVEMBER 14, 1970
WRITTEN BY BOB RODGERS
DIRECTED BY PETER BALDWIN
GUESTS: DICK PATTERSON AS M.C., HENRY CORDEN AS MR. HARTUNIAN, AND GREG MULLAVEY AS BOB

This episode introduces the Teddy Awards to the viewer, a local TV award that calls for a dinner and appropriate entertainment. Ted Baxter creates an obsession with the award that will run the length of the show's time on the air. In this particular version Mary has been nominated but is badly distracted by the fact that Rhoda's new boyfriend is far more attracted to her than to her closest friend.

10. ASSISTANT WANTED, FEMALE—NOVEMBER 21, 1970
WRITTEN BY TREVA SILVERMAN
DIRECTED BY PETER BALDWIN
GUEST: JOHN AMOS

In an improbable twist, Phyllis, who is a constant irritant for Mary at home, wangles her way into the role of Mary's assistant at WJM. She antagonizes everyone at the station. John Amos, playing Gordy the Weatherman, is regularly mistaken by Phyllis as the sportscaster because he is black and big. This remained a running line of humor, a constant reminder of the folly of stereotyping, as long as Amos remained with the show.

11. 1040 OR FIGHT—NOVEMBER 28, 1970
WRITTEN BY DAVID DAVIS AND LORENZO MUSIC
DIRECTED BY JAY SANDRICH
GUEST: PAUL SAND

Paul Sand has a field day with the part of an IRS examiner auditing Mary's tax returns. He becomes attracted to her and invites her to dinner. Self-effacing throughout, he constantly apologizes as he spends more and more time with her. He takes her to a restaurant where he can get good service because he is auditing the manager. He excuses taking her to a movie on the grounds that he is auditing the taxes of the usher. Mary meanwhile keeps all her records in a shoe box and the result is somewhat less than good accounting procedures.

12. ANCHORMAN OVERBOARD—DECEMBER 5, 1970
WRITTEN BY LORENZO MUSIC
DIRECTED BY JAY SANDRICH
GUESTS: BILL FIORE, BOB DUGGAN AS CLOCK MAN

Phyllis persuades Mary to get Ted to speak to a group for which she serves as program chair. Against her better judgment, Mary gets Ted to agree. The engagement at the women's club is a disaster, with Ted unable to answer any questions, remaining silent for minutes on end. Mary must restore Ted's confidence in time for the news and placate an irate Phyllis.

13. HE'S ALL YOURS—DECEMBER 12, 1970
WRITTEN BY BOB RODGERS
DIRECTED BY JAY SANDRICH
GUEST: WES STERN AS ALLEN STEVENS

A new cameraman, Allen, at WJM seems far more interested in Mary than in his work. He is quite young and he tells Mary, "You don't know what it's like to feel like you're the only virgin in the whole college." Mary replies, "As a matter of fact, I do." Just as Mary has had enough, Lou tells her to look after the young man as a favor to him. It turns out that Allen is Lou's nephew. When Lou discovers Allen is trying to make time with Mary, he explodes, "Look, you, I want you to remember something and remember it forever. I think of this girl here as if she were my own daughter and that means she's your cousin, you get my meaning?" Lou Grant will expand on this protective role, continuing it into the final season.

A look at the newsroom staff during the first season.

14. CHRISTMAS AND THE HARD-LUCK KID—DECEMBER 19, 1970
WRITTEN BY JAMES L. BROOKS AND ALLAN BURNS
DIRECTED BY JAY SANDRICH
GUEST: NED WERTIMER

This is a pleasant, comfortable episode by the creators of the series. The premise is simple enough: Mary has to work on Christmas Day; after all, it's a newsroom. She initiates projects to instill Yule spirit at WJM, not always an easy task.

15. HOWARD'S GIRL—JANUARY, 2, 1971
WRITTEN BY TREVA SILVERMAN
DIRECTED BY JAY SANDRICH
GUESTS: RICHARD SCHAAL, HENRY JONES, MARY JACKSON

In this episode Mary decides to date her former boyfriend's brother, Paul, and ends up being entertained by his parents. It is one of the earlier efforts to pair Mary with a man, something that never really worked because, as Brooks and Burns said, they could never find the actor whom the audience would accept with Mary.

16. PARTY IS SUCH SWEET SORROW—JANUARY 9, 1971
WRITTEN BY MARTIN COHAN
DIRECTED BY JAY SANDRICH
GUESTS: DICK CLAIR, JOHN AMOS

We all know it can't happen, but the fun and pathos wrung from this episode make it worthwhile suspending belief. Mary accepts a better job at a larger station in the city. Obviously there must be a farewell party at WJM, and tears flow before Mary decides to stay with her friends. It is not clear that this was a good career move, but then Mary's career is never separated from her loving relationship with friends.

17. JUST A LUNCH—JANUARY 16, 1971
WRITTEN BY JAMES BROOKS AND ALLAN BURNS
DIRECTED BY BRUCE BILSON
GUESTS: MONTE MARKHAM, JOYCE BULIFANT

Mary becomes involved with a "dashing foreign correspondent" who is attracted to her and refuses to break off the relationship even after it is learned that he is married. This episode marks the first appearance of Joyce Bulifant as Murray's wife. In the coming seasons Marie will be mentioned more than seen, but she etched a special place in the series for seven years.

18. SECOND-STORY STORY—JANUARY 23, 1971
WRITTEN BY STEVE PRITZKER
DIRECTED BY JAY SANDRICH
GUESTS: BOB DISHY, BURT MUSTIN, VIC TAYBACK

The trauma of burglary is repeated for Mary on two succeeding days, leading to a buzz at the office and a comic effort to apprehend the culprit, who has escaped without a clue.

19. WE CLOSED IN MINNEAPOLIS—JANUARY 30, 1971
WRITTEN BY KENNY SOLMS AND GAIL PARENT
DIRECTED BY JAY SANDRICH
GUEST: JOYCE BULIFANT

Murray finally achieves the success he has sought when his play is produced in Minneapolis. We know it's going to be a disaster, made all the worse by the fact that since Ted made the deal, he will be the star. Murray's failure is played for laughs, but the underlying theme is support for a friend.

20. HI!—FEBRUARY 6, 1971
WRITTEN BY TREVA SILVERMAN
DIRECTED BY JAY SANDRICH
GUESTS: PAT CARROLL, BRUCE KIRBY, ROBERT CASPER, ARTHUR ADELSON

Mary is somewhat embarrassed when she has to go to the hospital to have one tonsil removed. Her roommate, played to the hilt by Pat Carroll, is an irascible grouch with a broken leg, an ulcer, and a sardonic wit. Visits from the WJM staff turn the hospital room upside down and Mary is at her wit's end trying to turn Mrs. Khune's good disposition on with a smile.

21. THE BOSS ISN'T COMING TO DINNER—FEBRUARY 13, 1971
WRITTEN BY DAVID DAVIS AND LORENZO MUSIC
DIRECTED BY JAY SANDRICH
GUESTS: JOHN AMOS, PAUL MICALE AS WAITER

Mary learns, after all the men in the newsroom, that Lou and Edie are having marital problems. Lou has to tell her because she expects the two of them for dinner. Thus, when Lou asks her to get Mrs.

Grant on the phone, she is thrilled. With excitement she calls to tell him his wife is waiting to speak to him. A moment later she enters Lou's office, all smiles at the thought of reconciliation. Actually Lou had called Edie to ask if she would do his laundry. She said no. Mary looks at the bag and takes it off to do the laundry herself. This episode has one of its most effective moments when Ted, Murray, Gordy, Lou, and Mary go to the bar to talk to Lou. We see Mary exerting her feminine perspective and seeking to help Lou in spite of himself. Finally Lou calls Edie, "If you're not doing anything tonight, I'm coming home." At the time the marital differences had to do with Edie going to school. Later Edie would leave Lou and a divorce would ensue.

22. A Friend In Deed—February 20, 1971
Written by Susan Silver
Directed by Jay Sandrich
Guest: Patte Finley as Twinks McFarland

The new receptionist at WJM-TV is Twinks, warm, gushy, and taking every advantage of the fact that she met Mary at camp—eighteen years ago. In fact, Mary hardly remembers, but tries to befriend Twinks, who asks Mary to be in her wedding. She also asks Rhoda. At the last minute a better friend arrives and Mary is out in the cold with an absurd dress. On the other hand, Rhoda participates in the wedding and has to wear the silly outfit.

23. Smokey the Bear Wants You—February 27, 1971
Written by Steve Pritzker
Directed by Jay Sandrich
Guest: Michael Callan as Chuck Pelligrini

Rhoda begins seeing Chuck and a romance seems in evidence. Yet Chuck has no obvious job and goes to strange meetings. In fact, he is a successful businessman who plans to become a forest ranger. Rhoda decides not to join him in the venture, but the option adds a new dimension to the Rhoda character.

24. The Forty-Five-Year-Old Man—March 6, 1971
Written by George Kirgo
Directed by Herbert Kenwith
Guests: John Amos, Slim Pickens, Richard Roat as Barry Phelps, Sid
    Clute as Everett Edwards, and Richard Libertini as Big Chicken

Slim Pickens plays Wild Jack Monroe, owner of WJM. The ratings for the news are poor, and management decides to fire Lou. Mary goes to see Monroe and pleads for Lou while Wild Jack sits on a life-size replica of a horse. He remembers being at a bar with Lou, and on the strength of Mary's plea, Lou gets his job back. This was probably the broadest comedy attempted by the company in its seven years.

Second Season

25. THE BIRDS . . . AND . . . UM . . . BEES—SEPTEMBER 18, 1971
WRITTEN BY TREVA SILVERMAN
DIRECTED BY JAY SANDRICH
GUESTS: LISA GERRITSEN, JOHN AMOS

This episode has two dimensions. First, Mary produces a documentary, "What's Your Sexual IQ?" The newsroom is astir and obscene phone calls begin to be received from viewers. Second, Phyllis decides Mary should tell Bess about the facts of life. Mary agrees, reluctantly, and the following exchange between Bess and Mary ensues:

> Bess: Well, sex I know about, but the whole thing about love, well, that I got to know, because of Howie. . . . He loves me but the thing is, I don't know whether I want to love him back or not.
> Mary: Well, Bess, you don't have to love him back if you don't feel it.
> Bess: Well, everybody says love and sex go together, right? . . . So if you love somebody, do you . . . ?
> Mary: Oh! Bess, no, of course not. Oh! Sweetheart, was that what you were worried about? You don't even have to think about that for a while. No, darling, you are allowed to love somebody and not even be concerned about the other thing.

26. I AM CURIOUS COOPER—SEPTEMBER 25, 1971
WRITTEN BY DAVID DAVIS AND LORENZO MUSIC
DIRECTED BY JAY SANDRICH
GUESTS: SHIZUKO IWAMATSU AS MAMA MOTO, MICHAEL CONSTANTINE AS MIKE COOPER

Lou makes one of his mishandled efforts to match Mary with a friend. Lou's conviction that they were made for each other is wildly out of line with the casual friendship the two establish. As *TV Guide* commented, ". . . when Lou plays Cupid, he comes on like a bull in a china shop."

27. HE'S NO HEAVY, HE'S MY BROTHER—OCTOBER 2, 1971
WRITTEN BY ALLAN BURNS
DIRECTED BY JERRY PARIS
GUESTS: JOHN AMOS, FRANK RAMIREZ AS GUSTAVO

Mary and Rhoda plan a winter vacation to Mexico and become involved in a strange plot concerning the owner of a Mexican restaurant and a waiter who holds the key to their vacation plans. If the waiter makes the wrong decision, Mary and Rhoda will stay in icy Minneapolis. After ample convolution the two friends do take their trip.

28. ROOM 223—OCTOBER 9, 1971
WRITTEN BY SUSAN SILVER
DIRECTED BY JAY SANDRICH
GUESTS: MICHAEL TOLAN AS DAN WHITFIELD, FLORIDA FRIEBUS AS MRS. MARSHALL, VAL BISOGLIO AS DEFOREST

Mary decides that in order to succeed at her profession at WJM, she needs journalistic skills. She enrolls in a TV journalism class and immediately becomes involved with her professor, Dan Whitfield, who dates her while he is grading her.

29. A GIRL'S BEST MOTHER IS NOT HER FRIEND—OCTOBER 16, 1971
WRITTEN BY DAVID DAVIS AND LORENZO MUSIC
DIRECTED BY JAY SANDRICH
GUEST: NANCY WALKER

TV Guide described this episode nicely: "You don't have to be Jewish to be a Jewish mother—anyone can elevate suffering to a fine art. Nancy Walker returns in the hilarious role of Rhoda's mother, whose relationship with her daughter can best be described as a truce. It won't last. Mrs. Morgenstern's now set on becoming Rhoda's best friend."

30. COVER BOY—OCTOBER 23, 1971
WRITTEN BY TREVA SILVERMAN
DIRECTED BY JAY SANDRICH
GUEST: JACK CASSIDY AS HAL BAXTER

Ted's brother threatens Ted's ego. The competition between them reaches high comic proportions. In an effort to impress Hal, Ted pretends that he and Mary are lovers.

31. DIDN'T YOU USED TO BE . . . WAIT . . . DON'T TELL ME!—OCTOBER 30, 1971
WRITTEN BY ALLAN BURNS
DIRECTED BY JAY SANDRICH
GUESTS: RICHARD SCHAAL AS HOWARD, JACK RILEY AS ELDON COLFAX, KERMIT MURDOCK AS VANDERMAST, RON MASAK AS ED MIMS, PIPPA SCOTT AS ESTELLE

Mary decides to attend her high school reunion, a serious error of judgment. The entire trip is fraught with chaos and mistakes, coupled with Mary meeting her old boyfriend, Howard Arnell. To put it mildly, Mary does not have a roaring good time and her memories are better than the leftovers.

32. THOROUGHLY UNMILITANT MARY—NOVEMBER 6, 1971
WRITTEN BY MARTIN COHAN
DIRECTED BY JAY SANDRICH
GUESTS: JOHN AMOS, DICK BALDUZZI AS AL, LARRY GELMAN AS HERB, PAUL MICALE AS THE WAITER

TV Guide did its first close-up on the show with this episode: "A good stiff belt might calm newsroom boss Lou Grant, but it won't save him. . . . His staff is split by a strike. Not so bad, since marble-mouth newscaster Ted Baxter is out of action. On the other hand . . . Mary's churning out copy (if you can call that copy), and Lou, with the finesse of a moose, is finishing it off on the air."

33. AND NOW, SITTING IN FOR TED BAXTER—NOVEMBER 13, 1971
WRITTEN BY STEVE PRITZKER
DIRECTED BY JERRY PARIS
GUESTS: JED ALLAN AS ROD PORTER, BILL WOODSON

Ted is to take an unwanted vacation. It is complicated by the fact that his replacement is more competent than he and has begun to turn the Six O'Clock News into a ratings success. The upshot is that Ted fears for his job.

34. Don't Break the Chain—November 20, 1971
Written by David Davis and Lorenzo Music
Directed by Jerry Paris
Guests: Jack DeMave as Armand, Gino Conforti as Roy Martoni

Lou sends a chain letter to his friends. Mary receives it and is warned by Lou not to break the chain. Against her better judgment she answers the letter that traps her with a "tiresome Romeo" and an overly enthusiastic cookware salesman.

35. The Six-and-a-Half-Year Itch—November 27, 1971
Written by Treva Silverman
Directed by Jay Sandrich
Guests: Lawrence Pressman as Bill, Elizabeth Berger

Lou sees his son-in-law at a movie with a strange woman. Lou reaches the correct conclusion and goes into a major tirade with the son-in-law over his philandering.

36. . . . Is a Friend In Need—December 4, 1971
Written by Susan Silver
Directed by Jay Sandrich
Guest: Beverly Sanders as Waitress

Rhoda gets fired. She begins by telling everyone she quit over the pay. Mary tries to help . . . to a point. When a job opens at WJM for which Rhoda is qualified, Mary lies about the job, telling Rhoda it is filled. Feeling guilty, she tells Lou, who enjoys the moment because Mary finally did something rotten. Mary was, according to Susan Silver, displaying a reluctance to work with a friend on a job. This is examined more closely in the text. In any event, Rhoda lands a job at Hempel's decorating their windows at a larger salary than Mary receives.

37. The Square-Shaped Room—December 11, 1971
Written by Susan Silver
Directed by Jay Sandrich

Lou quickly regrets asking Rhoda to redecorate his living room. Her tastes are not exactly what he had in mind, nor are the costs suited to his pocketbook.

38. Ted Over Heels—December 18, 1971—8:30 p.m.
Written by David Davis and Lorenzo Music
Directed by Peter Baldwin
Guest: Arlene Golonka as Betty

In episode 2 Phyllis asked Mary why she didn't date Ted Baxter. She replied that while he was good-looking, "he always looks to me like he's posing for a postage stamp." In the second season the producers determine to find ways to provide Ted some romance. He has a crush on the daughter of Chuckles the Clown.

39. The Five-Minute Dress—January 1, 1972
Written by Pat Nardo and Gloria Banta
Directed by Jay Sandrich

The continuing theme of Mary's love life receives another treatment when she becomes involved with a handsome government official who continually breaks their dates due to his busy schedule.

40. Feeb—January 8, 1972
Written by Dick Clair and Jenna McMahon
Directed by Peter Baldwin
Guest: Barbara Sharma

Mary complains about an incompetent waitress at a restaurant and as a result the woman is fired. Mary feels guilty and finds a job for her at WJM, where she is equally incompetent in the newsroom. What can the sympathetic Mary do now?

41. The Slaughter Affair—January 15, 1972
Written by Rick Mittleman
Directed by Peter Baldwin

Murray, the faithful and devoted husband, comes to work nearly asleep and Lou has no patience with his condition. Mary seeks to find out why Murray is so tired and discovers he is moonlighting as a cab driver in order to buy Marie a new car. Complicating the whole situation is the fact that Marie believes Murray is having an affair with Mary. The resolution restores everyone's trust and gets Marie a secondhand car that she loves.

42. BABY SITCOM—JANUARY 22, 1972
WRITTEN BY TREVA SILVERMAN
DIRECTED BY JAY SANDRICH
GUESTS: LISA GERRITSEN, JOSHUA BRYANT AS SANDY, LESLIE GRAVES AS DEE-DEE

Mary, having agreed to baby-sit with Bess, has to back out. She recruits Lou to fill in. As *TV Guide* suggests, "Picture the gruffest man in the world baby-sitting for a little girl."

43. MORE THAN NEIGHBORS—JANUARY 29, 1972
WRITTEN BY STEVE PRITZKER
DIRECTED BY JAY SANDRICH
GUEST: JACK BENDER AS MICHAEL LEE

Mary's apartment, the location for so much of the action in the episodes, particularly involving Rhoda, becomes the focus of attention once again as Ted considers moving into the building. Rhoda and Mary go overtime trying to discourage him.

44. THE CARE AND FEEDING OF PARENTS—FEBRUARY 5, 1972
WRITTEN BY DICK CLAIR AND JENNA MCMAHON
DIRECTED BY JAY SANDRICH
GUESTS: LISA GERRITSEN, JON LOCKE AS TURNER, BRAD TRUMBULL AS MITCHELL

Mary finds herself in a difficult situation with pushy Phyllis after Mary praises a school composition written by eleven-year-old Bess. Her mother decides Mary should attempt to get the essay published. Phyllis plays the "stage-door mother" bit with vigor.

45. WHERE THERE'S SMOKE, THERE'S RHODA—FEBRUARY 12, 1972
WRITTEN BY MARTIN COHAN
DIRECTED BY PETER BALDWIN
GUEST: JOHN AMOS, MICHAEL BELL AS FIREMAN

Rhoda's apartment is damaged by a fire. While repairs are being made Mary invites Rhoda to move in with her. It is supposed to be for a few days, but the two friends discover that friendship may not survive the roommate status. There are overtones of *The Odd Couple* in this funny episode.

46. YOU CERTAINLY ARE A BIG BOY—FEBRUARY 19, 1972
WRITTEN BY MARTIN COHAN
DIRECTED BY JAY SANDRICH
GUESTS: BRADFORD DILLMAN, JOHN RUBINSTEIN AS MATT, JR., BEVERLY
SANDERS

Mary has a new male companion whose unusual courting style raises questions that are answered when she discovers he has a son approximately her age. This causes Mary to rethink her relationship with the attractive architect.

47. SOME OF MY BEST FRIENDS ARE RHODA—FEBRUARY 26, 1972
WRITTEN BY STEVE PRITZKER
DIRECTED BY PETER BALDWIN
GUEST: MARY FRANN AS JOANNE

Mary's car is the victim of a minor accident and when she meets the driver, Joanne, they strike up a friendship. It is one that appears to be moving Rhoda out of the center of Mary's social life. The two play tennis and generally seem to enjoy each other. All the while Joanne puts off paying for the car damage. The plot sets up the final scene when, finding themselves in need of a fourth for tennis, liberal Mary discovers that Joanne doesn't want Rhoda at her club because Rhoda is Jewish. Mary ends the relationship with Joanne immediately, gets her check for the damage, and reaffirms her closeness to Rhoda. This is one of the few shows of the series where the message drives the script.

48. HIS TWO RIGHT ARMS—MARCH 4, 1972
WRITTEN BY JIM PARKER AND ARNOLD MARGOLIN
DIRECTED BY JAY SANDRICH
GUESTS: BILL DAILY AS PETE PETERSON, CAROL ANDROSKY AS JENNIFER
RILEY, JANET MACLACHLAN AS SHERRY WILSON, WALLY TAYLOR AS
WALTER ELLIS, ISABEL SANFORD AS MRS. WILSON, PHILLIPPA HARRIS AS
WOMAN FROM AUDIENCE, DAVIS ROBERTS AS MAN FROM AUDIENCE

Mary has to plan a WJM talk show. She schedules a thoroughly incompetent and excessively eager politician who is ignorant of all current events. Of course this is a perfect match for Ted, who must interview the councilman.

Third Season

49. THE GOOD-TIME NEWS—SEPTEMBER 16, 1972—9:00 P.M.
WRITTEN BY JAMES BROOKS AND ALLAN BURNS
DIRECTED BY HAL COOPER
GUESTS: ROBERT HOGAN, JACK STONEHAM, JOHN AMOS

Lou is decidedly *un*happy about happy news, a format Mary has been assigned to create for the Six O'Clock News. Her problem is complicated by the specter of the humorless Ted Baxter as the anchor of this effort. When this show was aired "happy news" was a fairly new concept. Seventeen years later it is still around and still as silly as this episode depicts it.

50. WHAT IS MARY RICHARDS REALLY LIKE?—SEPTEMBER 23, 1972
WRITTEN BY SUSAN SILVER
DIRECTED BY JERRY BELSON
GUEST: PETER HASKELL AS MARK WILLIAMS

Mary is asked, as the only woman in the newsroom, for an interview by Mark Williams, a local columnist whom Lou is convinced is out only to destroy people's reputations. He reluctantly agrees to the interview and Mary spends extra time finding just the right outfit for the meeting. She decides on a checkered brown pants suit. Second thoughts about her choice occur at the office. "I'm being interviewed as the only woman at WJM and here I am dressed like a man." Lou warns her about Williams's penchant for romancing beautiful women. The entire interview is high comedy and the result is a devastating portrayal of Lou as a drunk. Mary comes out unscathed in the paper and does see Williams socially. Lou gets to tell Mary, "I told you so."

51. WHO'S IN CHARGE HERE?—SEPTEMBER 30, 1972
WRITTEN BY MARTIN COHAN
DIRECTED BY JAY SANDRICH
GUEST: JOAN TOMPKINS AS MRS. THORN

Lou receives a promotion to the position of program director. This places Murray in charge in the newsroom, a task for which he is most certainly unqualified. The newsroom staff is a "comic study in blue" as the chaos grows.

52. ENTER RHODA'S PARENTS—OCTOBER 7, 1972
WRITTEN BY MARTIN COHAN
DIRECTED BY JAY SANDRICH
GUESTS: NANCY WALKER, HAROLD GOULD, LEANNA ROBERTS

TV Guide did its second close-up on the series with this episode: "Into each life some rain must fall, but Rhoda's been hit by a cloudburst named Mother. After thirty-five years of marriage, Mrs. Morgenstern knows hubby's out chasing skirts, and she's determined to drag Rhoda through every minute of those he-doesn't-love-me-anymore blues. Comedienne Nancy Walker returns as Rhoda's mother."

53. IT'S WHETHER YOU WIN OR LOSE—OCTOBER 14, 1972
WRITTEN BY MARTIN DONOVAN
DIRECTED BY JAY SANDRICH
GUEST: PATRICK CAMPBELL AS PAT

Master director Jay Sandrich won an Emmy for this episode, which deals with the severe problems created by a gambling fever. Murray is the compulsive gambler, for some time recovered from the habit. He is caught up in a poker game planned by Mary, and before the show concludes Murray is betting a great deal on Ted's inability to read the script correctly on the news.

54. RHODA THE BEAUTIFUL—OCTOBER 21, 1972
WRITTEN BY TREVA SILVERMAN
DIRECTED BY JAY SANDRICH

As we have noted in Chapters 4 and 6, Treva Silverman was particularly gifted with her treatment of Rhoda. This episode addresses Rhoda's sense of self-esteem, a crash diet, and an invitation by Hempel's, where Rhoda works, to enter a beauty contest. The exchanges with Phyllis are delightful and the "happy" ending with Rhoda actually winning the contest is great fun.

55. JUST AROUND THE CORNER—OCTOBER 28, 1972
WRITTEN BY STEVE PRITZKER
DIRECTED BY JAY SANDRICH
GUESTS: NANETTE FABRAY, BILL QUINN

Mary's parents decide to move to Minneapolis to be near their daughter. While nowhere as extreme as the tale of Rhoda's mother, this episode makes it clear that mother/daughter relations are not defined by ethnic background. Mary has to find out how to tell her mother to mind her own business.

56. BUT SERIOUSLY FOLKS—NOVEMBER 4, 1972
WRITTEN BY ED. WEINBERGER
DIRECTED BY PETER BALDWIN
GUESTS: JERRY VAN DYKE AS WES CALLISON, JOHN FOX AS BOWLER, BOB DUGGAN AS STAGE MANAGER, RUDY DELUCA AS NIGHTCLUB MANAGER, ETHEL REDA LEOPOLD AS WOMAN

This was the first show to be aired written by the new producer, Ed. Weinberger. It relates the story of Wes Callison, who writes for Chuckles the Clown. He wants more, perhaps a shot at an on-air spot on the news. He doesn't get the job, but Mary sees him through the problems, including an absurd comedy routine delivered to a bowling alley lounge crowd.

57. FARMER TED AND THE NEWS—NOVEMBER 11, 1972
WRITTEN BY MARTIN DONOVAN
DIRECTED BY JAY SANDRICH
GUESTS: LURENE TUTTLE AS BELLA SWANN, PATRICK CAMPBELL AS ANNOUNCER'S VOICE

Ted hires an agent who gets Lou to approve a new contract allowing Ted to do commercials. Lou is frustrated as Ted's voice and face show up pushing all manner of sappy products. Ted even plays the part of a dog. It is all great fun, with Lou finally telling Ted he will rearrange his face unless he stops the ads. With a small raise as compensation, Ted agrees to desist.

58. HAVE I FOUND A GUY FOR YOU—NOVEMBER 18, 1972
WRITTEN BY CHARLOTTE BROWN
DIRECTED BY HAL COOPER
GUESTS: BERT CONVEY AS JACK FOSTER, BETH HOWLAND AS LINDA FOSTER, DAN KEOUGH AS ARTHUR PRICE

Mary has two friends, Jack and Linda, who are, she presumes, happily married. As the threesome find more time for each other, Mary quickly discovers the marriage is coming to an end. Jack wants to date Mary after the separation, but Beth, who is seeing other men, doesn't want her good friend Mary to see Jack.

The plot allows Mary and Rhoda to talk a bit about divorce. Mary comments, "Everybody takes divorce so lightly." Rhoda has the best line: "I like Pat and Dick Nixon's marriage . . . you know he can't fool around."

59. YOU'VE GOT A FRIEND—NOVEMBER 25, 1972
WRITTEN BY STEVE PRITZKER
DIRECTED BY JERRY BELSON
GUESTS: NANETTE FABRAY, BILL QUINN, BEVERLY SANDERS AS WAITRESS

Mary's father is retired. Feeling he needs a male friend, she tries to find one for her dad. The most likely prospect is Lou. Mary's good intentions create the humorous characteristics of this episode.

60. IT WAS FASCINATION, I KNOW—DECEMBER 2, 1972
WRITTEN BY ED. WEINBERGER
DIRECTED BY JAY SANDRICH
GUESTS: GERALD MICHENAUD AS WILLIAM, LISA GERRITSEN, JACK MAN-NING AS MAÎTRE D', MURRAY KORDA AS VIOLINIST

Mary finds herself faced with a romance she can do without. Bess's boyfriend, all of fifteen, decides he will go for a relationship with Mary. Mary's sensitivity makes the resolution work without serious embarrassment to William.

61. OPERATION: LOU—DECEMBER 9, 1972
WRITTEN BY ELIAS DAVIS AND DAVID POLLOCK
DIRECTED BY JAY SANDRICH
GUESTS: FLORIDA FRIEBUS AS NUN, LINDA SUBLETTE AS NURSE

Lou is hospitalized for the removal of some World War II shrapnel. Mary and Murray are left in charge of the newsroom and the result is not a pretty picture. The two end up fighting while Lou does some unlikely male bonding with Ted, who shares "guy" talk with him.

62. RHODA MORGENSTERN: MINNEAPOLIS TO NEW YORK—DECEMBER 16, 1972
WRITTEN BY TREVA SILVERMAN
DIRECTED BY JAY SANDRICH
GUESTS: JACK RILEY AS BARRY BARLOW, ROBERT CASPER AS ROB, GEORGIA ENGEL AS GEORGETTE

This show foreshadows Rhoda's later departure to her own series.

Her plans to move to New York devastate Mary. Of course there has to be a farewell party, at which Rhoda changes her mind. What to do with the gifts? Georgette enters the cast as a romantic interest for Ted.

63. THE COURTSHIP OF MARY'S FATHER'S DAUGHTER—DECEMBER 23, 1972
WRITTEN BY DAVID POLLOCK AND ELIAS DAVIS
DIRECTED BY JAY SANDRICH
GUESTS: MICHAEL TOLAN AS DAN WHITFIELD, BILL QUINN AS WALTER RICHARDS, BARRA GRANT AS JUDY CONRAD, STEVE FRANKEN AS JONAS LASSER, GORDON JUMP AS JUDY'S FATHER, ARTHUR ABELSON AS MAN IN ELEVATOR, MOLLY DODD AS WOMAN AT PARTY

Mary's former journalism teacher is getting married. He invites Mary to the engagement party since they had dated previously. Rhoda and Mary find themselves the objects of strange stares as a fight erupts between Dan and his new love over Mary being there. Mary's efforts to exit the party are particularly delightful.

64. LOU'S PLACE—JANUARY 6, 1973
WRITTEN BY ED. WEINBERGER
DIRECTED BY JAY SANDRICH
GUESTS: DICK BALDUZZI AS PHILLY, JACK SPRITT AS AL, ARTHUR ABELSON AS TIM, LEW HORN AS RICK, RUSS GRIEVE AS HENRY, RHODA GMIGNANI AS ALICE, KATHLEEN O'MALLEY AS BETTY

Lou and Ted decide to buy a bar they frequent. Lou's efforts as a tavern keeper quickly evacuate all the customers who were regulars and made the investment seem a good one. Lou gives orders to the few customers in an effort to create a "fun" atmosphere and the results are disastrous.

65. MY BROTHER'S KEEPER—JANUARY 13, 1973
WRITTEN BY DICK CLAIR AND JENNA MCMAHON
DIRECTED BY JAY SANDRICH
GUEST: ROBERT MOORE AS BEN SUTHERLAND

This episode gets its "kick" from a Wednesday night fix described earlier by Jim Brooks. Phyllis wants her brother, a musician, to meet and marry Mary. She uses a party at Mary's apartment to achieve this goal. However, by the time of the party Ben has taken up with Rhoda. The result is one of the several "disastrous" parties that Mary typically gives in ensuing seasons. This one is the setting for an emotional outburst by Phyllis facing Rhoda as a sister-in-law and great relief when she discovers Ben is gay.

66. THE GEORGETTE STORY—JANUARY 20, 1973
WRITTEN BY ED. WEINBERGER
DIRECTED BY PETER BALDWIN

Georgette is now established as Ted's "girl." But Ted is not inclined to thoughtfulness, something that angers Mary, who sets out to stop Ted from taking advantage of Georgette. The show has some feminist language and attitudes. It was earlier commented upon in the section on Georgette.

67. ROMEO AND MARY—JANUARY 27, 1973
WRITTEN BY JIM MULHOLLAND AND MIKE BARRIE
DIRECTED BY PETER BALDWIN
GUESTS: STUART MARGOLIN AS WARREN STURGES, BO KAPRALL AS LOWELL, JOE WARFIELD AS PETER, BARBARA BROWNELL AS PEGGY

Rhoda discovers someone for Mary to date. It is an unmitigated disaster as the new acquaintance, "a boring clod," insists upon marrying Mary, using all kinds of crazy antics to win her over.

68. WHAT DO YOU DO WHEN THE BOSS SAYS, "I LOVE YOU"—FEBRUARY 3, 1973
WRITTEN BY DAVID POLLOCK AND ELIAS DAVIS
DIRECTED BY JAY SANDRICH
GUESTS: LOIS NETTLETON AS BARBARA COLEMAN, DICK BALDUZZI AS PHILLY, CAROL WORTHINGTON AS DORIS

Mary is smug as she informs Lou that the new station manager is a woman. It is obvious that Mary feels good about this changing status of women in society. Lou is a bit uneasy at first, but things get downright tough when the boss makes a play for Lou. He rejects, quite gently, the overture and proclaims his love for Edie.

69. MURRAY FACES LIFE—FEBRUARY 10, 1973
WRITTEN BY MARTIN COHAN
DIRECTED BY JAY SANDRICH

The task in the newsroom is to give some ego reinforcement to Murray, who has decided life has passed him by. Depressed beyond toleration, the staff has to find the means to shore up Murray and make him feel confident and good about himself once again.

70. REMEMBRANCE OF THINGS PAST—FEBRUARY 17, 1973
WRITTEN BY DICK CLAIR AND JENNA MCMAHON
DIRECTED BY JAY SANDRICH
GUEST: JOSEPH CAMPANELLA AS TOM VERNON

In the continuing saga of Mary's love life we meet another old friend. Tom Vernon returns and the flame is rekindled until Mary remembers why the love affair failed in the first place. There is no place in Tom's life for Mary as an independent person. He expects her to roll with his own peculiarities and be the loving companion. It is not enough for Mary.

71. PUT ON A HAPPY FACE—FEBRUARY 24, 1973
WRITTEN BY MARILYN SUZANNE MILLER AND MONICA MAGOWAN
DIRECTED BY JAY SANDRICH
GUESTS: STEVE FRANKEN AS JONAS LASSER, ART GILMORE AS NORMAN, HERBIE FAYE AS CLEANING MAN, EDDY CARROLL AS EMCEE

A very funny episode centering on the Teddy Awards dinner. Mary has been nominated but everything goes wrong for her, including the wearing of one shoe and one fuzzy slipper to the dinner.

72. MARY RICHARDS AND THE INCREDIBLE PLANT LADY—MARCH 3, 1973
WRITTEN BY MARTIN COHAN
DIRECTED BY JOHN C. CHULAY
GUESTS: LOUISE LASSER AS ANNE ADAMS, ROBERT KARVELAS AS BOB, HENRY CORDEN AS HARRY, CRAIG NELSON AS CHARLIE, BOB ROSS AS SALESMAN

The bank scene when Mary goes for a loan to Anne Adams, played brilliantly by Louise Lasser, is a classic moment. Mary needs the money because she is lending it to Rhoda for a new business—a plant store. Having borrowed $1,295, Rhoda hires an assistant and her business thrives, but is not mentioning paying off the loan to Mary. Of course she does, and in a spectacular way, by arranging to get Mary a new car she really wants.

Fourth Season
73. THE LARS AFFAIR—SEPTEMBER 15, 1973
WRITTEN BY ED. WEINBERGER
DIRECTED BY JAY SANDRICH
GUEST: BETTY WHITE

Lars, the never-seen husband of Phyllis, is fooling around with "a pert TV homemaking expert." Thus enters Sue Ann Nivens, played by Betty White. Phyllis, of course, is out for blood. In an interesting comment on the opening of this fourth season, *TV Guide* wrote, "Thirty-three, unmarried and unworried—Mary is the liberated woman's ideal." This reflects a growing awareness of the connections being made between the character of Mary Richards and women her age entering the male-dominated work force.

74. ANGELS IN THE SNOW—SEPTEMBER 22, 1973
WRITTEN BY MARILYN SUZANNE MILLER AND MONICA MAGOWAN JOHNSON
DIRECTED BY JAY SANDRICH
GUESTS: PETER STRAUSS AS STEPHEN, ELAYNE HEILVEIL AS SALESGIRL, CAROLE ITA WHITE AS GIRL AT PARTY, JON KORKES AS BECK WILSON

Mary's friends are concerned over her budding romance with a young man in his twenties. She ignores them until she attends a swinging party that reminds her of the gap that separates his friends from hers. In some ways the portrayal of Stephen is a caricature of twenty-year-olds in the seventies.

75. RHODA'S SISTER GETS MARRIED—SEPTEMBER 29, 1973
WRITTEN BY KARYL GELD
DIRECTED BY JERRY BELSON
GUESTS: LIBERTY WILLIAMS AS DEBBIE MORGENSTERN, NANCY WALKER, HAROLD GOULD, BRET SOMERS AS AUNT ROSE

Rhoda's sister is getting married and Mary goes to New York with her friend to attend the wedding. The comedy grows from the exchanges between mother and daughter and Mary's role as mediator. The mother is sure Rhoda is extremely jealous of her sister.

76. THE LOU AND EDIE STORY—OCTOBER 6, 1973
WRITTEN BY TREVA SILVERMAN
DIRECTED BY JAY SANDRICH
GUESTS: PRISCILLA MORRILL, DARREL ZWERLING AS MR. CHARNEY

The beginning of the end for the Grant marriage is treated with sensitivity by Treva Silverman. *TV Guide* expounded at some length on this episode: "Something a little different for *The Mary Tyler Moore Show*—a touching story about a middle-age marriage in trouble. Ironically, it's the tyrant of the newsroom, Lou Grant, who is helplessly watching his marriage totter. There are still light moments: namely Ted, knowing nothing of the problem, making a pass at Lou's wife. [*TV Guide* misstated Ted's action.] But the heart of the show is the sensitive acting of Edward Asner as Lou—confused, angry and heartbroken."

In a series that nearly "wasn't" because it began with a divorce premise that CBS rejected, the producers had finally introduced the subject . . . and with dignity.

77. HI THERE, SPORTS FANS—OCTOBER 13, 1973
WRITTEN BY JERRY MAYER
DIRECTED BY JAY SANDRICH
GUESTS: DICK GAUTIER AS ED CAVANAUGH, GORDON JUMP AS HANK MOR-
 TON, JOHN GABRIEL AS ANDY RIVERS

Mary has been after Lou for months to give her greater responsibility. He finally agrees, telling her she has the job of firing the current WJM sportscaster before finding a new one.

78. FATHER'S DAY—OCTOBER 20, 1973
WRITTEN BY ED. WEINBERGER AND STAN DANIELS
DIRECTED BY JAY SANDRICH
GUESTS: LIAM DUNN AS MR. BAXTER, JOHN HOLLAND AS CALDWELL

This episode has a degree of comic relief, but it is really about Ted coming to terms with his father, who abandoned him when Ted was a baby. It is a gentle show, with Ted's humanity almost showing.

79. SON OF "BUT SERIOUSLY, FOLKS"—OCTOBER 27, 1973
WRITTEN BY PHIL MISHKIN
DIRECTED BY JAY SANDRICH
GUEST: JERRY VAN DYKE AS WES CALLISON

Wes Callison, on an earlier show a writer for Chuckles, returns to work in the newsroom. Wes is in love with Mary and that fact makes him unable to leave his personal feelings out of his work. Van Dyke once more plays the bumbling Wes with style.

80. LOU'S FIRST DATE—NOVEMBER 3, 1973
WRITTEN BY ED. WEINBERGER AND STAN DANIELS
DIRECTED BY JAY SANDRICH
GUESTS: FLORENCE LAKE AS MARTHA, PRISCILLA MORRILL AS EDIE, JEFF
 THOMPSON AS MIKE MONTGOMERY

We know now that the marriage is at an end. Lou seeks Mary's assistance in getting him a date. The occasion is an awards dinner and Mary mixes up the names and gets Lou a date with an eighty-year-old woman.

81. LOVE BLOOMS AT HEMPEL'S—NOVEMBER 10, 1973
WRITTEN BY SYBIL ADELMAN AND BARBARA GALLAGHER
DIRECTED BY JAY SANDRICH
GUESTS: WILLIAM BURNS AS DOUG HEMPEL, BARBARA BARRETT AS MARGA-
RET KELLOGG, MEG WYLLIE AS EVE BAYLESS, ROY WEST

A love story for Rhoda. She falls in love with the manager of the store where she works. She wants to tell Doug of her feelings, but Mary cautions her to slow down and not make herself so obvious.

82. THE DINNER PARTY—NOVEMBER 17, 1973
WRITTEN BY ED. WEINBERGER
DIRECTED BY JAY SANDRICH
GUESTS: IRENE TEDROW AS MRS. GEDDES, HENRY WINKLER AS STEVE
WALDMAN

By now all Mary fans know that she gives the worst parties in Minneapolis. Her reputation in that regard does not help as she is drawn into planning a dinner party for a congresswoman.

83. JUST FRIENDS—NOVEMBER 24, 1973
WRITTEN BY WILLIAM WOOD
DIRECTED BY NANCY WALKER
GUEST: PRISCILLA MORRILL

Lou is depressed over his marital breakup and has been spending great amounts of time at Mary's apartment. Mary decides to solve her problem by reuniting Edie and Lou. Each such episode reinforces the inevitable fact that Lou is alone.

84. WE WANT BAXTER—DECEMBER 1, 1973
WRITTEN BY DAVID LLOYD
DIRECTED BY JAY SANDRICH
GUEST: JOHN AMOS

Phyllis has always liked Ted. She tried to talk Mary into dating him in the second episode of the first season. Now she has the notion to have Ted run for city council. This is the first of David Lloyd's scripts. He would write more than a third of the remaining episodes.

85. I Gave at the Office—December 8, 1973
Written by Don Reo and Allan Katz
Directed by Jay Sandrich
Guests: Tammi Bula as Bonnie Slaughter, Bruce Boxleitner

Murray has arranged for his teenage daughter to work in the newsroom. While her father is hovering over her every action, Lou is a nervous wreck, unable even to swear in the office.

86. Almost a Nun's Story—December 15, 1973
Written by Ed. Weinberger and Stan Daniels
Directed by Jay Sandrich
Guest: Gail Strickland as Sister Ann

Ted has not yet adjusted to being faithful to Georgette, and this results in her seeing him with another woman. Hurt, Georgette decides to enter a convent. (One is tempted to explore the possibilities of a spin-off based on this premise.)

87. Happy Birthday, Lou—December 22, 1973
Written by David Lloyd
Directed by George Tyne
Guests: John Amos, Priscilla Morrill

Ed. Weinberger has related the source of this plot in Chapter 4. Mary tries to throw a surprise birthday party for Lou, who hates both surprises and public displays of affection. Lou was not quite as persistent in refusing such a party as Weinberger had been.

88. WJM Tries Harder—January 5, 1974
Written by Karyl Geld
Directed by Jay Sandrich
Guests: Anthony Eisley, Ned Wertimer, Regis Cordic

Mary dates the anchor of a news show from another station, leading to serious questions in her mind about the quality of her own WJM news offering.

89. COTTAGE FOR SALE—JANUARY 12, 1974
WRITTEN BY GEORGE ATKINS
DIRECTED BY JAY SANDRICH
GUESTS: MICHELE NICHOLS AS RENA, DAVID HASKELL AS DAVID

Phyllis decides to go into business and gets a real estate license. She uses Mary's office to solicit business and tries to talk Lou into selling his house.

90. THE CO-PRODUCERS—JANUARY 19, 1974
WRITTEN BY DAVID POLLOCK AND ELIAS DAVIS
DIRECTED BY JAY SANDRICH

To her surprise Mary is given the green light to develop a discussion show with Rhoda, who initiated the idea. All seems in good shape until it is determined that the hosts will be Sue Ann and Ted. The negotiations about the format feature the hosts' egos, Rhoda's bluntness, and Mary's usual attempts to reconcile the irreconcilable.

91. BEST OF ENEMIES—JANUARY 26, 1974
WRITTEN BY MARILYN SUZANNE MILLER AND MONICA JOHNSON
DIRECTED BY JAY SANDRICH

An interesting study of a profound friendship places Mary and Rhoda at odds with each other to such an extent that the relationship is threatened. Mary thinks Rhoda should apologize for the argument and Rhoda refuses.

92. BETTER LATE . . . THAT'S A PUN . . . THAN NEVER—FEBRUARY 2, 1974
WRITTEN BY TREVA SILVERMAN
DIRECTED BY JOHN CHULAY
GUEST: JENNIFER LEAK AS ERICA

One of the few episodes directed by the late John Chulay, who served for seven years as the assistant director, this may be Silverman's funniest effort. Returning to the Rhoda/Mary relationship, she has them writing silly obituaries late into the night. As fate would have it, one of the subjects dies and Ted snatches the comic obit from Mary's desk and reads it on the news. Lou reprimands Mary and then, because she will not accept suspension, fires her. She returns days later to find her desk occupied. However, Lou has a quick solution to that and the newsroom staff is reunited.

93. TED BAXTER MEETS WALTER CRONKITE—FEBRUARY 9, 1974
WRITTEN BY ED. WEINBERGER
DIRECTED BY JAY SANDRICH
GUESTS: WALTER CRONKITE, JOHN GABRIEL AS ANDY, JOHN PRINGLE

Ted is campaigning for a local news award, something he has lost
eight times but finally wins. He now feels ready to move up, maybe
co-anchor with Walter Cronkite. Lou and Walter go back many years
as friends, and on a visit to Minneapolis, Cronkite stops by to see
his old pal. Mary's reaction to an introduction to him is hilarious,
and Ted immediately puts the move on the famous newsman. It
leads Cronkite to say to Lou, "I'm gonna get you for this."

94. LOU'S SECOND DATE—FEBRUARY 16, 1974
WRITTEN BY ED. WEINBERGER
DIRECTED BY JERRY LONDON

In Valerie Harper's last appearance on the series as a regular, she
portrays Rhoda as dating Lou. After two dates together the newsroom
staff assume love is blooming. It was an effective way to wrap up
the relationships as Rhoda departs.

95. TWO WRONGS DON'T MAKE A WRITER—FEBRUARY 23, 1974
WRITTEN BY DAVID LLOYD
DIRECTED BY NANCY WALKER
GUEST: SHIRLEY O'HARA AS MRS. MALONE

Mary goes back to school, this time to attend a creative writing class.
Ted has visions of writing his own copy and enrolls in the class,
where his behavior is outrageous. If that isn't bad enough, he steals
Mary's idea for a composition and tells it as his own. This leaves
Mary to construct on the spot a new idea, which she does with just
the right touch of nervous stammering.

96. I WAS A SINGLE FOR WJM—MARCH 2, 1974
WRITTEN BY TREVA SILVERMAN
DIRECTED BY MEL FERBER
GUESTS: RICHARD SCHAAL AS DINO, PENNY MARSHALL AS TONI, ARLENE
    GOLONKA AS ALICE, ROBERT RIESEL AS BARTENDER, RANDY KIRBY AS
    STAGE MANAGER

Searching for new material and a new angle for the news, a meeting
of the staff results in live coverage of a singles bar. WJM cameras

drive almost everyone from the bar, leaving Murray and Mary and Lou to ad-lib with hilarious ineffectiveness after the departure of the customers.

Fifth Season

97. WILL MARY RICHARDS GO TO JAIL?—SEPTEMBER 14, 1974
WRITTEN BY ED. WEINBERGER AND STAN DANIELS
DIRECTED BY JAY SANDRICH
GUESTS: BARBARA COLBY AS SHERRY, JAMES RANDOLPH AS HARRISON, MARY
    ANN CHINN AS KIM, DARLENE CONLEY AS MATRON, DON MACON AS
    REPORTER, CHARLES WOOLF AS MR. EVERETT

Unquestionably one of the best episodes of the entire series, this story has to do with Mary's refusal to reveal her news source. She is threatened with jail by the judge. In Lou's office she blurts out, in

Scene from "Will Mary Richards Go to Jail?"

response to Lou's ringing defense of a free press, "I know it's the right thing to do. There's just one problem, Mr. Grant—I don't want to go to jail!"

In prison she meets a couple of prostitutes, one played brilliantly by the late Barbara Colby. The scenes in the cell with the three women and Lou are exceptional comedy. Released pending a trial for contempt, Mary must wait until episode 152 for a resolution.

98. NOT JUST ANOTHER PRETTY FACE—SEPTEMBER 21, 1974
WRITTEN BY ED. WEINBERGER AND STAN DANIELS
DIRECTED BY JAY SANDRICH
GUESTS: LISA GERRITSEN, ROBERT WOLDERS AS PAUL VAN DILLEN, LOU
   CUTELL AS NICE LITTLE MAN, JULIE ROGERS AS WAITRESS, CATHY BACO
   AS WAITRESS

Mary is dating a handsome ski instructor, Paul Van Dillen. Her friends don't understand what she sees in him. Mary works through this with Paul, who says he just enjoys her company and that, if she enjoys his, they should continue to see each other. Steven Scheuer, serving a brief stint as reviewer for *TV Guide*, wrote at the time, "The sharp, disparate styles of *The Mary Tyler Moore Show*'s Greek chorus of regulars—Cloris Leachman's pseudo-intellectual Phyllis, Georgia Engel's utterly naive Georgette and Betty White's brittle Sue Ann—allow them to emerge as more than the customary TV carica-tures. In this well-written entry, they accuse Mary of being shallow because of the man she's dating." Jay Sandrich observes that for her friends the only thing she could possibly like in this man, who had never heard of *Gone With the Wind*, was that he was good in bed.

99. YOU SOMETIMES HURT THE ONE YOU HATE—SEPTEMBER 28, 1974
WRITTEN BY DAVID LLOYD
DIRECTED BY JACKIE COOPER

We've been told that directing this episode was a nightmare for Jackie Cooper because he was unable to accept the injection of guidance from the sidelines by the producers and writers during the entire week. As we have noted earlier, it was a style of production that encouraged constant change and suggestions.

The episode centers on an angry Lou, frustrated with Ted's bum-bling, pushing him through a door and causing some slight injuries. Remorseful, Lou becomes Ted's defender as Mary and Murray can only gawk in disbelief. Ted's neck brace adds to Lou's discomfort.

100. Lou and That Woman—October 5, 1974
Written by David Lloyd
Directed by Jay Sandrich
Guests: Sheree North, Fred Festinger as Drunk

Steven Scheuer in *TV Guide* described this episode nicely: "Guest Sheree North scores on *The MTM Show,* turning on a faded warmth as a bar singer who picks up with a beady-eyed Lou Grant, still feeling pangs of his long separation from his wife." In fact, Lou gets a great deal of advice and kidding from his friends, who think that the stories he relates about her past make her unsuitable for him.

101. The Outsider—October 12, 1974
Written by Jack Winter
Directed by Peter Bonerz
Guest: Richard Masur

Trading on the popular scam of expert consultants, the writers have WJM seek an efficient young man to "shape up the news." He makes minor changes, insults everyone, and succeeds in increasing the ratings by one point. He then leaves WJM, telling the newsroom staff they are without talent and that he must advance his own career.

102. I Love a Piano—October 19, 1974
Written by Treva Silverman
Directed by Jay Sandrich
Guest: Barbara Barrie as Judith

Murray faces middle-age fantasy and nearly turns it into an affair with an attractive musician. The comedy is often a function of Murray's own good nature and his intention to be faithful to Marie.

103. A New Sue Ann—October 26, 1974
Written by David Lloyd
Directed by Jay Sandrich
Guests: Linda Kelsey as Gloria, Ron Rifkin

While Mary is preparing for Rhoda's wedding, Sue Ann is facing an uncertain future when the Happy Homemaker is threatened with replacement by a designing young woman dear to the heart of the station manager. It might be noted that station managers at WJM served the same purpose as security guards on *Star Trek*—they fulfilled their function and were eliminated. Whether this was intended to be a comment upon the position of station manager by the producers, we haven't asked.

104. MÉNAGE À PHYLLIS—NOVEMBER 2, 1974
WRITTEN BY TREVA SILVERMAN
DIRECTED BY JAY SANDRICH
GUEST: JOHN SAXON

As only Phyllis would, she develops a "platonic" relationship with a young man for intellectual stimulation. Nevertheless, she is less than pleased when he shows an interest in dating Mary.

105. NOT A CHRISTMAS STORY—NOVEMBER 9, 1974
WRITTEN BY ED. WEINBERGER AND STAN DANIELS
DIRECTED BY JOHN C. CHULAY

Snowbound in November at WJM, the staff is far from cordial as they face the long ordeal. Once again snow is the perfect plot device and was a major reason for setting this series in Minneapolis. Sue Ann is having none of this depression and organizes a Christmas party to inject some cheer.

106. WHAT ARE FRIENDS FOR?—NOVEMBER 16, 1974
WRITTEN BY DAVID LLOYD
DIRECTED BY ALAN RAFKIN
GUESTS: NOBLE WILLINGHAM AS HAL, DAVID HUDDLESTON AS FREDDY,
    DAN BARROWS AS BELLHOP, ROBERT KARVELAS AS WAITER

Mary is selected to attend a broadcasters' convention in Chicago, something that becomes far less appealing when she discovers Sue Ann will be her companion. Naturally Sue Ann seeks to involve Mary in some man hunting, and the results are as funny as they were intended to be.

107. A BOY'S BEST FRIEND—NOVEMBER 23, 1974
WRITTEN BY DAVID LLOYD
DIRECTED BY MARY TYLER MOORE
GUEST: NOLAN LEARY AS GEORGE TEWKSBURY

Mary Tyler Moore chose to direct this one episode, a rather gentle revelation of Ted's insecurity and his concern over the relationship between his mother and her companion with whom she is living. Ted has some delightful scenes with the prospective new father and accepts the situation when he discovers the man is rich.

108. A Son for Murray—November 30, 1974
Written by Ed. Weinberger and Stan Daniels
Directed by Jay Sandrich
Guests: Michael Higa as Le Chan, John Gabriel as Andy Rivers, David Frescoe as Phil Kramer

Murray desperately wants a son. He and Marie have three daughters and Marie is not keen on having another child. The episode allows Murray to understand Marie's position while becoming attached to a young Vietnamese, Le Chan, whom the Slaughters adopt.

109. Neighbors—December 7, 1974
Written by Ziggy Steinberg
Directed by James Burrows and John C. Chulay
Guest: Clifford David as David

Lou finally decides to sell his house. Mary is not so pleased when she discovers he is thinking about renting Rhoda's old apartment. How do you tell your boss you don't want him as a neighbor? And if you get him, will there be any privacy for Mary?

110. A Girl Like Mary—December 14, 1974
Written by Ann Gibbs and Joel Kimmel
Directed by Jay Sandrich
Guests: Rosalind Cash as Enid, Judie Stein as First Auditioner

Lou decides to have a female co-anchor for the news. The humor of Mary and Sue Ann competing for this position, neither qualified, might undermine the central message of the entire series as, in the end, it leaves Ted to "make it on his own."

111. An Affair to Forget—December 21, 1974
Written by Ed. Weinberger and Stan Daniels
Directed by Jay Sandrich

Ted, the lady-killer, decides to convince the newsroom staff that he and Mary are having an affair. Vince Waldron described the results well: "We are able to sympathize with Ted's desperate plight just as much as we can identify with Mary's utter mortification. The entire embarrassing situation is made funny largely because we are convinced it could happen to any one of us."

112. MARY RICHARDS: PRODUCER—JANUARY 4, 1975
WRITTEN BY DAVID LLOYD
DIRECTED BY NORMAN CAMPBELL
GUESTS: ANTHONY HOLLAND AS MEL PETERS, PHILLIP R. ALLEN AS GUS BRUBAKER, FRED FESTINGER AS DRUNK, JOE SCOTT AS BARTENDER

Mary finally decides to press for the responsibility of producing the news. Lou agrees and the ensuing trauma as Mary tries to prove herself capable is the source of some high humor.

113. THE SYSTEM—JANUARY 11, 1975
WRITTEN BY ED. WEINBERGER AND STAN DANIELS
DIRECTED BY JAY SANDRICH
GUEST: JOHN GABRIEL AS ANDY RIVERS

Lou bets on football as a way of life. He is losing far too much money and is impressed by what appears to be a winning system devised by Ted. They join in a partnership that ends in disaster. This award-winning episode (an Emmy for Jay Sandrich) was based on the real-life experience related in the section on Stan Daniels.

114. PHYLLIS WHIPS INFLATION—JANUARY 18, 1975
WRITTEN BY ED. WEINBERGER AND STAN DANIELS
DIRECTED BY JAY SANDRICH
GUESTS: DORIS ROBERTS AS HELEN FARRELL, LISA GERRITSEN, GEORGE MEMMOLI AS BREWSTER

Cloris Leachman will leave after this episode to star in her own series. The plot concerns the never-to-be-seen Lars commanding Phyllis to cut back on her spending. Losing her credit cards, she contemplates work. A similar plot on *My World and Welcome to It* provided reinforcement for the notion of male wisdom and economic authority as all the women on that series accepted dependency. In this case the irony comes from the fact that Lars meets an untimely end and Phyllis gets a job on the first episode of her new show in the fall of 1975.

115. THE SHAME OF THE CITIES—JANUARY 25, 1975
WRITTEN BY MICHAEL ELIAS AND ARNIE KOGEN
DIRECTED BY JAY SANDRICH
GUESTS: SHEREE NORTH AS CHARLENE, ROBERT EMHARDT AS MAN, CHUCK
   BERGANSKY AS BARTENDER, JAMES JETER AS CUSTOMER

Lou remembers his glory days in journalism and, lusting for a great
story, decides to expose a municipal leader who, it turns out, has a
flawless record of competence and responsibility.

116. MARRIAGE: MINNEAPOLIS STYLE—FEBRUARY 1, 1975
WRITTEN BY PAMELA RUSSELL
DIRECTED BY JAY SANDRICH
GUEST: EILEEN MCDONOUGH AS ELLEN

Murray and Marie celebrate their twentieth wedding anniversary.
Ted, lonely, proposes to Georgette, as *TV Guide* described it, "in the
middle of his newscast. The soul-searching that prompted Ted's
decision, and his case of cold feet afterward, are a blend of outstanding comedy writing and top-flight character acting."

117. YOU TRY TO BE A NICE GUY—FEBRUARY 8, 1975
WRITTEN BY MICHAEL LEESON
DIRECTED BY JAY SANDRICH
GUEST: BARBARA COLBY

Remember when Mary was in jail? (#97) She met a prostitute,
played by Barbara Colby, with a heart of gold. The woman reap-
pears, seeking to have Mary sponsor her while she seeks a job.
Otherwise, she will have to go back to jail. Of course Mary does it.
Her friend tries several jobs, but the funniest is as a clothes de-
signer. It gives Mary a chance to model the tackiest, sexiest outfit
one can imagine—for Lou.

118. YOU CAN'T LOSE THEM ALL—FEBRUARY 15, 1975
WRITTEN BY DAVID LLOYD
DIRECTED BY MARJORIE MULLEN

While Lou is receiving an award he doesn't want, he must console
Ted, who is devastated by the news that he has not been nominated
for the newscaster award.

119. TED BAXTER'S FAMOUS BROADCASTERS SCHOOL—FEBRUARY 22, 1975
WRITTEN BY MICHAEL ZINBERG
DIRECTED BY JAY SANDRICH
GUESTS: BERNIE KOPELL, LEONARD FREY AS LAWRENCE HANNON, NORMAN BARTOLD AS ALAN MARSH

Ted joins a partnership to open a Famous Broadcasters School, which turns out to be a scam. When he is faced with teaching the course he bails out, and Lou, Mary, and Murray share the lecturing load for a class with a single student.

120. ANYONE WHO HATES KIDS AND DOGS—MARCH 8, 1975
WRITTEN BY JERRY MAYER
DIRECTED BY JAY SANDRICH
GUESTS: LAURENCE LUCKINBILL AS KEN, LEE H. MONTGOMERY AS STEVIE, MABEL ALBERTSON AS ETHEL, IAN WOLFE AS GRANDFATHER, CAROLE KING LARKEY AS AUNT HELEN

Yet again Mary seeks male companionship, this time with Ken, whose chief drawback is a twelve-year-old son whom she cannot stand.

Sixth Season

121. EDIE GETS MARRIED—SEPTEMBER 13, 1975
WRITTEN BY BOB ELLISON
DIRECTED BY JAY SANDRICH
GUESTS: PRISCILLA MORRILL, NORA HEFLIN AS JANEY

The sixth season is opened by Bob Ellison's first script. He would write thirteen more and collaborate on the last show. Edie is getting married and Lou cannot decide how to react. Tears flow at the bar as the staff seeks to comfort Mr. Grant. CBS advertised, "It's trauma time for Lou when his former wife decides to remarry. Mary and the newsroom gang have a tough time making him face facts and the impending ceremony." Reviewing the episode, *TV Guide* noted, "Edward Asner as Lou pulls it off, running the gamut of anger and sorrow in a believable and touching performance."

122. MARY MOVES OUT—SEPTEMBER 20, 1975
WRITTEN BY DAVID LLOYD
DIRECTED BY JAY SANDRICH
GUEST: JOHN LEHNE

Mary is depressed, so she decides to rent a new apartment. We have it on good authority that the move was concocted by Jay Sandrich, who was tired of the old set. Producers felt new neighbors might be a source of new plots. But it didn't work out that way—the old family was still the most workable and would generate ample fresh ideas. The move merely serves to remind us that the old format— home and work—has been set aside and now all of Mary's friends work at WJM. Symbolic of the non-change is the ceremony of her decorating her high rise with the big wooden M that was so much a part of the old environment.

123. MARY'S FATHER—SEPTEMBER 27, 1975
WRITTEN BY EARL POMERANTZ
DIRECTED BY JAY SANDRICH
GUEST: ED FLANDERS AS FATHER BRIAN

A really fine episode built around a serious misreading of intentions by Mary. It was well described by the critic at *TV Guide*: "A funny episode of *The MTM Show* concerns Mary's belief that her new friend Father Brian (well played by Ed Flanders) wants to leave the priest-hood because he has fallen in love with her. The scenes of Mary's shock and embarrassment are good, but the best moments belong to Betty White as the predatory Sue Ann, who begins to stalk the father before realizing that he's a priest."

124. MURRAY IN LOVE—OCTOBER 4, 1975
WRITTEN BY DAVID LLOYD
DIRECTED BY JAY SANDRICH
GUESTS: PENNY MARSHALL AS PAULA KOVACKS, MARY KAY PLACE AS SALLY JO HOTCHKISS, BARRY COE AS STEVE, PETER HOBBS AS BARTENDER

From the moment that Murray knocks at Mary's door with a gift, a goldfish, we know there's a problem. It turns out Murray is in love with Mary and he wants to know how she feels. Lou tells him not to ask, but Murray observes, "Just suppose she feels the same way and I never asked." The moment of encounter is adroitly directed and nicely played by both actors.

125. TED'S MOMENT OF GLORY—OCTOBER 11, 1975
WRITTEN BY CHARLES LEE AND GIG HENRY
DIRECTED BY JAY SANDRICH
GUESTS: RICHARD BALIN AS PRODUCER, MARILYN ROBERTS

A show written particularly for Ted Knight, it is, as *TV Guide* observed, "a comedic tour de force. . . . Ted Knight dominates this episode, which finds him flying to New York to audition for quizmaster on a new TV game show. And he may land the job. His mentality seems just right for 'The Fifty Thousand Dollar Steeplechase,' a game in which contestants sit on wooden horses and wear jockey caps while trying to answer stumpers like, 'True or false: Hubert Humphrey was once Vice President of the United States.' " Given his ego and desire for money, we might find his rejection of the job a little unbelievable. But, of course, he must remain on *The Mary Tyler Moore Show*.

126. MARY'S AUNT—OCTOBER 18, 1975
WRITTEN BY DAVID LLOYD
DIRECTED BY JAY SANDRICH
GUESTS: EILEEN HECKART, GEORGE CONRAD AS BARTENDER

Eileen Heckart makes her first appearance as Mary's Aunt Flo. She is a globe-hopping, name-dropping journalistic success. Lou is impressed to learn of Mary's relationship with the famous personality, but upon meeting the two become highly competitive, making Mary a most uncomfortable third party at dinner.

127. CHUCKLES BITES THE DUST—OCTOBER 25, 1975
WRITTEN BY DAVID LLOYD
DIRECTED BY JOAN DARLING
GUEST: JOHN HARKINS AS REVEREND BURNS

There is probably no "best" episode of this series, but if one were to be chosen, this one would be a finalist in the voting. Chuckles, dressed like a peanut, is "shelled" by a rogue elephant in a circus parade. The obvious jokes about the absurd situation run through the newsroom, but they do not amuse Mary, who feels outrage at the insensitive remarks of Lou and Murray. Then comes the funeral. Properly redressed, the newsroom staff sits quietly and reverently as the minister begins the eulogy. At that moment Mary begins to laugh as Rev. Burns names some of the characters on Chuckles's show. She tries to hide the laughter, but it finally becomes uncontrollable. The ending leaves the viewer limp from laughter.

128. MARY'S DELINQUENT—NOVEMBER 1, 1975
WRITTEN BY MARY KAY PLACE AND VALERIE CURTIN
DIRECTED BY JAY SANDRICH
GUESTS: MACKENZIE PHILLIPS, TAMU, PHILLIP R. ALLEN

Mary and Sue Ann volunteer as big sisters for two streetwise girls. The contrast between the personalities makes this sequence work well.

129. TED'S WEDDING—NOVEMBER 8, 1975
WRITTEN BY DAVID LLOYD
DIRECTED BY JAY SANDRICH
GUEST: JOHN RITTER

Ted proposes once again to Georgette, and this time she tells him to marry her in the next half hour or forget their relationship. The newsroom crowd gathers at Mary's, where the minister, John Ritter, appears in tennis attire to tie the knot.

Scene from "Ted's Wedding."

130. Lou Douses an Old Flame—November 15, 1975
Written by David Lloyd
Directed by Jay Sandrich
Guest: Beverly Garland as Veronica

Thirty years ago, during the war, Lou's girl wrote him a "Dear John" letter. Suddenly she appears in Minneapolis and Lou is not sure he should see her. But he has fond memories and he is curious about her and why she wrote the letter. They meet in a restaurant where the purpose of her visit is revealed—she wants to borrow some money. She gets the money and a sticky dessert dumped on her head by Lou, making him feel a lot better.

131. Mary Richards Falls in Love—November 22, 1975
Written by Ed. Weinberger and Stan Daniels
Directed by Jay Sandrich
Guests: Ted Bessell as Joe Warner, Valerie Harper, David Groh, Beth Howland, Michael Perrotta

Mary meets a new man, Joe Warner, played by Ted Bessell, who also played Ann Marie's love interest in *That Girl*. It seems to be the best casting yet discovered for a companion for Mary. Sandrich says that had Bessell been available the producers probably would have incorporated Joe as a regular character. In their early encounters he embarrasses her by public displays of affection. Rhoda appears with her husband, crossing over from her own series.

132. Ted's Tax Refund—November 29, 1975
Written by Bob Ellison
Directed by Marjorie Mullen
Guest: Paul Lichman as Irv Gevins

A play centered on Ted, who receives a $6,000 tax refund to which he is not entitled. He spends it and then discovers he will have to repay the IRS.

133. The Happy Homemaker Takes Lou Home—December 6, 1975
Written by David Lloyd
Directed by James Burrows
Guests: Wynn Irwin, Titos Vandis as Lazlo Kralic

In one of the funnier scenes developed on the show, Sue Ann eavesdrops as Mary goes through with a promise to get her a date with Lou. The exchanges between Lou and Sue Ann thereafter are a delight.

134. ONE BOYFRIEND TOO MANY—DECEMBER 13, 1975
WRITTEN BY DAVID LLOYD
DIRECTED BY JAY SANDRICH
GUESTS: MICHAEL TOLAN, TED BESSELL

This is a touching episode that involves Mary with current loyalty and past romance. When she agrees to go out with her former teacher, her new love, Joe, is angry. Mary tells him he is overreacting. He reminds her that she was upset when he saw someone else earlier in the year. "That was different," Mary says, "you didn't cry your eyes out." "No," says Joe, "I did the male version of crying—pretending that it doesn't hurt." It is a nice touch and leaves Mary unsure of the rules of the "dating game" in 1975.

135. WHAT DO YOU WANT TO DO WHEN YOU PRODUCE?—DECEMBER 20, 1975
WRITTEN BY SHELLEY NELBERT AND CRAIG ALLEN HAFNER
DIRECTED BY JAY SANDRICH

Murray gets a chance to increase his salary, but the cost is high as he accepts the role of producer for the "Happy Homemaker Show." Sue Ann makes life absolutely terrible for him, forcing him into demeaning tasks that make him long for the newsroom.

136. NOT WITH MY WIFE, I DON'T—JANUARY 3, 1976
WRITTEN BY BOB ELLISON
DIRECTED BY JAY SANDRICH
GUEST: ALLAN MANSON AS PSYCHIATRIST

Georgette is distressed about her marriage. She tells Mary that Ted is sleeping on the couch in the living room and she is thinking about leaving him. This leads to professional counseling and an explanation.

137. THE SEMINAR—JANUARY 10, 1976
WRITTEN BY JAMES MACDONALD AND ROBERT GERLACH
DIRECTED BY STUART MARGOLIN
GUESTS: BETTY FORD, DABNEY COLEMAN

Asner, Sandrich, MacLeod, Weinberger.

Mary and Lou attend a political seminar in Washington. Mary wants to see the city, but Lou asks her to wait for invitations he is sure he will receive from old friends in the Capital. Mary goes out, and when she returns Lou tells her about a party with celebrities that he hosted, with guests including President and Mrs. Ford. Mary laughs in a disbelieving manner, only to be stunned when the phone rings and she has an impromptu conversation with Betty Ford.

138. ONCE I HAD A SECRET LOVE—JANUARY 17, 1976
WRITTEN BY PAT NARDO AND GLORIA BANTA
DIRECTED BY JAY SANDRICH

We think this is one of the best. Lou somehow finds himself in Sue Ann's apartment overnight. He comes to the office bearded and disarranged and without socks. Mary finally extracts the truth from Lou, upon the promise she will tell no one. Murray, sensing something strange, then gets the story out of Mary. In a give-and-take in the newsroom Lou discovers Mary has talked and he tells her he's no longer her friend. The final scene, when that assertion is laid to rest, is a classic comic bit.

139. MÉNAGE À LOU—JANUARY 24, 1976
WRITTEN BY BOB ELLISON
DIRECTED BY JAY SANDRICH
GUESTS: JANIS PAIGE AS CHARLENE, PENNY MARSHALL AS PAULA, JEFF CONAWAY

The departure of Sheree North to another show left a gap that is filled here by Janis Paige. Charlene starts dating a younger man and Lou decides to get even by dating Mary's neighbor, Paula, played by Penny Marshall.

140. MURRAY TAKES A STAND—JANUARY 31, 1976
WRITTEN BY DAVID LLOYD
DIRECTED BY JAY SANDRICH

The station owner has some policies Murray finds objectionable. He makes this known and launches a vigorous protest. For his courage he is fired. Then the task becomes one of restoring Murray to the team.

141. MARY'S AUNT RETURNS—FEBRUARY 7, 1976
WRITTEN BY DAVID LLOYD
DIRECTED BY JAY SANDRICH
GUEST: EILEEN HECKART

Aunt Flo returns with an idea for a partnership with Lou on a PBS project. They begin, find no grounds for agreement concerning the journalistic integrity of the show, and discuss the matter with Mary and Murray. The result—Mary and Lou team up to compete with Flo and Murray for the best concept. The victory of Mary and Lou in this contest is sweet but it doesn't faze Flo.

142. A RELIABLE SOURCE—FEBRUARY 21, 1976
WRITTEN BY RICHARD M. POWELL
DIRECTED BY JAY SANDRICH
GUEST: EDWARD WINTER

Mary and Lou are at odds when he decides to do an exposé on a political figure who happens to be Mary's idol.

143. SUE ANN FALLS IN LOVE—FEBRUARY 28, 1976
WRITTEN BY BOB ELLISON
DIRECTED BY DOUG ROGERS
GUESTS: JAMES LUISI AS DOUG KELLUM, PAT GAYNOR, LARRY WILDE

Says *TV Guide*, "A funny-sad episode of *The MTM Show* belongs to Betty White. As Happy Homemaker Sue Ann Nivens, she's desperately in love with a fellow who's definitely not worth it: He makes a play for Mary and schemes to exploit the Happy Homemaker financially." It is also a week in which Sue Ann is nominated for a Teddy Award.

144. TED AND THE KID—MARCH 6, 1976
WRITTEN BY BOB ELLISON
DIRECTED BY MARJORIE MULLEN
GUEST: ROBBIE RIST AS DAVID

Ted discovers that the reason he and Georgette cannot have children lies with him. After initial embarrassment the couple decide to adopt a son, a boy who turns out to be extremely bright. At the end of the episode Georgette announces that she is pregnant.

Seventh Season

145. MARY MIDWIFE—SEPTEMBER 25, 1976
WRITTEN BY DAVID LLOYD
DIRECTED BY JAY SANDRICH
GUEST: FORD RAINEY AS DR. RAINEY

Sue Ann plans a party for the WJM staff at Mary's place to try out her low-calorie éclairs. Mary makes Lou unhappy by suggesting he is overweight. But before that issue can be developed, Georgette decides she is in labor. She is right and Lou finally delivers the baby, with Mary's help. Everyone else goes to pieces except Sue Ann, who continues blithely to watch her show on television. CBS advertised the episode with an eye to the Women's Movement with the following line: "Mary and Lou as midpersons." Now the Baxters have two children, an adopted boy and an infant daughter.

146. MARY THE WRITER—OCTOBER 2, 1976
WRITTEN BY BURT PRELUTSKY
DIRECTED BY JAMES BURROWS

Lou makes some critical remarks about Mary's writing that do not please her. Hurt, she pretends her story has been accepted by *Cosmopolitan*. Lou knows better, but plays along until she confesses. She asks why he was so frank with her and then praised a book Ted had written that Lou thought was terrible. He explains, "I respect you." He doesn't respect Ted so Ted has not learned the truth.

147. SUE ANN'S SISTER—OCTOBER 9, 1976
WRITTEN BY DAVID LLOYD
DIRECTED BY JAY SANDRICH
GUEST: PAT PRIEST AS LILA NIVENS

Sue Ann's sister comes to visit, strikes up a good relationship with Lou, and lands a job at a competing station in the city. She is going to move to Minneapolis. Sue Ann's depression at this culmination of their lifelong rivalry ends in the bed scene described in Chapter 6. The audience for that show arrived to find half the stage blocked from view. The summer audience saw the bedroom only at the same moment as the viewing audience did. There was a wild uproar in Sound Stage 2.

148. WHAT'S WRONG WITH SWIMMING?—OCTOBER 16, 1976
WRITTEN BY DAVID LLOYD
DIRECTED BY MARJORIE MULLEN
GUEST: CAREN KAYE AS BARBARA JEAN SMATHERS

Lou and the other men at WJM are not happy with the idea, but Lou agrees to Mary's request that she hire B. J. Smathers as sportscaster. She is a devotée of swimming. Mary is delighted and invites Lou to dinner along with B.J. Lou quickly discovers that on the sports that evening she has covered international diving instead of the Vikings. Livid, he fires her. Mary tells him he can't do that, that she will handle it and to go home. Then Mary confronts B.J., who refuses to budge in not reporting violent sports. Mary says in her firmest voice, "B.J., you're fired."

149. TED'S CHANGE OF HEART—OCTOBER 23, 1976
WRITTEN BY EARL POMERANTZ
DIRECTED BY JAY SANDRICH
GUESTS: HARVEY VERNON, JERRY FOGEL

Ted has a mild heart attack and decides to smell the roses. This new sweetness is driving the newsroom straight up the wall. One scene is particularly memorable—Lou, Mary, and Murray staring out the window at the sunset, trying to get a grip on the new approach to life.

Scene from "One Producer Too Many." Lou brings dinner as a peace offering.

150. ONE PRODUCER TOO MANY—OCTOBER 30, 1976
WRITTEN BY BOB ELLISON
DIRECTED BY JAY SANDRICH
GUESTS: RICHARD SELF, MURRAY KORDA

Lou agrees to make Murray co-producer of the evening news in order to keep him from taking another job. There's just one problem—he hasn't told Mary. He takes her to a fine restaurant and sets her up for making a wonderful gesture on Murray's behalf. A sign of the growth of Mary Richards is that she is having no part in that arrangement and she lets Lou know it. Nevertheless, Lou forces the issue by threatening to replace Mary. In fact Lou is manipulating both Murray and Mary, who does retain her job.

151. MY SON, THE GENIUS—NOVEMBER 6, 1976—8:00 P.M.
WRITTEN BY BOB ELLISON
DIRECTED BY JAY SANDRICH
GUESTS: ROBBIE RIST AS DAVID, WILLIAM BOGART, NED GLASS AS MORRIS
    BENDER

Georgette and Ted are worried about their son David's weak performance in school. Seeking answers, they go to a psychologist, who tests the child and tells them David is in the genius category. The absurdity of this situation cannot be missed by anyone familiar with the couple involved. And yet the less-than-genius parents become capable of asserting their authority when their son acts like a normal, willful child.

152. MARY GETS A LAWYER—NOVEMBER 13, 1976
WRITTEN BY BURT PRELUTSKY
DIRECTED BY JAY SANDRICH
GUEST: JOHN MCMARTIN

Mary's stand for journalistic integrity, a position that caused her to go to jail, is finally in court. Her big problem now is that her lawyer is so infatuated with her, he cannot seem to do a professional job.

153. LOU PROPOSES—NOVEMBER 20, 1976
WRITTEN BY DAVID LLOYD
DIRECTED BY JAY SANDRICH
GUESTS: EILEEN HECKART, T. J. CASTRONOVA

Outtake from "Lou Proposes."

CBS touted this episode with the headline "Lou's long-burning passion for Mary's Aunt Flo reaches the boiling point." Indeed, Lou does decide to propose to Flo. Her decision to refuse is cast in terms of mutual respect that makes her final appearance on the series memorable. In 1988 she returned to television with Mary, as her mother in *Annie McGuire*.

insert photo #61

154. MURRAY CAN'T LOSE—NOVEMBER 27, 1976
WRITTEN BY DAVID LLOYD
DIRECTED BY JAY SANDRICH
GUESTS: LARRY WILDE AS M.C., LISA PARKES AS PRESENTER

As the Teddy Awards ceremony approaches Lou gets an inside tip that Murray, who has been nominated, is going to win. Try as they will, his newsroom friends cannot resist telling Murray. Unfortunately, someone made a mistake and Murray doesn't win. The group repairs to Mary's apartment, where Murray delivers his acceptance speech to an appreciative audience.

155. MARY'S INSOMNIA—DECEMBER 4, 1976
WRITTEN BY DAVID LLOYD
DIRECTED BY JAMES BURROWS
GUESTS: SHERRY HURSEY AS BONNIE SLAUGHTER, TED LEHMAN AS THE JANITOR

A serious subject, adroitly written by David Lloyd, becomes a fine comedic experience. Mary is taking sleeping pills in order to overcome insomnia. Lou tries to break her of the habit. As Ted listens, totally unaware of the subject, Mary says to Lou, "All right, Mr. Grant, I won't take my pill tonight." Efforts to aid Mary in her fight against barbituates include the entire male cast visiting her while she is taking a bath. Finally Lou puts her to sleep by telling her a story, sitting up with her all night as she rests on his numb left arm.

156. TED'S TEMPTATION—DECEMBER 11, 1976
WRITTEN BY BOB ELLISON
DIRECTED BY HARRY MASTROGEORGE
GUEST: TRISHA NOBLE AS WHITNEY LEWIS

Mary and Ted are attending a broadcasters' convention in Hollywood where an attractive young woman wants Ted to allow her to interview him and much more. Ted's faithfulness to Georgette is tested and remains secure.

157. LOOK AT US, WE'RE WALKING—DECEMBER 25, 1976
WRITTEN BY BOB ELLISON
DIRECTED BY JAY SANDRICH
GUEST: DAVID OGDEN STIERS AS MEL PRICE

Yet another new station manager appears as a focus of rebellion by Mary and Lou, who feel a pay raise is in order. They are told to either take the small amount offered or leave.

158. THE CRITIC—JANUARY 8, 1977
WRITTEN BY DAVID LLOYD
DIRECTED BY MARTIN COHAN
GUESTS: ERIC BRAEDON AS KARL HELLER, DAVID OGDEN STIERS AS MEL PRICE

In a rare twist the station manager keeps his job for two weeks, and this time he wants to improve ratings by hiring a critic-at-large, a pompous bore whose mean spirit and venomous prose cut to ribbons everyone in and out of the newsroom. A particularly intriguing moment is the date with Mary, when he reduces her to total embarrassment by making vicious attacks on the entire restaurant staff. This Morton Downey before his time does get his comeuppance.

159. LOU'S ARMY REUNION—JANUARY 15, 1977
WRITTEN BY BOB ELLISON
DIRECTED BY JAY SANDRICH
GUEST: ALEX ROCCO AS BEN

An old Army buddy meets Lou at a reunion and immediately sets his sights on Mary. He expects to make a sexual conquest, and before Mary can throw him out, Lou knocks him out of the apartment. Now Mary is really angry at Lou for failing to trust her to take care of herself. Lou reminds her that for him she is still that wide-eyed young woman who came to his office seven years ago and he thinks of her as his daughter.

160. THE TED AND GEORGETTE SHOW—JANUARY 22, 1977
WRITTEN BY DAVID LLOYD
DIRECTED BY JAY SANDRICH
GUESTS: DAVID OGDEN STIERS AS MEL PRICE, ALEX HENTELOFF AS ELLIOT

Mel Price is back again as manager, this time happy over the fine success of a variety show hosted by the Baxters. Ted loves it, but Georgette becomes quite unhappy with the limelight.

161. SUE ANN GETS THE AX—JANUARY 29, 1977
WRITTEN BY BOB ELLISON
DIRECTED BY JAY SANDRICH
GUEST: LOUIS GUSS AS SAM, LINDEN CHILES AS GELSON

Sue Ann gets fired twice in this last season. *TV Guide* did a good close-up: "Sue Ann Nivens loses her *Happy Homemaker* show because of poor ratings, and the next thing to go is her pride. She begs Lou for a newsroom job, and when that gambit fails she resolves to hang out at WJM for the two years left on her contract— even though the station manager promises to make her life miserable. Which he does. Sue Ann's humiliations begin with a job reading spot announcements ('Tonight on *Gilligan's Island* two lonely men catch a young mermaid and throw half of her back'). And they end with a true mortification: dressed like a daisy, she plays straight woman to a pair of wisecracking puppets."

Scene from "Sue Ann Gets the Ax."

162. HAIL THE CONQUERING GORDY—FEBRUARY 5, 1977
WRITTEN BY EARL POMERANTZ
DIRECTED BY JAY SANDRICH
GUEST: JOHN AMOS

Gordy, the weatherman of previous seasons, returns to WJM for a visit after achieving success hosting a New York talk show. Ted tries to get consideration for a spot as co-host, something Gordy has little trouble resisting.

163. MARY AND THE SEXAGENARIAN—FEBRUARY 12, 1977
WRITTEN BY LES CHARLES AND GLEN CHARLES
DIRECTED BY JAY SANDRICH
GUESTS: LEW AYRES AS DOUG, JON LORMER

Mary's dating becomes a regular theme in the final episodes. In this outing she is the object of considerable ridicule when she dates an older man—Murray's father.

164. MURRAY GHOSTS FOR TED—FEBRUARY 19, 1977
WRITTEN BY DAVID LLOYD
DIRECTED BY JAY SANDRICH
GUEST: HELEN HUNT AS LAURIE SLAUGHTER

Ted has been asked to write a newspaper article on freedom of the press. He pays Murray to write it for him and extracts the promise that Murray won't tell. The article is so good that *Reader's Digest* offers to buy it. Lou and Mary find out who wrote the article and pressure Ted to tell Murray's daughter and Marie the truth. They even convince Ted to share the money, but Murray is so pleased about the recognition in front of his family that he rejects the offer. It is Ted's turn to be pleased.

165. MARY'S THREE HUSBANDS—FEBRUARY 26, 1977
WRITTEN BY BOB ELLISON
DIRECTED BY JAY SANDRICH
GUEST: BILL DARTH

The show, which features the fantasies of her three friends about her as they talk at a bar, includes Mary as Murray's devoted, pregnant wife, Ted's newlywed bride, and Lou's newsroom partner of fifty years. It was a particularly difficult show to shoot because of the makeup problems, which were complicated by the presence of an audience.

166. MARY'S BIG PARTY—MARCH 5, 1977
WRITTEN BY BOB ELLISON
DIRECTED BY JAY SANDRICH
GUESTS: JOHNNY CARSON, IRENE TEDROW AS CONGRESSWOMAN GEDDES

Mary's final party, disastrous like all the rest, ends with the lights going out and people unable to see her guest of honor, Johnny Carson. Clips from earlier seasons fill out the episode as each guest remembers the past.

167. LOU DATES MARY—MARCH 12, 1977
WRITTEN BY DAVID LLOYD
DIRECTED BY JAY SANDRICH
GUESTS: JOHN REILLY AS JAKE, KENNY WALLER AS HARVEY

Mary arrives at her apartment with a date who immediately starts to take his clothes off. In anger she throws him out and begins to muse on the number of dates, thousands, she estimates, she has had and the boring nature of most of them. It is the catalyst for her, prodded by Georgette, to ask Lou for a date. They give it a try, laugh over a kiss, enjoy the evening meal, and recognize, "This would never work."

Scene from "The Last Show."

168. THE LAST SHOW—MARCH 19, 1977
WRITTEN BY ALLAN BURNS, JAMES L. BROOKS, ED. WEINBERGER, STAN
 DANIELS, DAVID LLOYD, BOB ELLISON
DIRECTED BY JAY SANDRICH
GUESTS: ROBBIE RIST AS DAVID, VINCENT GARDENIA AS FRANK COLEMAN,
 CLORIS LEACHMAN, VALERIE HARPER

For details of this episode see Chapter 7. *TV Guide* gave it a good
send-off with the following note: *"The MTM Show*—winner of 26
Emmys in seven years and mother of two spin-off series—airs its
final first-run show tonight. Cloris Leachman and Valerie Harper
appear in the funny and poignant episode, in which a new station
manager fires everyone on the newsroom staff—except Ted."

2. WRITERS' CREDITS

An alphabetical list of those women and men who contributed the all-important written word, from which the special quality of *The Mary Tyler Moore Show* emerged. Emmy Award–winning scripts are noted. Reference numbers correspond to episodes listed in the previous section of this chapter.

Sybil Adelman, Barbara Gallagher

#81, Love Blooms at Hempel's

George Atkins

#89, Cottage for Sale

John D. F. Black

#3, Bess, You Is My Daughter Now
#96, I Was a Single for WJM

Jim Brooks and Allan Burns

#1, Love Is All Around
#6, Support Your Local Mother (Emmy Award, Outstanding Writing Achievement in Comedy, 1970–71)
#14, Christmas and the Hard-Luck Kid
#17, Just a Lunch
#49, The Good-Time News
#168, The Last Show (Emmy Award, Outstanding Writing in a Comedy Series, 1976–77)

Charlotte Brown

#58, Have I Found a Guy for You

Allan Burns

#27, He's No Heavy, He's My Brother
#31, Didn't You Used to Be . . . Wait . . . Don't Tell Me!

Les Charles, Glen Charles

#163, Mary and the Sexagenarian

Dick Clair, Jenna McMahon

#40, Feeb
#44, The Care and Feeding of Parents
#65, My Brother's Keeper
#70, Remembrance of Things Past

Martin Cohan

#16, Party Is Such Sweet Sorrow
#32, Thoroughly Unmilitant Mary
#45, Where There's Smoke, There's Rhoda
#46, You Certainly Are a Big Boy
#51, Who's in Charge Here?
#52, Enter Rhoda's Parents
#69, Murray Faces Life
#72, Mary Richards and the Incredible Plant Lady

David Davis, Lorenzo Music

 #8, The Show Must Go On
#34, Don't Break the Chain
#11, 1040 or Fight
#21, The Boss Isn't Coming to Dinner
#26, I Am Curious Cooper
#29, A Girl's Best Mother Is Not Her Friend
#38, Ted Over Heels

Elias Davis, David Pollock

#61, Operation: Lou
#63, The Courtship of Mary's Father's Daughter
#68, What Do You Do When the Boss Says, "I Love You"?
#90, The Co-Producers

Martin Donovan

#53, It's Whether You Win or Lose

#57, Farmer Ted and the News

Michael Elias, Arnie Kogen

#115, The Shame of the Cities

Bob Ellison

#121, Edie Gets Married
#132, Ted's Tax Refund
#136, Not with My Wife, I Don't
#139, Ménage à Lou
#143, Sue Ann Falls in Love
#144, Ted and the Kid
#150, One Producer Too Many
#151, My Son, the Genius
#156, Ted's Temptation
#157, Look at Us, We're Walking
#159, Lou's Army Reunion
#161, Sue Ann Gets the Ax
#165, Mary's Three Husbands
#166, Mary's Big Party
#168, The Last Show (Emmy Award, Outstanding Writing in a Comedy Series, 1976–77)

Karyl Geld

#75, Rhoda's Sister Gets Married
#88, WJM Tries Harder

Ann Gibbs, Joel Kimmel

#110, A Girl Like Mary

George Kirgo

#24, The Forty-Five-Year-Old Man

Charles Lee, Gig Henry

#125, Ted's Moment of Glory

Michael Leeson

#117, You Try to Be a Nice Guy

David Lloyd

#84, We Want Baxter
#87, Happy Birthday, Lou

#95, Two Wrongs Don't Make a Writer
#99, You Sometimes Hurt the One You Hate
#100, Lou and That Woman
#103, A New Sue Ann
#106, What Are Friends For?
#107, A Boy's Best Friend
#112, Mary Richards: Producer
#118, You Can't Lose Them All
#122, Mary Moves Out
#124, Murray in Love
#126, Mary's Aunt
#127, Chuckles Bites the Dust (Emmy Award, Outstanding Writing in a Comedy Series, 1975–76)
#129, Ted's Wedding
#130, Lou Douses an Old Flame
#133, The Happy Homemaker Takes Lou Home
#134, One Boyfriend Too Many
#140, Murray Takes a Stand
#141, Mary's Aunt Returns
#145, Mary Midwife
#147, Sue Ann's Sister
#148, What's Wrong with Swimming?
#153, Lou Proposes
#154, Murray Can't Lose
#155, Mary's Insomnia
#158, The Critic
#160, The Ted and Georgette Show
#164, Murray Ghosts for Ted
#167, Lou Dates Mary
#168, The Last Show (Emmy Award, Outstanding Writing in a Comedy Series, 1976–77)

James MacDonald, Robert Gerlach

#137, The Seminar

Jerry Mayer

#77, Hi There, Sports Fans
#120, Anyone Who Hates Kids and Dogs

Marilyn Suzanne Miller, Monica Magowan (later Johnson)

#71, Put On a Happy Face
#74, Angels in the Snow
#91, Best of Enemies

Phil Mishkin

#79, Son of "But Seriously, Folks"

Rick Mittleman

#41, The Slaughter Affair

Jim Mulholland, Mike Barrie

#67, Romeo and Mary

Lorenzo Music

#12, Anchorman Overboard

Pat Nardo, Gloria Banta

#39, The Five-Minute Dress
#138, Once I Had a Secret Love

Shelley Nelbert, Craig Allen Hafner

#135, What Do You Want to Do When You Produce?

Jim Parker, Arnold Margolin

#48, His Two Right Arms

Mary Kay Place, Valerie Curtin

#128, Mary's Delinquent

Earl Pomerantz

#123, Mary's Father
#149, Ted's Change of Heart
#162, Hail the Conquering Gordy

Richard M. Powell

#142, A Reliable Source

Burt Prelutsky

#146, Mary the Writer
#152, Mary Gets a Lawyer

Steve Pritzker

#5, Keep Your Guard Up
#18, Second-Story Story
#23, Smokey the Bear Wants You
#33, And Now, Sitting In for Ted Baxter
#43, More Than Neighbors

#47, Some of My Best Friends Are Rhoda
#55, Just Around the Corner
#59, You've Got a Friend

Don Reo, Allan Katz

#85, I Gave at the Office

Bob Rodgers

#9, Bob and Rhoda and Teddy and Mary
#13, He's All Yours

Pamela Russell

#116, Marriage: Minneapolis Style

Kenny Solms, Gail Parent

#19, We Closed in Minneapolis

Susan Silver

#22, A Friend In Deed
#28, Room 223
#36, . . . Is a Friend In Need
#37, The Square-Shaped Room
#50, What Is Mary Richards Really Like?

Treva Silverman

#2, Today I Am a Ma'am
#4, Divorce Isn't Everything
#10, Assistant Wanted, Female
#15, Howard's Girl
#20, Hi!
#25, The Birds . . . and . . . um . . . Bees
#30, Cover Boy
#35, The Six-and-a-Half-Year Itch
#42, Baby Sitcom
#54, Rhoda the Beautiful
#62, Rhoda Morgenstern: Minneapolis to New York
#76, The Lou and Edie Story (Emmy Award, Best Writing in
      Comedy, 1973–74; Emmy Award, Writer of the Year, Series,
      1973–74)
#92, Better Late . . . That's a Pun . . . Than Never
#102, I Love a Piano
#104, Ménage à Phyllis

Ziggy Steinberg

#109, Neighbors

Lloyd Turner, Gordon Mitchell

#7, Toulouse-Lautrec Is One of My Favorite Artists

Ed. Weinberger

#56, But Seriously, Folks
#60, It was Fascination, I Know
#64, Lou's Place
#66, The Georgette Story
#73, The Lars Affair
#82, The Dinner Party
#93, Ted Baxter Meets Walter Cronkite
#94, Lou's Second Date

Ed. Weinberger, Stan Daniels

#78, Father's Day
#80, Lou's First Date
#86, Almost a Nun's Story
#97, Will Mary Richards Go to Jail? (Emmy Award, Outstanding Writing in a Comedy Series, 1974–75)
#98, Not Just Another Pretty Face
#105, Not a Christmas Story
#108, A Son for Murray
#111, An Affair to Forget
#113, The System
#114, Phyllis Whips Inflation
#131, Mary Richards Falls in Love
#168, The Last Show (Emmy Award, Outstanding Writing in a Comedy Series, 1976–77)

Jack Winter

#101, The Outsider

William Wood

#83, Just Friends

Michael Zinberg

#119, Ted Baxter's Famous Broadcasters School

3. EMMY AWARDS

The following is a complete listing of the Emmy Awards given to *The Mary Tyler Show* and its creative artists by the National Academy of Television Arts and Sciences.

1970–71

Outstanding Performance by an Actor in a Supporting Role in Comedy: **Edward Asner**

Outstanding Performance by an Actress in a Supporting Role in Comedy: **Valerie Harper**

Outstanding Directorial Achievement in Comedy (Series): **Jay Sandrich,** "Toulouse-Lautrec is One of My Favorite Artists"

Outstanding Writing Achievement in Comedy: **James L. Brooks, Allan Burns,** "Support Your Local Mother"

1971–72

Outstanding Performance by an Actor in a Supporting Role in Comedy: **Edward Asner**

Outstanding Performance by an Actress in a Supporting Role in Comedy: **Valerie Harper** (tied with Sally Struthers)

1972–73

Outstanding Continued Performance by an Actress in a Leading Role in a Comedy Series: **Mary Tyler Moore**

Outstanding Performance by an Actor in a Supporting Role in Comedy: **Ted Knight**

Outstanding Performance by an Actress in a Supporting Role in Comedy: **Valerie Harper**

Outstanding Directorial Achievement in Comedy: **Jay Sandrich,** "It's Whether You Win or Lose"

1973–74

Best Lead Actress in a Comedy Series: **Mary Tyler Moore**

Actress of the Year, Series: **Mary Tyler Moore**

Best Supporting Actress in Comedy: **Cloris Leachman,** "The Lars Affair"

Best Writing in Comedy: **Treva Silverman,** "The Lou and Edie Story"

Writer of the Year, Series: **Treva Silverman**

1974–75

Outstanding Comedy Series: **The Mary Tyler Moore Show**

Outstanding Continuing Performance by a Supporting Actor in a Comedy Series: **Edward Asner**

Outstanding Continuing Performance by a Supporting Actress in a Comedy Series: **Betty White**

Outstanding Single Performance by a Supporting Actress in a Comedy or Drama Series: **Cloris Leachman,** "Phyllis Whips Inflation"

Outstanding Writing in a Comedy Series: **Ed. Weinberger, Stan Daniels,** "Mary Richards Goes to Jail"

1975–76

Outstanding Comedy Series: **The Mary Tyler Moore Show**

Outstanding Lead Actress in a Comedy Series: **Mary Tyler Moore**

Outstanding Continuing Performance by a Supporting Actor in a Comedy Series: **Ted Knight**

Outstanding Continuing Performance by a Supporting Actress in a Comedy Series: **Betty White**

Outstanding Writing in a Comedy Series: **David Lloyd,** "Chuckles Bites the Dust"

1976–77

Outstanding Comedy Series: **The Mary Tyler Moore Show**

Outstanding Writing in a Comedy Series: **Allan Burns, James L. Brooks, Ed. Weinberger, Stan Daniels, David Lloyd, Bob Ellison,** "The Last Show"

9

EPILOGUE

Twenty years after its conception *The Mary Tyler Moore Show* is generally considered a magic moment in television history. It was never at the top of the ratings chart, yet was always respectably placed, and now time has led to the critical assessment that it stands as the "classic" television comedy. Of course it is a "classic" in terms of a medium exactly fifty years old, the period of time since David Sarnoff introduced television to the American public in April 1939 at the New York World's Fair.

Some two hundred pages ago we offered the reader a celebration of this classic. In the interim we have listened to the voices of creators at work reflecting upon their quests for quality. Among the themes most often expressed was that concerning women in society. In 1975, Jim Brooks, referring to MTM, commented that their "timing was very fortunate" in relation to the evolution of the Women's Movement. He was quick to insist that he and Burns were not "espousing women's rights" but rather seeking to show "a woman from Mary Richards's background being in a world where women's rights are being talked about and having an impact." In Brooks's view it had a far different impact on Rhoda than on Mary. But both Brooks and Burns insist the show was not issue oriented. Burns commented in 1982, "We dealt with problems of a day-to-day type. Our issues were the small ones."

Was the intent of the creators totally without social content?

229

"Well, that gets tricky," they say, "because part of the fun of doing the show was a chance to try out your ideas, a chance to put your values out there. One of the dangers is that you become so self-indulgent that you're representing yourself and not the characters on the show. But you have to call on your own experience."

Brooks believes that the best thing about all the shows was "that in one way or another, no matter how absurd, they all tended to be love relationships. It's about people being interdependent, not dependent." Perhaps that is what caught Alan Alda's attention in 1976 when he spoke to us concerning the sensitivity of the show about Lou and Edie separating. In that context Alda observed, "I think in our best moments we try to show human behavior which, because of who we are and how we feel, reflects a particular value system, rather than presenting a logical codified argument of some specific issue." He concluded, "If a person proves an argument in a scene, it is not as theatrically satisfying as if that person goes through an experience and grows in some way. I think the audience vicariously grows with you and receives more benefit than by merely intellectually comprehending a point. You can't defend yourself against how you've grown."

For us the advantage of writing from a humanistic perspective is that you don't have to provide data. One can address feelings and motivations without a control group. By the same token, conclusions are slippery, albeit perhaps, in truth, no more slippery than social science "facts." So we are not concerned with demonstrating the social impact of *The Mary Tyler Moore Show*. Rather we ask about its content and the creative intent. In those terms was the show about Women's Liberation? We think so!

The times and the premise required either a genuine treatment of the changing role of women in society or a caricature going for the cheap laugh. While the show did have its share of farce, it ultimately was about people with whom the audience could and did identify. The Nielsen demographics tell us, if we choose to believe them, that Mary's viewers included a major component of the female audience ranging in age from twenty-five to fifty. Long after 1977, random sampling of opinion makes it obvious that those viewers respected Mary and believed in her as a decent human being.

The series was about a woman in her thirties, reared in rural Protestant Minnesota, conditioned by all the male perspectives on society, propriety, and vocation. And what did Mary Richards do? She championed equality with precisely that quaver in her voice and manner one might expect from persons of her generation. She never quite got used to Mr. Grant being Lou, and her vocation was largely

defined by a male perspective. But there were important moments that looked to a future when women who refused to be assigned roles by men would be on the cutting edge of a more humane society. A 1971 *TV Guide* article showed understanding of the possibilities when Diane Rosen wrote, "The miracle of *The Mary Tyler Moore Show* is that the heroine, Mary Richards, and her best friend, Rhoda Morgenstern, are unattached 30-year-olds. Valerie Harper plays Brooklyn-bred [sic] Rhoda with enough healthy cynicism to balance Mary's unflagging good cheer. Both of them have jobs and each seems to be surviving without the comfort of a brood of children or a steady boyfriend."

True enough, the show was developed and produced by men. But their sensitivities, coupled with the strong influence of such women as Treva Silverman, Marge Mullen, Ethel Winant, Valerie Harper, and Mary Tyler Moore, kept the series moving on its initial premise with an eye toward reality. The bumbling attempts by Lou to come to terms with Women's Liberation were not only fun, they made it clear that the stereotypes of the past were in need of replacement. And, as Alda rightly observed, as the character grew, so perhaps did the audience.

If Lou was growing, Ted never outgrew his basic sexism, and Bob Ellison made use of that fact in the last season. Through the words of Ted Baxter all of the absurd reactions to the Women's Movement were verbalized and made to be ridiculous. Ted, angry that Mary had added to "his" news show a short segment on local restaurants to be aired once a week and hosted by Sue Ann, identifies the grand female conspiracy:

> Put a chick on the news and gradually give her a bigger and bigger spot, before I know it you've got her taking over my job. . . . They want to take over the world . . . the secret organization that every chick on earth belongs to . . . whenever they go to the bathroom they never go alone. . . . That's where they hold their meetings. And have you noticed they're always asking for quarters? *Dues!* . . . They're clever, won't let you hear anything. They keep flushing!

Murray turns to Mary and in mock derision says, "Shame on you, Mary." She replies, "Yes, well, I guess the jig's up." There was a statement, one that reduces to folly all those antifeminist stances predicated upon fear and ignorance.

In 1970 there were a few female producers, but for the most part women were confined to acting and writing and lower-level administrative jobs. Susan Silver reminds us that there were only a small number of female writers, and of those only a few felt an obligation to explore a "feminine perspective." We understand that term as describing an attitude of mind and spirit at present represented largely by women. Socially prescribed sex roles, long ago established by men, have created a system of male-defined social structures. Women became the keepers of a humane tradition, one that emphasized a caring, sustaining, nurturing spirit—with all those "unmanly" traits. Since, as we believe, women and men have the

potential to enjoy the full range of human expression, both sexes may escape from the trap of confinement created by a socialization process constructed by our forefathers. But that escape is possible only through the transformation of existing social structures, and then only as women reach a critical mass in every aspect of culture, effecting serious challenges to the myriad of man-made systems dominating current society.

In its time and in its way *The Mary Tyler Moore Show* communicated attitudes consistent with the movement for equal rights for women. Further, through its sensitive portrayals it offered a glimpse of a new perspective on vocation and the relationships between men and women in the work force. Whatever its "impact," the force of its points of view affirmed for millions of viewers, male and female, something exciting about the changes in society.

Distinguished producer and current president of Women in Film, Marian Rees, observed recently that Grant Tinker, when presiding over NBC, was honest and fair in dealing with gender issues. Listening to a delegation of women making a case for a different perspective in network television, Tinker was responsive, and as Rees noted, he "urged the women to continue their efforts and to be themselves." After all is written, isn't that what Rhoda and Mary were attempting in the uneasy world of the 1970s? And in spite of the theme song, they didn't really make it on their own, they made it as part of a caring community defined in Mary's closing soliloquy, "What is a family anyway? It is a place where you feel less alone and really loved."

We can hear you now, Allan and Jim, asking, "What is this? An *epilogue*, yet! We create the classic television *comedy* of all time and you guys end on Women's Lib. Come on."

Well, Allan and Jim, we'd better offer an apologia. Why don't we blame it on Jim? After all, you did tell us in 1976, "We never think about the show in that way, being about the Women's Movement. I mean we never think about it like that. But when you talk about it, it is there." You even dared speculate that Maude Findlay and Mary Richards "probably would be friends." Taking a couple of breaths, you brought this point together with your belief that you were "trying to be true to characters and to be funny." The two of you gave us the clue: "If we treat a separation in a marriage realistically and find the humor in that, then we are doing something pretty spectacular."

We celebrate *The Mary Tyler Moore Show* as a "spectacular" example of high art in television comedy. As we have peeled back the layers to expose the predispositions that led to the pro-social "messages," we have labored to keep the fun in the foreground. Because the last word for us on *The Mary Tyler Moore Show* is precisely that. Grant Tinker began this volume by speaking of our enjoyment of "the fun of it." Fun born of good feelings, unmatched talent, a wry sense of human nature, and a good dose of shared friendships.

Commemorative plaque at the entrance to Sound Stage 2.